THE PATH

by

Malcolm McKay

A BASELINE PAPERBACK

© Copyright 2015
Malcolm McKay

ISBN–9781511924139

For those who walk

For
Elio.
Thanks for all your
help.
Best wishes
Mallon

INTERNET REVIEWS

* This is an absolute gem of a story. The richness of the characters, their stories and their different reasons for embarking on the Camino de Santiago are delightfully woven together and teased out in a way that kept me turning the pages long into the night on more than one occasion. I was enchanted, amused, enraged and saddened in turn by their all too human failings as they desperately seek answers that mostly evade them and often leave them wondering if they are asking the right questions. The book offers a wryly humorous, engaging, well observed and occasionally profound insight into the greater journey that, one way or another, we are all on.

* I loved this book. I was hooked from the first page and wanted to know how each of the characters developed and progressed. The descriptions of the Camino itself are magnificent and very inspiring. It made me want to strap on my backpack and get going! Definitely recommend this as a great read.

* Malcolm McKay's modern-day pilgrims set out with nothing in common but an urge to submit themselves to one of the most ancient and arduous challenges in the western world. The Camino de Compostela winds more than five hundred miles over mountains, across sierras, through landscapes ancient and modern. Just as Chaucer's Prologue to The Canterbury Tales reads at times as a very modern text, so The Path has ancient resonances--people have been walking this path for well over a thousand years. The Camino has always been, to some

necessary and mysterious degree, an ordeal. Chaucer's pilgrims tell stories to pass the time. The Path is full of stories too--but these are the stories of the pilgrims themselves. The Camino tests and reveals character. It engenders intense intimacies and hostilities. It strips away the carefully cultivated lies that people live by, and leaves the truth of their shared humanity.

* Whatever the question is, in the end, what is most important is that they put one foot in front of the other to find their own answers.

* I found it very inspirational and intend to walk The Path before I die.

* My kindle's got blisters.

* This is an absorbing book that I have just read for the second time. I've no doubt that, if I were to attempt the Camino, I would find a similar assortment of backgrounds, nationalities and personalities amongst those characterised. It's a very tempting prospect, as is the physical challenge, and one that I very much doubt anyone who completes it will ever forget.

* Oh what a lovely book !! So perceptive and touching . I read it on my phone! It was so compulsive I hardly noticed the tiny screen. Why do people of all ages and levels of fitness embark on this strenuous trek ? This elegantly written account goes a long way to answering this question. You are gripped by the characters and when you reach the brilliant ending you are loath to leave them.

* I awarded this book five stars because I found it totally absorbing,to the point where I did not want to put it down, but neither did I want to finish it.

* By the end-an amazing, transcendent ending-I felt privileged to have traveled with them. McKay is an infallible guide.

* Malcolm McKay skilfully weaves the thoughts and emotions

of his characters into a story of huge significance to all of us. I've now read the book so, where's the film?! A 'must read'. Highly recommended.

* This is another wonderful book by Malcolm McKay. Having read his fascinating novel The Lack Brothers, I was anxious to read The Path, and was not disappointed.

* A wonderful, touching and laugh-out-loud in places read. it both soothes and feeds a pilgrim's post-Camino blues. sigh. a sequel, please!

* Although it is fiction I read this whilst walking the Camino. It realistically captures the difficulties and fun of the journey and the inner strivings that people will make as they struggle with the challenges and demands.

* A wonderful insight into various characters in lives and their individual journeys along this pilgrimage route. I have set myself a challenge to do this when I turn 50 and can't wait. Great read.

* A Twenty First Century "Canterbury Tales" for the post-freudian generation.

* If you enjoyed the film "The Way" , you will probably enjoy this book.

MALCOLM McKAY

Malcolm McKay has been writer/director of several successful television films including the award winning A Wanted Man trilogy, Redemption and adaptations of Emil Zola's La Bete Humaine and Mervyn Peake's Gormenghast. He has had three novels published, The Lack Brothers, Breaking Up and Thistown for children.

THE CAMINO DE SANTIAGO

The Camino is the way. The Camino de Santiago is the ancient pilgrimage to the remains of Saint James in the Cathedral of Santiago de Compostella in the northwest of Spain.

Over the past thirteen hundred years millions of pilgrims have trod the Path, the Way of Saint James. Although the religious purpose of the camino remains a motive for many, it has evolved over the years until now in the Twenty-first century, it is undertaken by men and women of all denominations and none.

They come from all over the world to do the camino. They are of all ages, all types, all professions and occupations. It is regarded by many as a journey of a lifetime for self discovery; perhaps psychological, perhaps spiritual, or maybe purely physical. As it is said on the camino, everybody has their own question to ask.

PART ONE

ST JEAN PIED DE PORT

Around eighty pilgrims had gathered that night in Saint Jean Pied de Port in the French Pyrenees in late September to begin their camino. That figure was low. In the height of summer there would have been hundreds. In addition to these there would have been many who started from Le Puy, or Lyons in France; others would have begun in Paris, Geneva or any number of European cities, towns or villages where a man or woman felt compelled to heave a pack onto their back and take to the Path. Most of these trails converged on St. Jean, the last French town before the eight hundred kilometre walk across northern Spain to Santiago de Compostella.

At the beginning of August Werner Schmidt had walked out of his home in Vienna; three weeks after that Fabian Laurent had slung his miniature guitar on his back, closed his front door behind him in Nancy, and headed south to the Pyrenees - and he intended to walk back again. Others had flown in to Biarritz, Bilbao or Pamplona and taken the train to St Jean. Rhoda and Deena Dunne had boarded a plane from Toronto, Paul Kramer and Harry Hook had started out from Minnesota, and Ingrid Sorensen had taken a flight from Copenhagen via London. They were all nervous, exhilarated and scared that they didn't have what it takes to get them over the plains, the valleys, the rolling hills and the two mountain ranges they would have to cross to reach the great city and its ancient cathedral containing the last remains of the apostle, James. Not that they were all there for religious reasons; every one of them had their own thoughts, worries about the future, and questions to ask.

Peter Donald had taken a flight from Stansted to Biarritz. Frankly, as he'd told anyone who'd asked, he hardly knew why he was there. The most obvious reason was that his brother had told him to go. That in it itself was irritating enough but he had to admit he needed time to think, or maybe not to think; either way to allow the decision as to what to do next with his life to surface and become known to him. He had to face it sometime, the future was blank. A full life, or what had seemed like a full life (although he had doubts about that too) had come to a full stop. Now what?

He shifted uncomfortably in his seat. He was tall and his body cramped more easily and frequently then it used to - the idea that his discomfort may have been a reflection of his state of mind never occurred to him. At least, not then. He was a man unused to such considerations. The world for him was what he saw in front of him, a series of practical propositions; problems and their solutions. The unobvious, unclear, or unanswerable were left as just that. Those who knew him thought him charming, a little vain, with interested eyes, and an easy smile. They weren't deceived. These qualities were as profoundly part of him as were the unwanted thoughts, sudden insights and inexplicable feelings that would rise and be concealed again, as much from himself as from those who knew him.

He looked down through the window as the plane banked over the Atlantic coast of France and slowly began its descent into Biarritz. He remembered a camping holiday he'd had with his wife and son on the Isle de Roi not too far to the south of where he was now. That was eight years ago. He'd had a four week leave plus two weeks compassionate as his father had died. Within days of the funeral they'd gone on holiday. Gemma had said, don't you want some time? What for? Grieve? What was the point? Anyway after his four months away in Basra Sam was showing signs of needing him. Not that the holiday had done much for that. All that Peter could remember was the kind of sulk that only a fourteen year old could deliver. It went on for days. He felt later that it was the beginning of his son's rejection of him; the awful and unconscious revenge of a teenager. He turned in his seat again. No thank you, he didn't want to think about that now. Or his father. Although he was irritated to discover that as these thoughts came, so did a tightening of his stomach and a subtle, ridiculous anxiety, as though he didn't know what he was doing for Christ's sake. He pushed his blond hair back from his forehead and sat straighter. It was done. They were divorced. The army was behind him. Sam was...? He didn't know.

The stewardess brought the scotch he'd ordered. He smiled, she smiled back. He was tempted to start the conversation. It had happened once on a flight to Bangkok and he'd met the stewardess later in a hotel. He let his mind wander for a second and had a brief image of her naked on the room's balcony. He dismissed the thought with some difficulty and looked down at the guidebook in his lap. Never in his life had he been this unprepared for anything. The thought gave him the first inclination (of many that were to come) as to how things, or at least his view of them, were beginning to shift in him. He turned to the introduction.

Santiago. San Tiago. Saint James. Apparently his relics were in the sepulchre of the Cathedral. He took a sip of the scotch and wondered what Gemma would be thinking of him doing this. She would know of course; she seemed to know everything. Not that she ever spoke to him now. But if she did? She'd smile quizzically as if he was beyond all comprehension. You, a pilgrim? He was beginning to agree with her. But if he'd known then what he knew later, he'd have told her that the pilgrimage had as many meanings as the number of people who went on it. For most, religion was hardly the heart of the matter; it was the hard road of change they walked, and for some it revealed the darkest and most difficult challenges they'd ever faced. For now he bent his head down and forced himself to read the legend, the ancient beginning of it all.

The apostle, James, son of Zebedee and Salome, brother of John, was a fisherman who'd left Galilee on hearing the call of the

Lord. He'd been a faithful follower throughout the three years of Christ's public life, had witnessed the crucifixion, been present at the resurrection, on the day of the Pentecost had received the holy spirit and been commanded by the Holy Ghost to travel the known world and teach the one true gospel. He was known as the Son of Thunder, apparently, because of his zeal. Peter smiled. Sam would have liked that. At least the old Sam would have done.

James had preached first in Judea and afterwards sailed to Spain. He'd landed on the Atlantic coast and had only been saved from the tumultuous seas by the intervention of the Virgin Mary who had sent a stone barque to rescue him. He'd come ashore in Muxia - good for the tourist trade, thought Peter - and from there travelled all over northern Spain proselytising as he went, and experienced another vision of the Blessed Virgin in Zarragossa. She appeared on a marble pillar and commanded him to build a church on the spot, which he'd done. Peter wondered how long that took. Then James and his, by then, band of disciples had returned to Jerusalem.

Peter sipped his drink. His father had been an absolute unbeliever and, although it would have been different if his mother had been strong enough to have her way, neither he nor his brother had ever been christened. It had caused a raised eyebrow when he'd put down atheist under religion on his entrance to Sandhurst. 'Why don't you put down C of E?' barked a sergeant. 'Makes things fucking easier on a Sunday, don't it?' He could easily have changed it. But maybe he didn't want to reveal the vacuum he felt, so he'd stuck with atheist; at least it had the advantage of being set, done, and he wouldn't have to think about it again. Not that different from his father, he thought. He read on.

James was nothing if not fervent and, having returned to the Holy Land, continued as an uncompromising and passionate advocate of the teachings of his Master. In 44 AD within months of his arrival in Jerusalem Herod Agrippa had him beheaded as a revolutionary and threat to the state; the first of the twelve apostles to be publicly martyred. His disciples managed to retrieve both his torso and head, and decided to return them to Spain for burial. They found a ship, crossed the Mediterranean and according to the legend reached Spain at Iria Flavia on the mouth of the River Ulla. The idea was to bury him at Finnis Terre, world's end, but the great Queen Lupa conspiring with the Roman Legate based nearby tried to seize the body and destroy it. The disciples escaped over a bridge on the River Tambre which collapsed as soon as they'd crossed it, cutting off the pursuing Romans and the frustrated Queen gave up the chase. A few days later at Libredon the wild bulls pulling the cart stopped of their own accord and the disciples decided to lay James to rest where they'd halted. The Celtic Druids of the surrounding district had other ideas and attacked them, killing several. The remaining two buried James before they too were slaughtered and interred either side of him, although by whom wasn't made clear as all the disciples were by now dead or fled. And there the body or bodies lay undisturbed for eight hundred years.

He skipped over the fall of the Roman Empire and the establishment of Western Islamic rule - although it did occur to him how indebted the present Spanish character must be to Moorish genes. In 813 an old shepherd called Pelagius saw a bright star in the sky and lights flickering around an oak tree. (At this point Peter nearly gave up.) The shepherd immediately reported this to the local bishop, Theodonis. And lo and behold the bodies of James and his disciples were discovered in this field under the stars - the compostella. A church was built to house the remains, was destroyed, a replacement erected, was destroyed again - he passed over another page of medieval brutality and vandalism including the establishment and dissolution of the Grand Inquisition - until finally the present cathedral began to slowly take shape. It took a thousand years to become what it is today, which even he had to admit was impressive. He studied the aerial photograph. The great entrance, the dome, and the hulk of the cathedral itself, with its two defending towers, was a mass of baroque stone standing solid and inviolable against a smoky sky; the whole edifice surrounded and further guarded by the ancient, and then modern, city of Santiago de Compostella.

He finished his scotch. The stewardess smiled as she took his glass. He looked down at the picture again. Even if the beginnings of this history had been little more than the fevered imaginings of the medieval mind, and the legend created more by desire than fact - Peter's brother in his student philosophy days had labelled him empiricist down to his cadet boot straps - the enduring bulk and permanence of the cathedral were real enough. All that sheer effort, stubbornness, invention, heaving the stone, the intricacy of the design, the argument, the politics, the amount of time it had taken, the blood in the walls, it must all mean - he hesitated to continue - it must all mean something. He glanced down through the window. He could see Biarritz to his left, and beyond it the Pyrenees. Tomorrow he'd be walking across them.

* * * *

Bayonne was quiet and almost deserted in the afternoon sun. The train to Saint Jean standing in the station consisted of only three carriages, so it didn't take long for Ingrid Sorensen to walk the length of the platform peering in through all the windows. She wasn't looking for anyone she knew. She'd travelled alone from Copenhagen, and unknowingly taken the same plane from Stansted as Peter, and then a taxi from Biarritz airport, whereas he'd caught the bus. What she was looking for was a companion. To look at Ingrid you wouldn't guess that she had such a need. She was a lithe and strong woman in her early forties, (although she looked younger), with a good figure, brown bobbed hair, a round, faintly freckled face, full pink lips and hooded pale blue eyes that could be fascinated by you, or nervous, depending on her mood. She carried her pack comfortably and walked down the platform with a natural physical confidence that masked her unease.

She stopped opposite a window and then walked back away from it. She saw Peter down the quickly emptying platform behind her pick up his rucksack and get onto the train through the first door he came to. She immediately weighed him up, as was her habit with men. (She prided herself on her accuracy.) His fair hair made her guess he was either English or German; he was good-looking, confident, carried himself well, and had an air of certainty about him. She was surprised that a man like this should be a pilgrim. She'd envisaged pilgrims to be at least a version of the ancients; bearded men with rough cloaks and wide-brimmed hats, carrying crucifixes.

She turned again and looked through the windows. She caught sight of her own reflection. She was in quarter profile and it seemed as if she was looking over her shoulder to see who was following her. Do I do that all the time? she thought. Well not anymore. The Path was going to change all that. She glanced through the window again and saw a woman sitting on the other side of the train. She seemed about the right age and type. Ingrid decided she'd sit close to her; not next to her, but close enough to start a conversation and find out if she was the companion she was looking for. She moved down the platform and stepped up into the carriage.

The woman Ingrid had seen was Eva Protin a corporate lawyer from Geneva. Her straight blond hair was pulled tightly back from her oval face. Her eyes were so dark, they seemed black; her lips, though not thin, were tightly compressed. She looked small and very neat, sitting by the window, holding herself erect, and looking forward as if trying to see something in the back of the seat ahead. Her telltale backpack and walking sticks were on the seat next to her.

Ingrid sat across the aisle. She'd left her pack in the rack by the door. She took a camino guide book from her pocket and began to read. After a minute she turned and glanced at Eva who hadn't moved. The train started. There was an announcement in French listing the stations the train would stop at. The last was St Jean de Pied Port. She turned towards Eva.

"Do you speak English?"

Eva smiled.

Ingrid smiled back. "Are you going on the Path?"

By the time the train had climbed the heavily wooded slopes and reached St Jean in the heart of the Pyrenees about an hour later, they'd become friends. As she looked out of the window and marvelled at what seemed the impossibly angled forests of fir, Ingrid talked well and listened carefully. She had a talent for both, especially with women. She opened up easily, wasn't afraid of letting slip slight confidences about herself and was receptive to, and non-judgemental about, anything the other might offer. There was also an air of vulnerability about her. She could seem like a little girl looking for a big sister, or sometimes, paradoxically, an equally naive, young protector looking for a child of her own to look after. She had a wonderfully forgiving smile.

Eva, nervous as she was, slowly unwound as they ascended into the higher cooler air of the mountains. Impossible thoughts had been going round in her mind for weeks and the questions, or more exactly question, that those thoughts were returning to, as if by the minute, as if by the second, was becoming so tight and unanswerable that it was becoming a throbbing pain at the back of her head. But now at least she was here, actually on the train to St Jean with her pack by her side. She arched back in her seat and smiled at Ingrid. One relief at least was to talk; talk about nothing, say nothing and give nothing away, at least until she'd decided on the answer to her question.

Not that Ingrid knew anything about this, and wouldn't until much later on the Path. What she saw next to her (after ten minutes they'd moved Eva's pack to the rack and Ingrid had taken the seat by her) was a charming, intelligent, to be sure watchful, but giving woman who seemed happy to chat. In the absence of anything much more than professional and domestic fact coming from Eva - she was thirty-eight, well-paid (unbelievably well-paid compared to Ingrid), lived alone, visited her parents once a month, had several good friends, liked to read psychology (but had given it up), and the great love of her life was her cat, at present being looked after by her mother - Ingrid did what she did best and talked about herself as the train pulled slowly up towards St Jean.

She told Eva about her daughter who was studying fashion at university. She said she was also alone and it was such a relief not to have him all over the house, making too much noise, watching football on TV, and leaving his clothes everywhere. Of course Eva was astute enough to realise that this somewhat stereotyped man that Ingrid was describing was probably a long way from the actual relationship or relationships that Ingrid was - Eva paused in her mind before she allowed the thought - running away from. The phrase remained a smile on her lips as Ingrid went happily on. She was the manager of a small chain of hairdressing salons. Her job was to make everything run smoothly, keep it all in its rightful place and everyone content. She even cleaned the windows because the cleaners they had were inefficient and she preferred to do it herself. The owner of the chain was very pleased with her.

"I like them all to be happy," she said. "And then no-one gets angry and the atmosphere is good." She shifted slightly in her seat as she said as if comforting herself.

Although Ingrid spoke ten words to Eva's one, it became slowly clear to the latter that Ingrid was giving away hardly more than she was. Eva thought of veils and masks and hooded cloaks as Ingrid regarded her with her opaque blue eyes. Eva decided that Ingrid was obviously a pleasant enough woman who had a talent for closeness (if not intimacy), and certainly loyalty, which in itself could be worrying as it might turn into need. But Eva decided to put her doubts aside. What she wanted to do was relax and let the Path unfold, and maybe this question in her mind would resolve itself and her headache would go.

They arrived in St Jean at dusk, climbed down from the train, and stood on the asphalt platform, their packs by their feet. Eva turned slowly, looking round. She could just see, caught in the last light of the sun, the snowcapped peaks further south and west. She breathed in deeply, allowing the cool air to calm her nerves.

Ingrid felt confident enough to ask - she wouldn't have done if instinctively she didn't already know the answer. "Shall we walk together?'

"You mean the Path?"

Ingrid shrugged, offering her most vulnerable smile.

"That will be OK."

"Good."

Ingrid had found her companion. She felt happy as she lifted her pack onto her shoulders and they followed Peter Donald up the road into St Jean.

* * * *

It was getting quite dark as Peter passed through the ramparts into the old town. The street was narrow and cobbled. To his right was a bar, empty in the early evening, but welcoming nevertheless. He thought about a drink but decided against it. That was something else he was going to have to deal with. In the past six months since leaving the army with time weighing heavily on his hands he'd spent most evenings in the pub. He'd told himself he needed to think, as if thinking could only be done leaning against the bar in the Duke. Why couldn't he work things out lying on the bed in that wonderfully dreary flat he called home? He'd convinced himself he needed people; their energy, laughter, inane chat and ridiculous opinions; maudlin men and flirty women. Somehow all this propped him up, and he had to admit it, stopped him thinking. Having been in the army helped. 'Served in Iraq mate, have one on me.' Even the occasional, 'Don't know why we went,' was useful. But best of all, 'Bet you looked nice in uniform. Still wear it sometimes, do you?' And Peter knew exactly when she wanted it on him, and off him. He'd known that all his life. It was his greatest talent. The thought made him smile, then for some reason he felt angry. He looked down the street to the bar and heard the pain and rage in Gemma's voice again. Half the time what she thought wasn't true anyway. Half the time? So the other half...? Stop right there. Another thought (another life) rammed back down. Must be like a pot of snakes in there.

10

Stop. Back on track please. At least in the army you knew who was who, what was what, and when to do it. As for the rest, cram a life (and a wife) into a four week leave, flowers for her, pay the bills, take the boy out, no time for thinking. Time. That was the real problem. What do you do with it? Go on a bloody walk for a month. He looked down at the cobbles shining in the lamplight. Is that what he thought? Go on a bloody walk? Waste some time? Six months in Basra, couple of weeks in Winchester, short tour in Dubai, Christmas at home, a course in London, quick holiday in France, back to Winchester, a bloody walk? Life in bits? Live in pieces? Someone was coming up the street behind him. He looked round as Ingrid and Eva passed him. He clocked Ingrid, no doubt about it, couldn't help it. Then he turned and went back down to the bar. A quick one wouldn't hurt.

* * * *

The two women continued up to the intersection. Ingrid looked at the map in her guidebook under the light of a street lamp. "I think it's here." She pointed left up the long narrow street cut by yellow shafts of light from windows either side piercing the early evening mist. They continued up the hill towards the pilgrim's office, past shadowy, dark beamed houses crowding and overhanging the street. The town smelt of age and evening. There was something welcoming about it which relaxed them both.

They were chatting easily now. Eva had begun to laugh and the tension in the back of her head was easing. Ingrid would have been surprised to know that Eva had decided to walk with her on the train, ten minutes before she'd asked. It was a foretaste of what was to come. Ingrid would talk, suggest, organise, and on the face of it control what they did, but Eva had already decided what they would do. Already she could feel herself slipping back to that place she disliked; the analysis of the fine print, detecting the holes in the argument, and with deadly accuracy redrafting the contract. That's why they paid her so much. This was the real mountain Eva had to climb, the hard rock face of her own

11

intellectual capacity which seemed to mock and flatten all other responses. Maybe she needed to let herself lose for once - and be happy as she did so.

"There it is," Ingrid was looking ahead of them towards the light coming from the pilgrim's office window.

They moved up the street passing the bright display of a small shop on their right. Eva noticed a large rubber bucket containing five foot high, wooden, pilgrim's staffs, their tops tied loosely to the wall by the shop doorway. On the other side of the door was a rack of scallop shells, the sign of the pilgrim, each with a small, ornate, red sword painted in the centre. These, as Eva knew, were the marks of the ancient order of the Knights Templar, the traditional protectors of the pilgrim. She'd read that everyone wore them tied to the back of their packs.

"I'd like to buy a shell." She stopped.

"Maybe we should later," said Ingrid, as always, worried about what was to come. "I don't know what time the office is closed."

Eva let it go. It was only seven o'clock and she'd read that the office stayed open late, and so therefore would the shop, to pick up the trade from the pilgrims. She glanced in through the doorway as they passed.

* * * *

Inside Llewellyn Lewis was, as usual, dithering, although you wouldn't have known it. He stood perfectly still with his feet connected at the heels and splayed outwards like a ballet dancer. His hands were held flat together and steepled as he pressed them lightly against the half smile of his lips. He was small, wiry, fair haired, and had managed to arrive at his thirty-ninth year without ever having held down a full time job for longer than two months. It wasn't that he was lazy. More disengaged. He certainly wasn't rebellious either; softly anarchic maybe, but with a demeanour that was always accommodating. It was Llewellyn's way, he liked to be liked, and usually was. If Peter was a drinker, he had nothing on Llewellyn, who was a heavy smoker too, forever stopping on the trail for a fag break. As a matter of fact that's how he met Werner Schmidt later, over a shared roll-up in Pamplona, and how he began to lose all sense of himself on the Path.

Even now he wasn't entirely sure of what was happening. On the face of it he was buying a T shirt. His collection of gear for the expedition, as he called it, was not yet complete. Not that it ever would be, because he would never have any real idea of what he needed until he noticed it wasn't there, and stood frozen on the plain, or wet in the hills, or without a cigarette paper outside a closed shop in siesta Spain in the afternoon sun.

He'd decided barely twenty-four hours ago to come on the Path. In the same way as he'd decided a week before that to walk out of his sister, Cindy's, house in Swansea, where he'd been staying for the previous month in his latest period of homelessness. The thought that Cindy still didn't know where he was, or why he'd left, still bothered him, but he put it aside, as he put everything else aside, and looked up at the T shirts displayed on the wall. Anyone else buying clothing for a five week walk might have considered its warmth, weight, or proof against the weather. Llewellyn was only really interested in its colour. He quite liked the various camino designs, but wasn't too keen on the cartoon characters with bandaged feet and stupid grins, mouthing in bubbles, no pain, no gain! He decided on a black T shirt with a bold, yellow arrow camino waymark across the chest. It would remind him of where he was going.

He was still half drunk from the wine he'd bought on the train. He'd sat with a couple of French blokes as far as - he couldn't remember where they'd got off - and they'd had a great old time despite one or two language difficulties. Llewellyn's life may well have stumbled from one disaster to another, but no-one could ever accuse him of lacking congeniality. As the wine went down, so would he, into a gentle, smiling, welcoming stupor, punctuated only by roll-ups and a light ripple of a laugh that made you feel protective towards him.

He'd walked out of Cindy's house at four in the morning - even now he wasn't entirely sure why. Maybe it was the finally overpowering feeling of dissatisfaction with the suffocating, jammed-in pettiness and chip shop stink of a terraced Welsh side-street, or perhaps it was the Guinness in the crowded old pub; that night mixed with port, cigarette smoke and too much rubbish chat, too loud too; he remembered being confused by the looming faces and what felt like their overlarge mouths laughing and chomping at him. Or maybe it was the fact that he'd started to pack his bag anyway to go and spend a few days with Robert in boring-as-hell Caerphilly for more alcohol, Chinese takeaways, and unwanted psychoanalysis from the no-hope brigade; or ultimately perhaps it was no more than he'd heard the shed door banging in the wind and decided to go down to the yard and shut it. Whatever it was, two hours later he'd found himself on the early train to London. On arrival, he'd walked from Paddington, wandered aimlessly for a few hours, and ended up in the Grays Inn Road, where he'd quite by chance discovered the Welsh club. Where else? Obviously he went in for a drink, obviously he was confused, and equally obviously someone had felt sorry for him and had offered him a sofabed for the night. This was the way of Llewellyn's life. More booze followed. He wasn't broke; his stash, still recently acquired, was holding up, and he was generous with it.

He spent four days in London, most of it draped over an old armchair in the Welsh club surrounded by the like-minded, with a continually replenished glass of beer and a sad but satisfied smile. He was vaguely aware of being propositioned by the owner of the sofabed, but such was his Llewellyn innocence projected, that he'd come through unscathed and the next morning on a whim had walked through the Covent Garden tourist market to Waterloo where he'd taken the Eurotunnel to Paris. Now he knew why he'd taken his passport with him when he'd left Cindy's house. Or maybe it was because he'd taken his passport with him that he'd left the country. Cause and effect in Llewellyn's life were never quite clear as separate entities and therefore easily and continually reversible. He followed his nose and somehow the world always seemed to provide. This time his nose led him straight out of the Gare du Nord and into a tobacco-stained bar where there was an Irishman sitting on a shiny stool at a strange angle, drinking a beer with a backpack by his chair. One thing led to another, more drinks were bought, laughs were laughed, Llewellyn adopted the reverse angle, and the Irishman, called Stephen, told him an incredible tale of the wonderful trek he'd just completed called the Camino de Santiago.

"It's a spiritual journey," said Stephen, "You'll discover yourself."

Which didn't seem like a bad idea to Llewellyn.

"And the craic is just something else."

Llewellyn unwound his money belt in the toilet, consulted his stash and estimated he still had plenty. Following the Irishman's directions he negotiated the metro with an instinct that always seemed faultless in times like these, and bought himself a ticket to St Jean Pied de Port. Having a couple of hours to spare, he went for a walk, dropped carelessly into another bar, then on the way back to the station found himself staring into the window of a magazin de sports. He went in and came out twenty blurred minutes later with a rucksack, a bright red walking jacket and a pair of trekking trainers. He stuffed the rest of his possessions into the rucksack and threw his old bag away. He heaved the pack onto his back. Something felt very right about it.

On his way back to the station he passed a milliners and saw in the window a wide-brimmed straw hat. Although the summer was over, it somehow fitted his mood. The stash was once again referred to. It was looking a little pilfered, but to hell with it, the Irishman had said the camino was cheap, and so with hat perched gloriously on head, and pack weighing not too heavily on back, Llewellyn had taken his seat on the train to the south of France and the Pyrenees. He'd negotiated two changes of trains, vaguely remembered drinking with the two Frenchmen (one was called Alphonse), and there he was in the Rue de Citadelle in St Jean buying a T shirt. As he came out of the shop he saw the knotted and whittled pilgrim staffs and had no doubt he should have one of those too. He picked a sturdy example, tried it out by leaning on it and thought he would decorate the bare wood sometime. Peter passed on the street and Llewellyn said, "Pardon, vous parlez...?

"I'm English."

"Oh hullo, do you know where...?"

"Bureau de pelerins? I understand it's up there on the left."

Llewellyn went back into the shop to pay for his staff.

* * * *

Rhoda and Deena Dunne were already in the cluttered, dimly lit, pilgrim's office when Ingrid and Eva came in. They'd been there for twenty minutes sitting on two of the chairs that lined the left-hand wall under a series of topographical maps of each stage of the Path, and staring at the long and vacant desks that ran along the other side of the room. Behind them were large colour posters of the snowcapped Pyrenees.

"It's not snowing up there, is it?" Rhoda, a sprightly, thin woman, full of her own energy and opinion, spoke too loudly as usual, embarrassing her daughter.

"No, Ma, it's still only the fall," Deena smiled at Ingrid who was dumping her pack by Eva's. "Hi," she said, trying to be friendly, and half apologising, as usual, for her mother. Big boned, like the father she couldn't remember, Deena was clumsy in both manner and form, and her big honk didn't help matters much either. She existed in a world of apology and retreat, and ended up being so nice to everybody that her saving grace, a considered and intelligent compassion, went unnoticed - except maybe by her mother who wasn't going to thank her for it.

"What's the point of the place being open if there's no-one here to serve you?" said Rhoda.

Deena knew that her mother was setting the tone for the weeks to come. First she'd be sceptical of the French, then critical of the Spanish and probably downright rude to any other nationality she met on the way. Anyone she liked would have the benefit of her life story in detail. 'I lived in five countries...' Deena could hear it

16

already. Why she'd agreed to this, God alone knew. Rhoda had heard about the Path from Edwina Matthews on the green at the bowls club, who had boasted that her niece, Scarlett, had done it, and do you know, it changed her, changed her from top to bottom. Rhoda had quite liked the idea of being different (for a while), and having questioned her friend and rival intently over a tomato juice on the sun terrace outside the bar, had deduced that she was more than a little reluctant, if not nervous, of undertaking this process of change personally. As night follows day it became apparent to Rhoda that here was a heaven sent opportunity to get one up on Edwina.

'Ma, you're seventy-two years old, you do not need to be a different person, you're quite good enough...well, you're who you are anyway,' Deena had told her, then wished she'd kept her mouth shut. Any argument with her mother always and absolutely reinforced her position.

'Don't you want me to go? Why not? I'm going.'

Within an hour Rhoda was on the internet; by the end of the evening she'd read everything there was to read and forgotten most of it, the next day she'd ordered five guide books from Amazon (two of them in German; she'd realised another one was in Korean just in time), and was starting the campaign to get Deena to go with her. 'Come on, you don't know who you'll meet,' she'd said with her usual deadly talent for saying exactly what the person she was talking to didn't want to hear.

'Ma, I'm very happy, thank you.'

'No, you're not, you don't have a career and you don't have a man. And you're thirty-five years old.' She said it as she'd been saying it for the past four months since Deena's birthday. 'Time's running out, honey.'

Deena had retreated to her room and cried, just as she'd been doing for what seemed like most of her existence on this earth. She was the youngest of Rhoda's five children by three husbands, or more exactly two, the last being not so hot in that department. Nevertheless Deena had got his name, Dunne. And how she cursed her mother for the Deena. Dunne was bad enough but the alliteration somehow increased the possibility of ridicule. 'Hey Deena, you done it?' Or at school, 'Yes, sir, Deena done it.' Had her mother named her with intent? She'd humiliated her from cradle to thirty-five anyway, so what was wrong with encouraging a few hundred schoolgirls, shop managers and gas station attendants to do it in her absence?

It's fate, let it happen, thought Deena in the pilgrim's office, as she lent her head back against the outline of the mountain she was going to have to climb the next day. It's a foreign country, new people, new everything. She turned to see Eva and Ingrid, a few feet along from her, talking seriously, heads bowed over a guidebook. Already a couple of interesting looking women. The door opened and Peter came in. She gave him a cursory glance. Too old. She looked away. Face it, Deena, you had no choice. How could you let your seventy year old mother do this on her own? This was a point Rhoda had made several times, once even with a hint of a tear, and again when she'd groaned getting out of an armchair. Deena leaned back on her own hard seat in the pilgrim's office. She knew why she was there, guilt; age-old, primitive, damn forever, infantile guilt. And gratitude. All I done for you! How many times had she heard that as Rhoda's campaign intensified, each dart spreading its poison in Deena's sentimental underside. She'd known from the moment the subject had come up that she wouldn't be able to withstand the assault. Her mother had become too big, too important, too all-consuming; a whole universe of Ma enveloping her child. What would she feel if Rhoda had died on some hillside, falling flat on her pack, legs in the air like a helpless beetle with her new extendable walking sticks clattering to the ground, while her daughter was sitting in some warm coffee house in Toronto jawing with Samantha - who, by the way, had warned her in some detail of what was to come. 'You're going to get so pissed off you'll never want to talk to her again. So go. Maybe it's the only way you'll ever find what it takes to move out of her house.'

But there was another thing buried even deeper than guilt or gratitude, or even her romantic dreams. It was this stuff about

God and fate. Even Rhoda had targeted the mystical element, as she'd called it. 'There are things down there in the spirit, Deena, that are just swirling around waiting to come out, not that Edwina Matthews knows anything about it, but you just got to give them time to reveal themselves.' As usual Rhoda struck a nerve.

Deena had always had a kind of unsayable idea, that there was something ahead of her that she wasn't responsible for. Deena's destiny, she called it when it floated up just close enough to the surface to be felt if not seen. She didn't know what it was, what shape or colour, what it would entail, even whether it was good or bad, but it was there, that's for sure. And it had nothing to do with men either. One night (the seventh of Rhoda's campaign) she'd had a dream about a child, she didn't know whether it was a boy or a girl, but whichever it was, it had given her such a warm beautiful, kind of thank you, loving smile that it seemed like an omen, her destiny calling her. When she woke up she knew she was going to walk the Path. Rhoda had punched the air, given her a hug and then said, maybe she was changing her mind and wouldn't go anyway. Deena said, she could please herself. She was going on her own if need be. Rhoda booked the flights.

* * * *

Llewellyn came out of the shop with his newly purchased T shirt and staff. He went downhill, and had gone fifty yards before he realised the houses either side seemed familiar. He turned round and went back up. By the time he'd got to the pilgrims office, Charles, the volunteer who was on duty that day, had appeared.

"About damn time," said Rhoda.

Deena stifled the 'Ma' and smiled at Charles, then at everyone else before looking down at her pack.

Possibly Charles, who was around the same age as Rhoda, hadn't heard her, or maybe he considered it acceptable septuagenarian behaviour, or perhaps his English wasn't good enough to understand; whatever it was he ignored it and turned with a charming smile to Llewellyn standing in the doorway and said, "Bienvenue pelerin."

"Hullo," Llewellyn came awkwardly into the room and after some indecision sat between Peter and Ingrid.

"Bienvenue a vous tous," Charles smiled again. "Qui parle Francais?"

"Un peu," said Peter.

"Je suis Suisse," said Eva.

"What?" said Rhoda.

"Ah so I will speak English. I am sorry I am late." Charles nodded towards Rhoda.

So he did hear her, thought Deena without looking up.

"It's OK, I'll forgive you this time," Rhoda smirked, already charmed by this French guy with the twinkling eyes.

Oh no, she's flirting now, thought Deena.

"This is your Carnet de Pelerin," said Charles as he picked up a small folded card from the desk. "Or in Espana, the Credencial del Peregrino. You take this to albergues on the Camino and they put a stamp ici." He indicated the spaces in the booklet. "Remember no carnet, no albergue."

"What?" Rhoda hadn't got it.

"You got to have one of those to get into the Albergs," said Deena patiently.

"They the places that cost three bucks a night?"

"Yes."

"Well, get one, Deena, don't just sit there."

"I will, Ma," Deena looked up at Charles. "Sorry, sir."

Charles went on as though nothing had happened. "A Carnet est two euros. If you want to stay in the refuge tonight it is eight euros with breakfast."

"Eight? How many dollars is that?"

"Ma, can you wait, please?"

"OK, I'll leave it to you. I got my small purse here anyway. Don't worry."

Charles moved towards them and pointed to the maps on the wall. "Voici le Camino," He pointed to the diagram behind

Rhoda's head that showed a mountain with what seemed to be an almost vertical ascent. "This the first day. Very long, very high. One thousand, three hundred metres. You will see the birds under you."

"Birds? Under? He mean, below us?"

There was such panic in Rhoda's voice that Peter laughed out loud.

So did Charles. "Don't worry, Madame, many people do this and when you are in Roncesvalles the other side, you know you can go all the way to Santiago."

"If the mountain don't kill you first?'" Rhoda looked at the map with horror.

"Madame, you will go to Roncavalles, I am sure of it."

"If you say so, mister."

Charles went back and sat behind the desk. "Who is first?"

* * * *

Fifteen minutes later Rhoda and Deena were on the cobbles again and going further up the hill towards the refuge, having paid their eight euros. It was dark now and they were walking in a misty lamplight that for some reason reminded Deena of Christmas. Maybe it was the cool air.

"Well that wasn't so bad, was it honey? What a sweet old guy. I just hope when I get to his age I can be as absolutely charming as he was."

Deena didn't think it necessary to comment. "Well here it is."

They'd stopped outside the heavy wooden, black, studded door of an old and low, grey stone, terraced house. Deena knocked then pushed the door open.

"What he call it? A refuge? That make us, refugees?" Rhoda was happy again.

They went in and were greeted by the stony, unyielding face of Madame Phillippe, a short, squat woman with an almost exactly square face. She was dressed in black and standing behind a small bar. She spoke quickly in French.

"What?" Rhoda didn't know what was going on.

Deena shrugged and looked expectantly at Madame Phillippe who said, "Door close, ten. Matin, you go, eight."

"Did her lips move?"

"Ma, please."

"Well thank you, Madame," Rhoda creased her most grotesque smile. "You are most welcoming."

There were two tables rudimentarily laid for breakfast in front of the bar.

"Petit dejeuner ici." Madame Phillippe arched her eyebrows at the tables, and then said, "Chambre deux." She held up two fingers and pointed to the corridor.

"I guess that means number two, honey," Rhoda's good humour was evaporating fast. She picked up her pack, groaning as if to say where's the porter, and they went through the bar into a short corridor. Rhoda, no nonsense now, bumped the door open with her pack. The room was small and had once been painted pink. In it were three double bunk beds, two of them taken up, top and bottom, by four Koreans.

"Oh my God," Rhoda dropped the pack.

"Ma, please!" Deena pushed past Rhoda and stood in the middle of the room. "Hi, everybody, I'm Deena, and this is my mother, Rhoda." She gave her best smile.

The Koreans all grinned back. A cheerful young man with a black crewcut and cheeky air, was perched on a top bunk. "I am Chan-ja." He pointed to the woman on the bunk beneath him. "And this is Soon-ok."

"How you doing?" Rhoda still hadn't quite wiped the shock off her face. "Who are those?" She looked over at the other Koreans, an older man and another girl.

"I don't know," said Chan.

"Didn't you come together?"

"No, we only just met," Chan laughed. "Path very popular in Korea," he added helpfully.

"I bet it is," said Rhoda, inwardly cursing Edwina Matthews who'd let her in for all this. Was it a setup? She wouldn't put it past Edwina.

"OK, Ma, you take the bottom, I'll take the top, OK?" Deena was getting organised.

"You going to sleep now? It's not even eight o'clock?"

"We just unpack a little."

"Deena, we got to talk about his," said Rhoda in a low voice.

Deena looked around the other bunks. They'd all rolled out their sleeping bags. "Ma, open your pack and put your sleeping bag on the bed," she said through gritted teeth.

"I'm hungry. Aren't you hungry?"

"Get your bag out." Deena gave her mother a ferocious look and then smiled up at Chan who was watching it all happily. "We're not used to this kind of thing. We're from Canada."

Rhoda unfurled her sleeping bag. "I done it. What now?"

"OK, Ma, we go out and eat."

Rhoda picked up her pack.

"It's OK, we leave it here."

"You're kidding me." Rhoda looked round the room. They were all looking at her, apart from the old man who'd fallen asleep and was snoring quietly.

"It's OK, we look for bag," said Chan.

"Well that's very kind of you," said Rhoda still holding her pack. And then in a burst of international bonhomie, "Hey, you people eat?"

"Thank you. We go to the supermarket." Chan held up a tin.

"Tuna? Well that's nice."

Deena had had enough. "Come on, mother." She went to the door.

Rhoda followed as the old man began to snore more loudly.

"I hope he isn't going to do that all night," Rhoda tried to laugh. They went out into the corridor.

"Honey there are quite a few hotels in the town."

Deena ignored her and nodded to Ingrid and Eva as they came past them and went on into room four. They were pleased to find it empty. Eva took a bottom bunk, Ingrid the one above her.

* * * *

Peter had decided not to stay at the refuge. He wanted be alone to collect his thoughts and had seen a small hotel a few doors down from the pilgrim's office. He checked in, left his bag in the tiny room with a single bed and a shower built into the corner, and went back to the bar he'd been in before. He sat at a table, ordered a beer and decided to eat. He looked round at the well-used, dark, wooden furniture. It had obviously been a bar for a very long time; the walls, in some places rock, were extensions of the old town ramparts; where they'd been plastered they were nicotine stained and covered in faded posters for long-past local events. He could imagine soldiers congregating around the bar, laughing and singing, maybe in the second world war, including his own father perhaps. The thought caught him by surprise and he looked down at his hands, feeling for a second a powerful longing to see again an old man he'd largely ignored for the last years of his life.

The waitress brought him his drink and his first menu de pelerins. The guidebook had described these as an altruistic gesture to a shared faith, a contemporary extension of the age-old hospitality shown to the ancient pilgrim. She asked him to select one dish from the first five and another from the second; the dessert, bread and wine were all included in the fixed price, which was more than a medieval pilgrim earned in a lifetime. He sipped his beer trying to suppress his cynicism. He ordered a salad and what he knew would be a thin piece of beef and chips at tourist prices. How do you rid yourself of bile, he wondered as he pushed his knife around on the chipped table top? Push it down, let it go, pretend it isn't there? All of these he was perfectly capable of given a lifetime of English practice, but how do you not feel it in the first place? He sighed, then looked up. Ingrid and Eva had come in. They'd chatted briefly and inconsequentially in the pilgrim's office.

A problem for the well-mannered is that often they offer what they believe they should, but don't mean, and find to their dismay that it is accepted, not because it is wanted, but in order not to cause offence. And so it was with Peter. As courteous as the officer's mess expected, he smiled and indicated that the women were welcome to join him. They hadn't expected to see him anymore than he had them. Ingrid looked at Eva. This had already become the unconscious habit of their decision making. Ingrid would sense what Eva wanted and then act on it. This time she saw Eva smile which threw her. She hadn't wanted to eat with anyone else, she needed to get to know Eva better and cement what she'd begun. She said, "Thank you," and they sat down opposite Peter.

They introduced themselves. He passed them the menu and said, "Especially for Pilgrims." He stopped himself commenting and watched them as they read it. Eva was probably the better looking, he thought, but the more reserved of the two; there was something contained about her which was always compelling. But Ingrid was the attractive one. He could see she'd rather not be sitting with him, or maybe she was just being coy. She was contained too. Or at least the surface was; beneath it he sensed something neurotic, as if she wasn't quite sure of herself and offered a facade that seemed both invitation and rejection at the same time. He noticed that neither of them had handbags. He couldn't remember the last time he'd seen a woman out of the army without one.

Eva ordered and then translated for Ingrid. They didn't go for the menu de pelerin - wise probably, thought Peter - and both ordered salads.

"Shall we get a bottle?' he asked. "Toast the journey?"

Eva smiled again.

He noticed it was lighter, less of a strain than before.

"Why not?" said Ingrid. Then she took a mobile phone out of her pocket. "Excuse me." She began to text. "It's my daughter," she said. "I must tell her I have arrived."

Eva could see that Ingrid was showing her irritation at sharing a table with Peter by taking out the phone. She wasn't going to let it worry her. She looked out of the window at the half lit street.

She'd have preferred to have taken a short stroll and then slept, but was hungry and could see that Ingrid needed to be with her. Tomorrow she would walk - that's all she really wanted - and focus on nothing else. Ingrid had already told her that she went fast, a habit gained from cross-country skiing in the North where it was too cold to linger. She'd offered to go ahead each day and find them both a bed for the night. That suited Eva. She could walk alone with her thoughts and have some company for the evening. Ingrid wouldn't disturb her. She wasn't a questioner, she was a talker.

Peter ordered the wine and Ingrid put her phone away. He told them a story about his army life which made Ingrid laugh. She could see, had seen immediately on the platform at Bayonne if she wanted to admit it, that he was the kind of man she knew well. She tried not to laugh at him too much, not to engage, but years of habit were governing her responses. What else could she do? Be quiet? Sulk? She caught his eye for a fraction of a second. A look of recognition. She flicked her glance away.

Shit, Gemma's right, thought Peter, I do it all the time.

Ingrid's phone rang. She took it out of her pocket. It was a text. "She's gone to Ingmar!" She said it without thinking.

"Is that a problem?" asked Eva.

"No. I'm sorry. My daughter has gone to visit her father in Sweden," Ingrid explained to Peter, trying to smile. "It's not to worry about. I don't know." She looked down as she put her phone away. There was an uneasy silence.

"Children aren't always easy, are they?" said Peter.

"I have no children," said Eva.

"Ah well, you wait."

"I don't want children."

Something about the way she said it unnerved him. He shifted in his seat.

The food came. They spoke little as they ate. Eva was calm, Ingrid preoccupied. Peter not sure what to say.

Ingrid suddenly said, "She promised to me she would never see him!" There was the beginning of a tear in her eye.

Eva said, "That's why I don't want them. You never know what they do."

Or where they are, thought Peter, but kept his mouth shut.

"I must talk to her," Ingrid pushed her chair back, got up and went out onto the street to make the call.

"A problem?" asked Peter.

"I only met her a few hours ago."

"Ah."

Eva changed the subject. "I have heard the albergue in Roncesvalles is very big. The biggest one. It has two hundred beds."

"Well it won't bother me. Once you've been in a barracks."

"I've never slept with other people."

"Really?" he couldn't help the smile.

"I mean in a big room."

"Ah."

Eva looked down. He'd embarrassed her.

"Sorry, I didn't mean..."

"It doesn't matter." She sipped her wine.

Peter smiled, or tried to. Ingrid returned. She'd been crying. She sat down and Eva touched her shoulder. Nothing was said. The women finished their food. Peter offered to pay. They declined. Eva said she wanted to sleep and they left him to finish the wine.

He poured a glass, sat back in the now empty restaurant and opened his guidebook again. It described the ancient pilgrims as men and women, "...so secure in their devotion that they husbanded their resources for years to embark on the holy journey: a truly dangerous journey which cost many of them their lives if not everything they possessed. They walked hundreds of miles from every town and village in Europe to the place where the body of their Saint was encased beneath a monument to their faith far greater and grander than anything they'd ever seen or imagined, the Cathedral of Santiago de Compostella, where they could fall to their knees within a few feet of the remains of the man himself; James one of the original twelve, an actual apostle who had seen, heard and touched the living Christ."

He poured the last of the wine. The book went on, "This path has been beaten for a millennium, by foot, by horse, by the poor, the nobility, by Kings and Queens. They've crossed the plain, ascended the heights, cut their way through forests, been whipped by the wind, baked by the sun, and drenched by the rain; they've been robbed and beaten, but they've pushed on, never doubting their goal, themselves, or their purpose. And even now, a thousand years later there were still hundreds on the path every year...."

He sighed and closed the book. Thousands. Including him it seemed; ex-army officer, divorced, womaniser (let's not mess around anymore), the unsatisfactory (to say the least) father of a disappeared son, and confused unbeliever with no idea of what he was doing there. Well, yes he did know that. He too was going to be a pilgrim - whatever that meant.

* * * *

The first out of the refuge in the morning were the Koreans, Chan and Soon-ok. They stood on the cobbles drinking the last of their coffee out of paper cups and looked down the narrow street winding between the dark beamed, pink and grey plastered houses now bright and confident in the early morning sunlight. To walk beneath their windows was the beginning of the Path. They were both from Seoul but had only met the previous evening. He was a student and she, tall and very thin, an executive in the computer industry. They were laughing and excited. Soon-ok extended her new walking sticks for the first time. Chan had bought himself a pilgrim staff and tied a scallop shell to the top.

"Hey, Mission Impossible!" He wasn't as happy as he sounded. His legs were bowed (the long silver basketball shorts he wore made the problem look even worse) and he wasn't a great walker.

"What you guys talking about?" said Rhoda as she came out onto the narrow street. She'd decided she liked the Koreans after all, even if their language did sound like oral spaghetti. She liked them that is apart from the old guy snoring, he was clear enough alright, she'd nearly thrown something at him. But all in all she'd suffered the whole thing better than Deena had expected. She'd washed in the communal bathroom, foregone her morning shower, brushed her teeth and laughed with her mouth full of paste. "Watch out mountain, here comes Rhoda!" Everything was just fine until she saw the breakfast.

"What's that, bread and jam? Coffee no milk?"

Madame Phillippe stared unblinkingly.

"How about some eggs? Eggs?" Rhoda pushed her elbows in and out miming a chicken.

Madame Phillippe said with cold courtesy and an even icier smile, "Le petit dejeuner..." She slowly stretched her arm towards the table, '...est ici." She walked imperiously round the bar, put both hands flat on the top, straightened her back, sniffed and looked out of the window.

"Shit," said Rhoda.

"Merde," said Madame Phillippe.

"Damn French."

"Americain."

"Ma, will you cut it out?"

"Eight euros, Deena."

"And a bed for the night!"

"More like a hellhole."

"It was your idea to come over here." Deena sat down and poured herself a coffee.

"Hi, you guys!" Julia came into the room. She was Australian, very pretty, had thick, curly, light brown hair, a cute, bright smile, and had celebrated her twenty-second birthday just the day before. Deena thought that she reminded her of someone. Then she remembered the warm and beautiful smile that the kid in her dream had given her.

"I'm starving." Julia sat down at the table.

"Well you come to the wrong place. Come on Deena, we'll find a cafe." Rhoda stared at Madame Phillippe who was still standing immobile behind the bar. "Somewhere you get real food."

"Ma, I have a coffee, already."

"I'll wait outside. And talk to the Koreans. They make more sense.'" Rhoda stuck her chin in the air, "Good morning, Madam, I will not be back." She walked across the room dragging her pack behind her. "And you can tell me how to work these damn sticks, Deena." She left, leaving the door open.

"Sorry," said Deena.

"No worries," Julia laughed. "God! First day, hey! I'm so excited!"

"Can't wait," Deena said sourly. She was beginning to feel that she and Rhoda had made a very bad start.

"We all got mothers," Julia grinned.

What was more humiliating, dealing with Rhoda or having someone like Julia sympathise? Deena finished her coffee, said goodbye and left Julia eating a banana she'd taken out of her pack.

"Bon camino!"

It was the first time that Deena had heard the fraternal greeting. She repeated it to her mother outside.

"Bon camino, Ma. You taken your heart pills?"

* * * *

It was a quarter past eight when Llewellyn emerged. It was fifteen minutes after throwing out time and he wasn't expecting any breakfast. He was halfway across the bar when Madame Phillippe appeared. Llewellyn thought she was going to open the door to let him out.

"Sorry," he mumbled.

"Coffee," she said and pulled the bread basket and jam closer to him. Llewellyn looked at the food. He was dying for a cigarette, but thought it would be better to eat something for the old girl's sake if not his own. He was very hung over. He looked up at the sun in the window. Everything seemed a bit of a mystery to him since walking out of Cindy's. His pack was by his feet, he remembered buying that. His straw hat was on the table next to him, he'd bought that. He suddenly thought, 'Where did I change my money into euros?' He couldn't remember. He felt a surge in his stomach. Panic or joy? He didn't know. He eat the bread. Joy. He realised he was happy. Somehow through the fog of it all he'd arrived where he wanted to be.

He raised the bread. "Tres bon, Madame."

She wasn't there.

RONCESVALLES

By the time Llewellyn had left the refuge, Father Paul Kramer and Harry Hopper were ten kilometres ahead of him. They'd spent the night in the first albergue out of St Jean (it was the same place that Rhoda and Deena had stayed, but they'd made no connection), and were now going up the steep mountain road to the Pic D'Orisson. The first half of the climb had been through wooded valleys. Now they were at three thousand feet; the air was cool and sharp and the mountains spread around and beneath them were a bleak, dull, brown. Their peaks and ridges were massive and smooth, softly rising one after another into the distance, often with cloud between and below them. They looked absolutely immovable; like God's will, Paul thought.

He was a powerfully built man of average height and too many pounds. He had a round, battered face and short grey hair; an easy smile and an engaging laugh, neither of which could entirely hide the deep sadness etched into the lines around his eyes. He was breathless from the climb as he reached the shrine of the Vierge D'Orisson set back from the road on a rock outcrop overlooking a shallow valley. He'd promised himself and Our Lady a novena when he'd reached the shrine, but the truth was he needed a rest anyway. Sixty five is too damn old for hauling this paunch up mountains. He sat on his pack and looked up at the statue cemented into the pile of fallen rock. The Virgin was about four feet high, grey pitted stone. There were some dead flowers around her feet, and a few small pink living ones sprouting too. He didn't know the name of them. Her face was weathered down, with a chipped nose in profile against the panorama beyond. The valley at her feet sloped away with a few little white houses dotted around, and then, even smaller, tiny in the fall of the land, what could have been the wild ponies they'd been told about, but they were too distant to make out down there. Must be freezing here in winter, he thought. "Look at that," he said, gazing up at the statue.

"Are those vultures?" said Harry. "Down there. It's a protected habitat, you know that? I heard they drop dead sheep by helicopter for them to feed on."

"I was talking about the Virgin, Harry." Paul dropped his pack and felt the relief in his shoulders. "What are you going on about anyway? Dropping sheep by helicopter? I never heard so much crap."

"It's what I heard. Probably see a few kites and buzzards too." Harry wasn't offended. He was lean, tall and sixty. He knew who he was and took it as it came, and anyway Paul was a good friend of his.

"I'm going to pray a little," said the priest.

"OK, Paul."

"You?"

"What are they, Japanese?" Harry was looking down the hill and could see the Koreans coming up. They were still a long way down.

Paul turned and looked out at the deep folding curves of the range. They felt like they'd been there for all of time. A lot longer than the Virgin anyway.

"Long way from Missouri." Paul stretched his back wanting to uncramp the burn in his neck. He was a parish priest from Jefferson City and had managed to persuade his bishop to let him take this break for spiritual refreshment. Even as he'd said it he knew it was only half the truth. Fact is, he was worn out. Didn't know what hard work was until he'd got to be a priest, which he'd done late, gone into the seminary at fifty-two years old. Seemed right at that time, maybe still was. His wife had left him, the boys were at university, what in hell was he going to do anyway? Just sit there on his own? A lonely decomposure, some other

33

stranded old guy had called it. Then on top of it all someone had whispered in his ear the company was in trouble, there was the smell of closure in the air and he knew he'd be the first for the sympathy. He'd thought about going back to college, but how much education do you need? He had already had his masters in psychology and anyway the one thing that had kept him going through the mess of divorce and her damn unreasonableness wasn't anything intellectual, it was the church. He'd lost count of how many times he'd sat in there on his own in a pew up the back looking at the altar, praying for the strength to get through it all. Then it was done; she'd taken off down to Texas with another guy. Didn't want the house or the kids. God, that was some woman he'd married. And he didn't want another one. He'd waited a few years looking after the boys, trying to hold back the depression he knew was coming, then they went too. He'd celebrated his fiftieth birthday on his own. Not long after came the damn company rocking. He hated the job anyway. And so there he was back in that empty church again looking up at Christ on the cross trying to imagine how men could do that to a man. He kept going back, night after night, just sitting there, nowhere else to go. He'd offered Father Weizinski as much help as he could, read the gospels, bought the old guys into mass in his car. Weizinski had said, why don't you take a theology degree, become a deacon? No, it didn't have the bite he needed. So he sat there in the pew again, night after night, his hands clasped in his lap, feeling cold and about as useful as the dust on his shoe. Then he had an idea. Why didn't he just ask God? Ask Him what to do? Seemed simple enough. So he did. Please God, I'm asking you, what should I do? He got no answer. Just rows of empty pews and the sound of traffic on the road outside. He didn't give up. He went back and asked again. On the third night the answer came. Be a priest. It knocked him sideways. He almost ran out of the church. He asked again. Same answer, be a priest. On his way home he stopped the car, got out and took a walk. There was a wind blowing, some grit got in his eye. He sat back in the car and turned the radio on. There was a guy talking about a forthcoming city celebration. He turned the radio off. What in hell did he have to celebrate? 'Be a priest.' The voice was so loud he turned round to the back of the car and stared at the seat. He checked the radio. It was off. He looked out of the window at the storm brewing. "Oh my God," he said.

The boys were horrified. It was outside their range. They couldn't imagine having their Dad as a holy man. You wear those black skirt things? Even Dorothea called from Houston. Are you insane? But the worst was from his mother. She didn't speak to him for two years, even after he'd entered the seminary she put the phone down on him. And boy was that training tough. Three times he thought to leave, once even packed a bag. He was hopeless, thought his memory had gone, couldn't remember a damn thing. But he made it, took his vows and ended up back in Jefferson City where it all started. His mother came round, and even attended mass in his church until she died. He threw himself into it, births, marriages, deaths. He was popular; an older man, been around a little, right to the point, knew people, what they were going through. They came to him for advice. Made him feel good; at first.

'Don't you miss a woman, Dad?' his youngest asked him.

'Hell no, I've had more intimate conversations with women on that couch than you've had hotdogs. And sex? You can keep it. Look what came out of it.' He gave the boy a hug.

For a while, some years maybe, he was happy, then it got hard, sheer grind. He stopped seeing happy faces, grieving faces, worried faces, all he saw was need, and all he could think of was going back to a TV dinner and his bed. No-one gets it do they? All that stuff can wear you down. You try doing three funerals in a week. He knew himself well enough to see that old depression just round the corner. So finally when he went into the bishop's office it wasn't just spiritual refreshment he needed, it was a damn good holiday. Only problem was the one he'd chosen seemed to involve walking around fifteen miles a day.

He dropped to his knees at the foot of the statue. Maybe this was better than the back of that empty church, but he still needed to pray just as bad. He badly needed to hear that voice again. He clasped his hands and asked God what he needed to know.

At first the sound was low, barely whispered, as if unsure of itself. Slowly it rose, a woman's voice. He opened his eyes and looked up. He'd thought at first that the statue was singing to him. It wasn't. He turned round. Standing behind him were Harry, two Koreans and a very fat woman. She must have been well over two hundred pounds. She was singing Gounod's Ave Maria. Her voice, now loud, was as clear as a bell, echoing across the valleys and rising up into the cold air. He'd never heard anything so beautiful. The Koreans, a kid with a crewcut, and a young slim woman with black hair, shifting her feet, stood with their hands clasped looking up at the Virgin. Harry, looming over all of them, was smiling like hell. Paul's first thought was to sing with her, but what was his voice going to add to this? The woman's big round face was full of light and a kind of fervour Paul had forgotten, or if he was honest, had never truly known.

Two other women were coming up behind. One had blond hair pulled back tight from her face. She dropped to her knees behind the fat woman. The other, taller, with short bobbed hair, held back; she dropped her pack on the road and sat on it. Paul lowered his head and prayed until the song was over.

He heard Harry say, "God, that was something."

Paul raised his head and smiled, "Thank you."

He introduced himself. The woman bowed her head in acknowledgement when Harry told her Paul was a priest. Her name was Maria. She was Spanish and didn't speak much English. The Koreans wanted to shake his hand too. And so did the blond. She said her name was Eva Protin.

"Nice to meet you all." He turned to Maria, "And you, Ma'am. I'd love to hear you sing again. Would you all like a blessing?"

"Merci, Papa," Eva clasped her hands. The others followed suit.

"Glorious Lady, Mother of God, see us in our struggle. Help us focus all our strength on coming to your great servant, James, the apostle of our Lord in Santiago. May God bless you all, Amen."

They all crossed themselves. Maria reached down to take up her pack. Harry went to help her. It wasn't easy for her to bend her body she had so much fat on it.

"Don't you want a rest?" asked Paul.

Maria looked puzzled.

Harry said, "You want? Sit down?" He mimed it in his big clumsy way.

"No. Camino. Gracias." Maria moved slowly away using both sticks in a steady tap on the road. The Koreans said shy goodbyes and Eva went back to Ingrid waiting by the road.

Harry watched as Maria went slowly up the hill. "Goddam, look at that."

Maria's weight made Paul feel embarrassed about his own.

"Takes some guts," said Harry. "Five hundred miles carrying all that."

"Going to take her some time," said Paul.

* * * *

Three hours later Llewellyn arrived at the shrine. He was worn out already. They were right when they said the first day was the worst. He hoped so, he couldn't take much more of this. His feet were burning already. He sat on the short, dry grass around the rocks beneath the Virgin and rolled a cigarette. After a minute or two he saw coming up the road below was a man with a teenage boy trailing fifty metres behind him. They came level but didn't stop at the shrine. As the man passed, Llewellyn shouted out, "You seen the border? I'm looking for Spain."

The man laughed and replied with a German accent. "That way." He pointed up the hill ahead of them.

"It would be," said Llewellyn."

The man turned back to the boy and shouted, "Willi!" Then he moved briskly forward up the hill, his walking sticks clipping the tarmac. The boy with a brand new backpack and boots stomped sulkily after him as Llewellyn dragged on his roll up, enjoying the view. Ten minutes later, after his second cigarette, he stood up and looked at the statue as if for the first time. His right hand moved as if to cross himself, but then he thought better of it and picked up his pack instead. An hour later he crossed the cattle grid that marked the frontier with Spain. He looked at his guide. Now he was in Navarre. For some reason the thought cheered him up. He felt he was getting somewhere.

* * * *

Peter had found the climb difficult, but the descent into Roncavalles even more exhausting. It was four kilometres down a steep, rutted and narrow trail, covered in dead leaves as it wound beneath an autumnal canopy of red brown branches and dying foliage revealing flashes of a patchwork grey sky above the forest of beech. It was around three o'clock in the afternoon. He reckoned he'd come about fourteen miles since seven that morning, including an extended break for lunch at the albergue in Orisson and realised his strength was beginning to go as he frequently slipped on the wet mud. He wasn't as fit as he thought he was.

He'd struck out fast from St Jean, straight up the hill on the side of a wooded valley. Just about every house he passed carried the small yellow scallop, the sign of the Path; there was no chance of getting lost. He'd left early, before daybreak and wondered if he hadn't gone out in the dark ahead of everyone else, because he was unconsciously trying to get to Roncavalles before Ingrid, the cross country skier. He saw immediately that he was competing with her, which was exactly the kind of motive he didn't want. Years of reaching the objective and driving those in his charge, had become habit. If he couldn't do it, they wouldn't. And more to the point they'd see he couldn't do it, which was something, for some reason, he couldn't bear. The thought stopped him for the first time that day. He looked up at the dark fretwork of branches above him silhouetted against the light. Why would he feel so humiliated if he didn't get there first? The responsibility of the officer, sah, as Sergeant Clarkson had unnecessarily reminded him. You're fucking obliged to get there first aren't you? But I'm not a fucking officer now, am I, Clarkson? You'll always be one, sah. Well I'm very sorry but I want to look at the bloody scenery, enjoy the air for Christ's sake.

Before he could imagine Clarkson's reply Ingrid passed him, stepping quickly over the stones on the path as she wound her way down. Her feet were light. She didn't use sticks but had her hands tucked into her front pack straps as a man might have stuck his thumbs behind his braces.

"We heard a beautiful song," she shouted back over her shoulder as she skipped easily away from him. "At the shrine."

"What shrine?"

"Ask Eva."

"Save me a bed!"

"No need!"

And she'd gone. She was taller than he'd realised and her shape was good. He watched her red pack bobbing on her back as she rounded the next bend in the path ahead. Competition with Ingrid? He nearly laughed. She was leaving him flat. He went down a steep incline, slipped, stumbled, nearly fell. He had to save himself with an outstretched hand. He brushed the mud off his knee. At least he'd known enough to lengthen his sticks and tighten his boot laces to stop his toes bruising in the front of his boots on the descent. Had she done that? He bent and rubbed his legs. There wasn't much he could do about his knees. They'd always been a weakness and now they were hurting. Did her's? His pack was getting very heavy. He stood up and shifted its weight. What was that about a shrine?

* * * *

He remembered what Eva had said about the Roncesvalles albergue. It was huge. And Ingrid had been right about the beds. Once a pilgrim's hospital, it was a cavernous, stone built hall with great, stripped wooden beams arching twenty feet above. He sat on a chair by the entrance under a stuffed, unruly notice board and unlaced his boots. It was a relief to get them off. His feet were sore and his back ached. He looked down the empty, echoing space, trying to estimate how many black metal double bunkbeds there were. Lining the walls either side, end on to the stone, there was a row of between twenty and thirty, and running down the centre another two rows were pushed together of the same number. Eva had guessed it could sleep two hundred. Peter thought it was more. There were dim lights hanging in clusters from huge iron frames suspended by chains from the ceiling. The place had the smell of age and there were no windows, giving it the impression of being a centuries old church or barracks, or, and Peter didn't want to dwell on it, a concentration camp. It was ugly and uncomfortable, but later when it was full, it had a vital, even convivial feel to it. Extraordinary what human energy, chatter, laughter can do to even the most unwelcoming of places, he thought later as he lay on his bunk watching a hundred or so pilgrims of all nationalities and ages spilling the contents of their backs across the beds, spreading their rolls, hanging coloured jackets on the iron frames, stretching lightweight towels like flags wherever they could find a space, and speaking in any number of tongues; their heads bobbing up and down between the rows and ambling (hobbling, some of them) to the steps leading down to the showers; or others, like him lying flat on their bunks, their hot feet spread and finally rested.

He paid his six euros to the volunteer hospitalero behind the desk by the entrance and his credenciale was stamped with the first of the thirty-three brightly coloured and ornate official albergue crests it was to be decorated with daily on the Path. He walked with stockinged feet down through the rows of bunks carrying a pillow, his pack and sticks. He saw Ingrid sitting cross-legged on the top bed of a bunk at the end of the row on the right. She was looking down at her bare feet in a pose that was to become so familiar to him on the Path that after a while he didn't notice it. What else are you going to look at after a fifteen mile walk? She'd thrown her jacket on the bed below her, no doubt saving it for Eva.

Peter went to the last bunk on the far left. It was close enough to be friendly, but not too close. He waved to her across the two rows of bunks running down the centre of the room. She waved back, didn't smile, and looked down at her feet again. Peter being early had a choice as to the top or bottom bunk. As he realised later when his world had been entirely reduced to the demands and necessities of the Path, this was an important decision. The lower bunks were usually taken first to prevent the necessity of a climb to the top. On the other hand one of the advantages of the top bunk was the view. You could lie leisurely back and take in all the new arrivals and everything that was going on. But then again, the bottom bunk was cosier, darker and better for sleep; you were also in easier reach of your pack for anything you might need during the night. This was his first experience of the importance of these tiny decisions on the Path. Existence was little more than attention to such things, which he found curiously liberating. His life became everything and only what he carried in his pack: its contents and weight, its comfort; his choice of rainwear, how much water to carry and food to buy, whether to wear a fleece or pack it, and most of all the state of his feet and boots. Such details seemed to expand, comfort, and ultimately satisfy until they filled his entire conscious mind. He made his decision and sat on the bottom bunk. It also had the advantage of not being in direct view of Ingrid at the top on the other side of the room.

He pulled out his sleeping bag, spread it on the bed and lay back. He noticed that the other bunks in the centre of the room had been set together in pairs so that the beds on the top and bottom were jammed next to one another and you could end up sleeping within inches of an unknown neighbour. He wondered if any furtive sex ever happened in these places. A hand groping in the night, sliding quietly into a partner's sleeping bag, or even into the private space of a stranger who'd given the hint by a too accidental movement of a leg, or the lazy fall of a sleepy arm. He had no doubt that the thought would be somewhere at the back of most people's minds, but after a fifteen mile walk sex wasn't the first thing you'd think of. Anyway it was a pilgrimage, wouldn't the sacred displace the physical? No chance. The human animal, Peter. Clarkson again. He couldn't disagree. Sexual awareness, be it celebrated, ignored or repressed, was as fundamental as breath. No-one was immune, no monk or nun, no saint or pope. And as for the ordinary: these pilgrims. Was it possible that they could slip into bed next to each other and not for one second have the slightest sense of the carnal, or just the thought of the sense of it, or even the repression of the thought of...? Of course they couldn't, which meant anything could happen. He smiled to himself as he acknowledged the wisdom of Clarkson. Always the same twisted logic, my man. Always leading to the same place.

He fumbled in his bag for the book he'd bought with him. It was an extremely old (and short) history of philosophy. He'd had the idea that he'd use his spare time to catch up with his studious brother and stop all his damn nonsense about the rational mind, or at least be able to argue his own side with a sibling, in his opinion, more inclined to instinct than reason. He opened the bag and put his reading glasses on. It was too dark to read. Another disadvantage of the bottom bunk, he noted. He felt in his pack for the small torch he'd brought with him. He couldn't find it. Another drip in what was beginning to feel like an incessant flow of attention to detail. He reminded himself to give everything a home in the same place or pocket every day and he'd know where it was. After all that time in the military he thought he should have learned that by now, but there was something about this experience (including his impetuous decision to come to Spain in the first place), that was beginning to unravel what he would have previously considered the most ingrained habit. He discovered the torch in a side pouch of his pack and opened the book again. He didn't want to read; the torchlight seemed juvenile and reminded him of school. He also, to his amazement, felt too energised. How could that be after walking up and down a mountain for fifteen miles? He assumed it was the endorphins produced by the exercise increasing the dopamine in the brain which were making him feel good. It was why sportsmen half killed themselves training every day. At the end of it they were on a high. He put the book back into his pack, where despite one or two fruitless further efforts to read, it was to remain for the next month.

He sat up, and banged his head on the frame of the bed above. That wouldn't happen on the top bunk, would it? The place was filling. He noticed a group of Koreans take places in the same row as him but closer to the door. A boy in basketball shorts looked exhausted. What now? It was four thirty, he didn't want to read, his feet didn't feel like they needed examining, and was he actually going to write in the notebook he'd brought with him? He could see several pilgrims were already lying on their bunks putting their thoughts on the first day to paper. What was he going to write? Hard walk, great views, Ingrid overtook, missed shrine? He took his torch out again and read the guide on tomorrow's trek. He'd try not to miss any other landmarks, religious or otherwise. He read for five minutes. The next day wouldn't be as bad as today, flatter, not so far. He didn't want to read anymore. All this energy, sore feet and nothing to do. Why not talk to Ingrid? He got up to do so and saw Eva coming down the other aisle towards her. They greeted each other and he watched as Eva looked round the hall with a kind of shocked awe. She saw him, waved, and turned back to Ingrid. He thought he'd leave them to it, have a shower, a walk round the village, a lie down and then dinner. He fumbled in his back pack again looking for his towel. He couldn't find it. The interior of this bag has to be fundamentally replanned, he thought.

* * * *

Paul and Harry came down the hill into Roncesvalles at least four hours after Peter. It was nearly seven o'clock and dark already.

"Roncesvalles. Know it means valley of thorns?" said Harry. "It's where the Emperor Charlemagne got beat."

"He can't be as beat as I am." Paul was just too damned tired to talk about it. That walk had just about killed him.

"That the monastery? There's some cloisters here, any rate," said Harry as they came off the Path into a large car park. He looked up at the rough grey stone. "Wow, that's got to be a couple of hundred years old. Older."

"I don't care about the monastery, I got to sit down."

Harry could see Paul was suffering. Priest's got feet same as anyone else, he thought, ain't gonna damn fly. He was in better shape than Paul and a few years younger but he could feel it too. You get to the top of the mountain and you think it's over, just downhill all the way, but hell, if anything the last couple of miles had been the absolute worst; slipping and sliding everywhere. He knew Paul was having a bad time with it; he'd gone down twice, but had got straight back up and for his age, he'd done well, especially carrying that gut. Harry was leaner, made out of leather his mother had said; just more active he guessed, and Martha gave him better food, lot better anyhow than the junk Paul eat by himself in that priest's house. Never seemed to cook, just straight off the supermarket shelf into the microwave. No wonder he put the weight on. But Jeez compared to that Spanish woman, Maria, he was a spring chicken. Harry looked back, wondering if she might be behind them. They'd overtaken her fifteen minutes after the shrine. How in hell she was going to get over that mountain God alone knew. He looked up and did one of his short sharp prayers, "Oh Lord Almighty, give that brave woman a break will you?"

Harry was a stalwart of Paul's congregation. Retired now, time on his hands. He spent a lot of it down at the church helping out where he could. He also liked Paul, as a man as well as a priest, though in his opinion, he spent too much damn time thinking. Harry could see he was lonely. His intelligence had gone into himself which wasn't good. You'd think with a psychology masters he'd be able to work it all out. Maybe he could, but sometimes he'd look at Paul and see him sunk dead and reaching for the bottle of scotch. And he was broke which didn't help. Money doesn't buy you happiness, but seventy-five bucks a week ain't a helluva lot to take your mind off things. Harry had bought him an old Ford. He'd have bought something better only he knew it would have embarrassed him, so he got a couple of guys he knew to put a new engine and gearbox into a battered shell, new tyres on it, battery and all that. Paul never knew he had a virtually new car.

Not that all this was too difficult for Harry. Last time he looked he had around two point seven million dollars in cash and stocks to his name, plus his house fully paid for, the place on the lake, and a company pension. You'd think with all that he'd been some kind of speculator, money juggler, or entrepreneur, but as he liked to say, this is America, anyone can do it, all you got to do is work. And he had. He'd worked his way up from truck driver to vice-president of WMA (We Move Anything) one of the biggest trucking companies in the Midwest. And as he would be delighted to tell anyone who asked, he'd done it all by being honest. Nothing better, gets you everywhere. It had taken him forty years but by the time he'd retired they'd paid him in so many shares, the company had done well, and he was a millionaire twice over. He'd a good marriage, five girls, complained about every prospective spouse; in fact tested every one of them to the point where they'd have been happier to have murdered him than have him as a father-in-law, and then he'd put his arm round their shoulders and told them, OK buddy now you're a member of the family. He was a good man to have around, happy and successful and devout. He prayed to his Lord God about every half hour.

But like everybody else on the camino he had a question to ask. What do I do next with this life you've given me with, Lord? He'd been mulling this over when Paul had started talking about Spain. Paul said he was going to ask the bishop for the cash. Harry knew he had no hope with that old skinflint. So he beat Paul to it and got into the Bishop's office first. He cut a deal. He'd pay seventy-five percent of the money they were trying to raise to redecorate the Boys and Girls club and fifty percent of Paul's expenses if the bishop would give the priest the time off and not tell him where the money had come from. The bishop thought about it and thought about it some more, pushed the fifty for the expenses to seventy-five and agreed. He gave Paul a hard time, keeping him waiting for two months before giving him an answer, and then offered only half of his share of the expenses he'd agreed with Harry, which is how he'd scooped everything they needed for the Boys and Girls club. Harry didn't care. He knew he could supplement Paul's budget on the walk anyway - if he went with him.

He and Paul talked about it. Paul just wanted to get away, it seemed as if something was really bugging him. He'd heard about the Path from one of the parishioners whose brother had done it years ago. He'd also read the book by Shirley MacLaine, thought it was shit, but it didn't matter, it had given him enough of a kick to make him want to get out to Spain. It's a pilgrimage, he'd said, you're going somewhere. Didn't say where. He said he could have gone on a retreat, but sitting around with a lot of other priests wasn't his idea of a holiday, could be a damn penance. Harry thought the whole thing was a great idea, his confirmation name had been James, and asked Paul if he wouldn't mind if he tagged along. Paul had raised his glass and said, I was hoping you'd suggest it.

Of course Harry had his own motives. His answer to his own big question was another one. Should he start a charity? He had the drive, the business skills, but had to be clear in his mind that he was committed enough to carry it through. He knew Martha'd pick holes the hell out of the whole thing. She just wanted to sit up on the lake and have the grandkids round. He had too much get up and go for that, but he knew he'd have to be very careful and have the whole thing worked out before he even mentioned it. He was just a piece of glass as far as Martha was concerned, and one she'd occasionally shattered. But he managed to convince her to let him go, mainly through his concern for good old Paul. Martha was Catholic too and found it hard to argue against helping out a priest. So Harry was here, tall, grey cropped head, big voice, the good old boy. And the charity? Well that needed a lot of thought.

Paul slumped down in the albergue reception area. He'd taken one look at the bunkbed cavern and thought for a second that he was back in the navy. He was so tired he could hardly get his boots off. If Peter had received a boost from his endorphins, Paul had gotten the reverse, whatever that was. He was pooped. Total. His legs felt like lead, his back stiffer than a steel plate, his shoulders burnt, the back of his neck was one solid ache, and he didn't even want to think about the raw lumps of meat he once called feet - he had a brief image of one of Harry's sons-in-law using a mallet to tenderise a steak before a barbecue. And the whole damn lot of it was about to shake and shiver unless he could lie down. Harry grabbed a couple of pillows, stuffed them under his arm and carried both their bags down the left hand aisle between the bunks. There were no bottom bunks left.

"You're going to have to climb up, old buddy."

"Oh no, I can't, I really can't."

Harry looked round. He didn't have to look far. One of the Korean kids they'd met at the shrine jumped up.

"Please," said Chan, pointing to his bottom bunk.

Soon-ok had come off the one next to it and was offering that too.

"That is very kind of you," said Paul, in no position to refuse.

"No problem," said Chan.

Harry could see the kid had some problems of his own with his legs, but Soon-ok was already collecting her roll from her bunk and spreading it on the bunk above. The two Americans sat on the bottom bunks that had been pushed together. Paul lay back and closed his eyes, then opened them again. Chan was looking down on him.

"You OK, Father Paul?"

"I am son. Helluva hill." He closed his eyes again and slept for two hours.

* * * *

Eva was also sleeping. Ingrid had left her on her bunk and gone outside to look around the village. Roncesvalles was small, only a hundred inhabitants. Being the first stop in Spain on the Camino it was also the starting point for many Spanish pilgrims coming up from the South and Catalonia in the East, consequently it boasted a large hotel as well as the albergue. There was also the fourteenth century monastery and adjoining the cloisters was the Royal Collegiate Church of Santa Maria which had a bookshop and a small museum.

It had been dark when Ingrid had come out of the albergue. She'd joined the other pilgrims ambling around the grey stone buildings, and looking briefly into the church had seen the hunched backs of more of them kneeling for mass, and discreetly made her exit. She'd sat outside a bar with a glass of wine until the service was over and then gone back into the church to the bookshop and bought three postcards from which she would choose one to send to her daughter Siri, another to her mother, and the third she would keep. She was looking up at yet another statue of the Virgin and thinking it strange that such a whole culture and belief was so alien to her. She only knew, and that vaguely too, a hard and unforgiving Protestantism which existed on the edge of her life, (although it probably affected her more than she'd admit); but other than the occasional Christmas service, Christening, or burial she'd hardly been in a church, and certainly nothing as heavy as this. She didn't like it. She felt enclosed, claustrophobic, weighed down. It was like the air was too thick to breathe. And she didn't like these statues of this Virgin either. Why should an unavailable woman be so prized, put up on there a pedestal? What was wrong with women as they really were? And why were they all so stupid and forgiving about everything, or told you they were anyway? Didn't this Mother of Christ get angry sometime? Didn't she ever say what she thought? Ingrid didn't feel like worshipping anything so meek and so mild. She knew what it was like to be pregnant watching your belly and breasts bulge as something in you changed as the baby grew. She understood cradling the child, she knew what she'd felt about the newborn Siri, and the ache in the stomach reminded her of how much she missed

48

her now. All that was real. But a virgin birth, what did that mean? Mary never had a man? Why not? What was wrong with sex? Was a woman who had sex, who enjoyed sex, filthy and degraded? This was a man's idea of women and it made her angry, that somehow they could fuck you and then hold you up in contempt for being fucked. What were they talking about? She despised them, the men, and the women too, who accepted this shit. She'd had sex, a lot of it, and enjoyed it very much, thank you, and had a caesarean too, and that was reality; it was flesh and it was blood, a lot of it, and it was a mess, and painful; agony, if you wish to know Mary. And she'd been abandoned with the child also. You want to think about this. We don't all have faithful carpenters who don't want to fuck us and just fix things around the house. And why didn't he want to fuck you? What was wrong with you? What was wrong with him? This story don't work! She wanted to shout it. Don't tell me about ideals no woman can live to, or even want to live to. Tell me what's real!

"It's Our Lady of Roncesvalles. Fourteenth century," Peter was standing behind her with his guide book open.

"I know," said Ingrid. She didn't turn round. She'd already seen him in the church and knew he'd come to her. They always did.

"I missed the first one," said Peter. "I thought I'd better pay more attention."

"They're all the same."

"Don't you like it?"

"It doesn't matter." Ingrid was moving away.

"Did you know that once criminals were offered the Path as an alternative to jail?" Peter was reading from the guide again.

"Everybody is a criminal in some way."

"Are you alright?"

"I'm worried about my daughter. It's OK."

"Do you want to call her? I have a phone." Peter's hand went to his pocket, and then he remembered he'd left his mobile in his bag.

"I have a phone too. Everyone does." She sat in a pew and looked up at the altar.

"Ah? Do you mind?" Peter sat next to her and looked around. "You can't help admiring it, can you?"

"This place crush me."

"I don't feel much like being a tourist either."

"It's so dark."

"So your sins can't be seen," he smiled.

"So the priests can do what they want," she smirked.

"Did you see the hotel. I imagine it has a bar."

"I'm meeting Eva for dinner."

"We're all going to the same place, aren't we?

She looked at him. "Are we?"

"An aperitif?"

They went to the hotel which had an imposing three tiered facade of long ranks of windows looking out over the tiny village. They trod soft carpets and sat in deep and comfortable armchairs in the spacious bar. It was like the life they'd left, but they weren't far enough away from it yet to miss it. Ingrid told him briefly about Siri and how she'd tried to keep her away from her father who'd been abusive. Abusive it seemed not towards the daughter, but to Ingrid. As she sat opposite him like a child being hugged by the leather arms of the chair, sipping her campari and flicking her eyes to the door every time someone came in, Peter could easily imagine the frustration and confusion she'd created in the heart of the man she'd married. She'd show herself as vulnerable, indicate her needs and then decline all comfort, and at the same time intimate that if it wasn't offered again (and again) she'd feel doubly abandoned. Clarkson had described them as come-go women. She'd probably demand total commitment too, and then be incapable of any real engagement on her own part. He recognised that this perception probably belonged more to him than it was a fair reflection of her - even so he'd bet you ten pounds he was right, and also knew he probably wouldn't be strong enough to resist her. He asked her if she wanted another drink. She said no. They sat in silence for a while. He wondered what would happen next if they'd been sitting like this in a London hotel? He had the feeling he knew the answer to that. She thought that if they'd been sitting like this in a Copenhagen hotel, she'd make an excuse and leave - but then, why had she gone there in the first place?

On the way back to the restaurant they saw a small group of Italian actors outside the church of Santa Maria, entertaining a circle of pilgrims with their version of the story of Saint James. One of them, a tall, languid man, was very funny as he acted out several parts including that of the Saint himself. Another, smaller man, was obviously the clown. The story was narrated by a woman who seemed to be the dominant force in the group. They were all in their fifties. Playing for their supper, thought Peter. As they passed, the actors had taken an enormous man with a shaved head and huge face from the crowd to play the crucified Christ. They'd pushed him up against the stone wall of the church and the clown had produced a heavy hammer and six inch iron nails from his bag. Just for a moment it looked horribly real, but the enormous man had laughed his way through the whole thing and was himself very funny. Peter wondered if he'd been a stooge.

* * * *

They bought tickets for the meal in the albergue. It was served in a large, white-walled room adjoining a bar in another stone building over the road. In the room were ten round tables, each seating eight people. They were all empty. The pilgrims were made to wait outside until exactly eight o'clock when a stern-faced, middle-aged waitress opened the large double doors leading into the room. She seated them peremptorily, trying to fill the tables from one end of the room to the other in the order that the pilgrims entered.

Peter and Ingrid, with Eva who'd joined them in the queue, came in together and sat at an empty table. The waitress was about to order one of them to take a place still available at a previous table when Paul and Harry came in. Paul immediately recognised Eva from the shrine.

"Do you mind?" He and Harry sat down with them.

They were too old and heavy for the waitress to object and she showed the next pilgrim in, a Frenchman, to the vacant space she was so determined to fill. After him came the huge man with the shaved head who'd played Christ for the Italians. He had large and expressive hands which seemed quite independent of the rest of his body. But no stigmata, Peter smiled to himself. The force of the man's personality seemed to create an inviolable space around him. He stood towering over their table and picked up the menu.

"Ha! Menu peregrino!" He laughed and sat down, although the waitress had gestured him to another table. Whether he noticed her or not wasn't clear, either way he ignored her and Peter had the impression he'd sit exactly where he liked in any event.

Next in was a party of Koreans including Chan and Soon-ok. The waitress tried to direct two of them to the last places left at Peter's table, but they cheerily took no notice either and went to an empty table. The waitress was about to remonstrate when she was distracted by a group of Germans who also took their own table. She gave up and walked angrily towards the kitchens. The room was suddenly full of noise.

The huge man stood up, "Julia!" He waved to the young Australian who'd spoken to Deena and Rhoda in the refuge in St Jean.

"How you doing, Oskar?" she shouted back from the other end of the room.

"I am happy!" He sat down with a huge laugh and picked up one of the two opened bottles of wine that had been placed on the table. He began to pour for everybody without asking if they wanted any. Such was his energy and air of goodwill that no-one seemed to mind.

"I am Oskar from Munich," he said. "The food is crapola. Who is caring?" He looked round the table, his great mouth hanging open as if to guffaw. "But the vino tinto is everything. And crapola too!" He raised his glass. "Skol. And don't worry about the waiter! She is malfunction. You sir, what is your name?"

"Paul. You say you're from Germany?"

"Bavaria. I walk the mountains. No problem. My feet are big, but my hands are bigger!" He held them up, they were like huge flippers. "My mother said, you will build houses. I said, no, I prefer money!" He laughed again, then leaned forward and whispered theatrically, "And two places empty at our table. More wine for us!"

By this time, Ingrid and Eva were giggling, Peter smiling.

"Quite a guy," said Harry. He raised his glass, "Here's to ya."

"The Path!" Oskar roared. "And big feet!" He emptied his glass in one and filled it again. "Don't worry, we get more wine!" He continued unabated with his extraordinary energy and unique English as they all introduced themselves. To Peter he said, "Ah England. What downpour. You wet for us the whole Europe." He loved Switzerland too and asked Eva which she liked best, "Mountains, gnomes or cuckoo clocks? Or Orson Welles!"

A young waitress came over. Peter had the feeling that the older one, having decided that Oskar had the better of her, had delegated the table to the younger woman. Her fear was to prove well founded as the evening progressed. They all ordered from the pilgrim menu.

"Am I too late?" It was Llewellyn. He'd arrived in Roncesvalles a half an hour ago, which wasn't bad considering his fag breaks every twenty minutes. "I'm amazed I got here," he said, as he sat down.

"I guess. Irishman!" said Oskar.

"Wales."

"Wales? I know nothing. I will shut up. I am eating the air for everyone. I am in repose." Oskar sat back, mouth shut, looking comically relaxed.

"I'm starving," said Llewellyn.

They all were. Oskar was true to his word and remained in silence as they ate the first course. As he was to tell Peter later, he had studied chemistry in Frankfurt as a young man, but the only thing he'd built wasn't the house of his mother's prediction, or even the bank balance of his own (although he did both of these in time), but increasingly elaborate and intricate models of molecular structures. His big hands were surprisingly delicate and at first he enjoyed the almost mindless focus the work seemed to require, but slowly came to realise his own fascination for the ways in which the natural world fitted together; its unforced cohesion, and most of all how it developed and changed at its own pace and according to its own laws. He referred to these constructions as his hobby, but as he was working with the plastic balls, the tubes and the glue, he realised he was allowing his mind to focus on a far bigger and more interesting problem. This was how to see his fellow man and his society from a similar molecular viewpoint and how to encourage, without too much interference, an equivalent, natural process of development. It was a question, or at least a way of putting the question, which was to obsess him for the rest of his life.

He'd worked as a chemical engineer for a few years after university but wasn't happy or fulfilled. He needed a bigger map for his life and a bigger house too, although not one he had any intention of building himself. He took a second degree, this time in economics and inveigled himself into the finance department of AVIL, Germany's biggest pharmaceutical company. He was hugely (literally) popular and rapidly achieved promotion. Now at the age of forty-one, he was managing director with a seat on the board. His meteoric rise was due to his realisation that financial systems could be seen in the same way as he'd seen those chemical structures; given the right setting, culture, and what he called ambience, they'd grow organically. He'd also understood a very simple fact: that money was people; that the financial structure was only a frame for the molecular composition of the workers themselves; that the production system had to incorporate their desires and creativity, and even further that the success of their productivity depended absolutely on the understanding that the man was the product itself and therefore was the financial system.

There were no real distinctions between them, the one grew from the other and they fitted into each other in exactly the same way as the most complex chemical formations evolved within and without each other.

Such an extreme holistic approach was as difficult to sell as it was to achieve, so he'd started with very simple propositions. At first he'd merely tied productivity to financial incentives, encouraged, by slow but sure reorganisation, a greater degree of inter-reaction between the workers and management, and had strongly emphasised the value (and profitability) of commitment to both groups. Although unspoken, he gradually developed his idea that the worker was indeed the product and vice versa. He made it clear to the research chemists that their targets weren't to discover the solutions to the technical problems confronting them, but to achieve the maximum potential within themselves. He made the managers understand that the technicians, whose output they were responsible for, were capable of far more if allowed to integrate themselves, not only with the product, but in the development of the system by which they produced it. On the factory floor the simplest line workers were encouraged to innovate. He gave them a better, freer atmosphere to work in, and more responsibility. He made clear to anyone who'd listen that production depended on creativity and that there was no-one of whatever experience, training, education or intellect who wasn't able to innovate to some degree. What was the point, he asked, in having only one true creator if you could have ten, hundreds, if not thousands? In his dreams he would ask, why not the whole world?

None of this, of course, happened overnight. It took him fifteen years. At first he'd followed the money; the financial tentacles of any company are the weft and weave of its structure, they reach everywhere, bind it, and influence, then decide its direction. Follow them and you will discover the bright lights of creation (happiness) and the dark corners of stasis (depression). For Oskar these things weren't matters of high-flown theory, or new-age psychology, or prayers to the Sun God at dawn, they were intensely practical problems each with their own deep and unusual solution. Just knots that's all, he said, knots that needed to be untied; knots that had sometimes been pulled so tight that they'd become almost invisible in the rope that held all things together. Oskar followed that rope everywhere, crawling along it, inch by inch. Some of these knots had been tied a hundred years before in the minds of those who'd invented the basis of the process. He realised that these represented deep attitudes that needed to be dissolved, and applied an extraordinary invention, a joyous persuasiveness, and a frightening tenacity to re-imagine them.

He told the board, that mind and body rested on the spirit and that the combination of all of them was creativity, and creativity was production, and production was money. They had initially been uncomprehending, then mocking, and he was subjected to a fair amount of outright hostility. Spirit, what's that go to do with business? They'd wanted to know. Oskar had raised his big hands and then curled his long fingers as if he was grasping at heaven and pulling it down, "I don't know!" And he'd laughed his huge laugh. And then the chairman had laughed, and then the vice-chairman, and a sense of an unknown, indiscernible merriment had spread around the boardroom table. Oskar knew something and they knew he knew it. And whatever it was, it was reflected in steadily growing margins and increased production.

He was unstoppable. His huge personality infected the factory. He certainly wasn't a fool. He didn't just pat people on the back and ask them to do better. He made suggestions every day, not only to directly improve the process, but also to subtly shift the attitudes that underlay it; to point to a place where a manager, a scientist, a researcher, a technician, even a packager or driver could shine a light on his or her own possibility, and once they'd achieved it they found lying in wait one of Oskar's brilliant financial incentives to go even further. Not only were they happier, they were richer! He ceaselessly worked along the line, from worker to creativity to productivity to profit, and then back again, and every year the company's shares rose in value.

What had been a small firm in the nineties with hardly more than two hundred workers and management was now a huge and thriving international concern, registered on the stock exchange and employing over twelve thousand men and women. It was serious. And so was Oskar. Very. No-one doubted he was the next chairman, "Except maybe me!" He'd said to Peter and laughed his huge laugh.

"So what are you doing on the Path, Oskar?" asked Harry finishing his roast chicken.

"Walk!" Oskar let his huge mouth hang open again revealing the last of his pork. "One feet, another feet. Mountain beautiful. Air good." He tapped his head, "Here all get empty! And people!" He gestured to the table. "What else?"

Llewellyn sat back. He'd needed to eat like he'd never had before. Fifteen bloody miles up a bloody hill, then down. He'd never felt such a sense of satisfaction either. And now he needed a smoke. He looked around, half hoping he'd see someone else with a cigarette. He noticed the man with the boy he'd seen on the camino earlier. They were sitting at a table with a group of other Germans. The man was thin and wiry with quite magnetic green eyes. The boy was still stuffing his face; someone must have given him a second helping. His left arm lay protectively around his plate as if guarding it from some imaginary thief. His other hand was holding the fork and shovelling the food into his mouth before the theft could happen. There was something animal about him. He was tubby, didn't look starved, just a greedy bugger, thought Llewellyn, and his father doesn't seem to mind either. He was looking at the boy as if he was some kind of foreign object. The kid was responding with what he imagined was a look of grown-up bemusement.

Llewellyn decided to go out for a cigarette. He was getting up as Maria came in. She stood just inside the door slowly shifting her weight from one foot to the other. Everything about her signalled complete exhaustion. She sagged against the door frame, hardly having the strength to hold her head up, and looked as if she was about to collapse.

Harry got up quickly, "Hey, Maria, come and sit down." He pulled out the remaining chair at the table.

Maria smiled weakly. Tears weren't far away.

Harry helped her to the chair and she sat heavily. "Have some wine." He poured a glass, "You look like you need it." He looked around, "Hey Miss." The young waitress came over. "What do you want, Maria?" He put the menu in front of her.

"No," said the waitress.

"What do you mean, no? She just walked from Saint Jean," said Harry. "She's been going for fifteen hours!"

The waitress shrugged, "Demasiado tarde para comer."

"What?"

"Late," said the waitress. She turned away.

"What do you mean, late? You got to have something?" This was the kind of behaviour that really got Harry's goat.

The older waitress came over, pleased to have an opportunity to unequivocally express her authority. "La cocina está cerrada," she said with a triumphal air.

"I don't think so." Oskar leaned forward, put his hands flat on the table and pushed himself up. He towered over both waitresses. "Give this good pilgrim bread and pasta. And meat."

The older woman stood her ground. "Cocina cerrada. Closed."

Oskar raised his hands then lowered them, palms down, as if he was pushing down an imaginary cloud. "You mean go in cocina and there is nada?" He looked at the woman for a second and laughed.

"No hay comida," the woman turned to walk away.

"No food? I look,' said Oskar. He walked after her.

"No. No in cocina." She stopped barring Oskar's way.

"Senora, if there no food, why don't I look?" He lowered his face towards hers.

"No hay nadie en la cocina."

"So I look myself."

"No." The woman was beginning to feel nervous. She looked round, everyone was looking at her and Oskar, and there was no doubt where their sympathies lay.

"I cook for her," said Oskar.

"No."

"I am very good cooking." He raised his hands, his big face loomed above her.

The woman was now distinctly uneasy. "Por Favor," she turned to walk away again.

"Wait. One moment please." The woman stopped. "Why don't everybody cook? Warum nicht?" He spread his arms and shrugged as he looked around the room. "We very good cooking. I cook water. Everyone take one pasta and put it in! Simple!" The Germans laughed, so did the Koreans although they weren't entirely sure why. Oskar wasn't going to leave it there. He pointed at the Germans, "Die Deutschen müssen das Fleisch kochen." He winked at Harry and whispered, "Germans do the meat." He laughed and then waved his hands at his own table. "Stand up. Wir gehen in la cocina!"

"I'm with you there, my friend," Harry stood up.

Llewellyn was pleased he hadn't left. "I'll help." He stood.

Maria sat at the table looking down. She was beginning to cry.

The father to the boy stood at the German table, "Ich mache einen fantastische bolognese!"

"You see?" said Oskar.

Chan stood up, "You want tuna?"

"Mit ensalada!" Oskar laughed and then turned very seriously to the woman. "Senora, I understand. I like you mucho." Peter thought for a second he was going to kiss her hand. "For you es dificil." He nodded his head in full acknowledgement of the problem. "Por favor, I ask you." He paused with a hang dog look, then smiled. "Or we all vamos to la cocina!" He looked down at Maria, who still sat head bowed.

The woman looked around. Many were by now standing. Their eyes were on her. No-one said anything. After a second she said, "I look," and walked quickly back to the kitchen.

Oskar began to clap, Harry joined, then Llewellyn. By the time she got to the kitchen the whole room was applauding her. As she got to the door she turned and smiled for the first time that night.

* * * *

They got back to the albergue just before the ten o'clock curfew. The waitress had excelled herself. She'd obviously seen Maria's weight and had brought enough food for her to regain whatever carbohydrates she'd lost on that day's walk; a huge bowl of pasta, roast chicken and roast pork, a piled plate of potatoes, all after a sopa verdura, and followed by crème caramel and icecream. Maria ate all of it plus a large basket of bread. The waitress also treated Oskar and the table to two extra bottles of wine. Paul got up and shook her hand which moved her almost to tears, although she declined Oskar's invitation to sit and join them. She preferred to stand and watch as Maria cleaned the plates and the others emptied the bottles. She even ignored Llewellyn's sneaky roll-up at the table.

Ingrid lay on her top bunk and stared up at the beams above. She'd enjoyed her evening, her first real pilgrim's dinner. Oskar had fascinated her. He wasn't a good looking man, his face was bigger than any she'd seen, his body was powerful but too big, and where did he get those hands? But it was his energy. He seemed to have a life force that had no boundaries, and there were no inhibitions. His performance had been ridiculous. He played the fool with pantomime English, but underneath was a sincerity which frightened her for some reason. She wondered if he was married. She couldn't imagine what he'd be like in bed. It would be like sleeping with a giant octopus. She smiled at the thought and closed her eyes.

Beneath her, Eva prayed. She'd dismissed Oskar as un bouffon. The charade could have been embarrassing, and Maria humiliated. She heard Oskar laughing again somewhere down at the other end of the room. The lights went out. They'd been given fifteen minutes after the ten o'clock shut-in to wash and get into their beds. Quite a few hadn't made it and were still stumbling to their bunks in the emergency half light. Soon it was quietened. Nearly two hundred people lying side by side turning slowly to sleep on the iron bunks under the high vaulted brick

60

ceiling. Eva continued to pray. First for Ingrid, that she would find whatever it was she was looking for, and then for Peter that he would do the same, although she hoped it wasn't Ingrid. She thanked God for seeing her through the walk that day. She knew He'd been with her and knew He would be from now on. She was as tired as she'd ever been, but the exercise had cleared her head and the ache had gone. She drifted into sleep and dreamt of the shrine at Orisson, except now it was her singing and not Maria, but she kept forgetting the words, and then she was falling down the mountainside to the valley below. She found herself in a bare room in a small white farmhouse where she sat alone feeling perfectly content except her feet hurt.

Peter fell asleep quickly. He'd wondered what he'd have done for Maria if Oskar hadn't been there. Probably nothing. He'd have accepted the rules of the house. (As he always did? What stopped him breaking them? And why was he suddenly asking all these questions?) On the other hand he might, just might, yes, he probably would have, taken her up to the hotel and bought her dinner. Even if he hadn't done it, he would have felt he ought to.

* * * *

Deena and Rhoda Dunne hadn't made it to Roncesvalles. At first Rhoda had been all for trying but Deena had been reluctant to push her mother too hard on the first day. She suffered from arrhythmia and although she took pills by the handful, Deena couldn't even think about the day when the occasional comma in her mother's heartbeat became a full stop. The idea of suddenly being alone without her mother terrified her, even if she had to admit, it was a time she secretly longed for. And Rhoda's behaviour that morning hadn't changed anything. She hadn't liked the private albergue they'd stayed in and hadn't wanted to stop there in the first place.

"It's only eight kilos out of St Jean!"

"Kilometres, Ma. A kilo is a kilogram."

"What's the difference?"

And so it had gone on all night. She'd complained about the snoring even though Deena hadn't noticed any. (They'd been in a six bunk room for women only.)

"And you can't say it was cheap, Deena. Thirty-five euros isn't cheap."

"It included dinner." Deena had poured herself a coffee and sat at a bar table looking out at the mist on the mountains and how it kind of sunk down into the valleys around them. Soon they' d be above cloud level.

Rhoda hadn't finished, "And they made you introduce yourself all round. God I haven't done that since I was at those night classes for interior decor."

"Ma, you talked for about ten minutes. You were only supposed to say your name and where you came from."

"They ask, they get. And what's wrong with my life? Don't you want to hear it?"

"I live it."

"Don't take that tone. And what about those showers? Only give you five minutes hot water, I hardly got the shampoo on."

Although she wasn't going to admit it, Deena had to agree with what her mother was saying, the place was a rip-off. She stood up. "Get some breakfast, Ma." She took her coffee outside.

Rhoda followed. "I won't be coming back here, that's for sure."

So far every albergue, both of them, that Rhoda had stayed in, would not benefit from her patronage again, but as Deena mentioned, they were on a journey to Santiago, they weren't likely to backtrack.

"And they know it too, don't they?" Rhoda said.

"Ma, are you going to be like this all the...?"

"We'll get something to eat on the road."

"There isn't anywhere for ten miles."

"How many kilograms is that?"

Deena wanted to scream.

"Aren't those mountains just beautiful? How about we take a taxi?"

"We've only just started!"

"Didn't you say there was some company that would take your pack on for you?"

Deena had to admit she was more than a little relieved. She went back into the bar, apologised to the owner for not eating his breakfast, and got a couple of numbers for taxi firms. Maybe they'd jump a couple of stages. Get it over with quicker.

So Rhoda never saw Roncesvalles and the biggest albergue on the camino. She missed the six o'clock lights up and didn't hear the recording of Gregorian chants played through crackling speakers to wake everybody up. She also missed the woman laughing hysterically in the middle of the night because her husband had fallen off the top bunk, and didn't giggle at the snore stopper, an elderly German, who went around poking anyone who dared. The others missed none of this and some of them laughed about it as they queued outside the washrooms to soak themselves in plentiful hot water.

ZUBIRI

The next day was shorter and initially much easier. The first part was gently downhill into the valley of the Rio Urrobi, then it was up and down on a narrow but shaded woodland trail until the final and more difficult descent into Zubiri. After the tough climb and descent of the previous day it was a relief.

Peter got out of the Roncesvalles albergue early. He'd intended to repack his rucksack but the recorded choral accompaniment to his getting up drove him out more quickly than he'd intended. If there was one thing he didn't need in the morning it was a religious broadcast. A bugle was bad enough.

It was still dark when he'd started walking and he was soon on a dark path through a wood. He stumbled on a root and located his torch quickly. He'd decided to keep it in a pocket in his fleece and there it would stay; it had found its place - one detail secured. In the light of its beam he saw a large, dark figure walking ahead of him. His first thought was that it was Oskar and he nearly called out, but then he could see he wasn't tall or bulky enough. Then he realised it was a Pole who he'd seen walking around the albergue the night before dressed only in a T shirt and bright white, obviously new, Y-front underpants. At first Peter had thought he was gay and then that it was just some kind of macho display of his admittedly powerful physique, but once Llewellyn had told him he was from Poland, he realised that he'd misjudged him. Everybody had strolled about in their underwear, it was that kind of easy atmosphere - and anyway how were you going to fit a pair of pyjamas and a robe into a tightly packed bag - and where would you change, in a toilet cubicle? A Swedish woman who must have been in her late sixties had bent over in front of him wearing only a shirt and a pair of well-fitted black knickers. She was unconcerned about any impression she might have been giving and had no compunction to do anything other than what she did - she was merely fishing something out of her pack and didn't give a damn what anyone else thought.

Probably one of the most self-conscious in there was himself. At first he thought it was because of the presence of so many women - it certainly wasn't the men, he'd spent months in barracks with hundreds of them. He started to think that the root of his embarrassment could well be the fact that he was on the Path at all, and although before he came he'd been fairly dismissive of the whole project as not much more than a long walk, he was beginning to understand that the physical challenge was the least of it. His problem was, and was going to be attitude; his attitude to himself, to what he'd been, and to how he'd be changed by his involvement in the lives and opinions of those around him - and indeed to how much he'd allow himself to be involved. Somehow the size of the Roncesvalles albergue, its number of pilgrims, and the sheer irrepressible vivacity of the place once it had filled, had thrown him. He was surprised to discover that it had made him a little nervous, which was unusual for him - he'd always prided himself on a carapace at least, of certainty and confidence. Maybe it was as simple as the fact that it was a world strange to him, one where he couldn't predict reaction or response which left him in doubt as to his own behaviour.

He finally made himself walk down to the washroom in a pair of undershorts. As he did so the thought occurred to him that it wasn't only his clothes that were coming off, a few of those old conclusions were being checked in too, and how easily shed they were. The camino in common with the army was a great equaliser. He realised as he walked through the wood the next day that the judgement he'd made on the big Pole in front of him was probably made on the basis of all sorts of assumptions that he'd been led to accept for years but never really believed anyway. The man disappeared into the trees and the darkness ahead. As he came into Burguette he thought he'd stop for a coffee and some breakfast.

* * * *

Paul and Harry walked on in silence, often side by side, the priest placing his sticks rhythmically on the track in front of him, right stick, left foot, left stick, right foot, it was hypnotic. Harry carried his sticks most of the time in his right hand. They were slow but steady walkers.

"Hey, isn't that beech?" said Harry.

"I guess so," Paul walked on only stopping briefly at another small plaque to the Virgin and Child at Alto de Mezquiriz. He crossed himself, said a short prayer and continued. It was downhill again for a while and rough. His trainers squidged in the mud and wet leaves. Harry followed, keeping one eye on the priest and the other up at the golden panoply of the trees above them. They dripped raindrops on them as they walked. Harry kind of liked the freshness of it, reminded him of his place by the lake back home.

Paul was thinking about Oskar. He admired what he'd done for Maria, but couldn't work out where Oskar's heart was. Everything seemed so out front it was hard to see where the man was coming from. The woman was in desperate need of food, that much was obvious. Was Oskar's show, and he couldn't help but think of it in that way, a Christian act; what the pilgrimage was for, or was it just grandstanding? If nothing else it had thrown into light Paul's own reaction. What had he done for Maria? Just sat there. He was a priest for God's sake, he had some standing amongst these people. What was we he going to do, say a mass the next day, or what? What in hell was being a priest anyway? Sure, all the obvious, he led the worship, gave comfort. But what did that mean? Sitting next to a widow on her couch, holding her hand, after her often unloved husband had passed, and pretending it was just spiritual support he was offering? Not that he had in mind even the vestige of anything else, but he couldn't deny he

66

enjoyed the emotional intimacy of it, and the power of it too. They looked up to him, accepted his word, but why should he know anymore about it than anyone else? They thought he had a direct line into these things and trusted him when he spoke about them. In addition he was unavailable as a man, which made it all the more intriguing.

And he prayed, sure he prayed, God he prayed, he prayed for them, he prayed for the dead, the dying, the newborn, the old, the sick and the just plain unhappy. He prayed for himself, for Harry, even for the bishop, who if anybody didn't need it, he didn't. How many prayers could you pray? And anyway what was going on when he prayed? Was it just some self comfort? Was he just pretending and only really talking to himself, or was it all some trick of the mind, like hearing that voice in his car that night the storm blew? His congregation didn't think so. They got what they wanted. Just like Maria did from Oskar.

* * * *

Llewellyn arrived in Burguette at least an hour after they'd passed through it. It wasn't much of a place, quiet and dead that time of the morning and strung out along the main road. He stopped for his first coffee and fag break outside the hotel bearing the name of the village. Apparently Earnest Hemingway had stayed there and signed the piano. Llewellyn had heard of signing photographs, programmes and even plaster casts, but a piano, that was a bit grand, wasn't it? He'd read half of For Whom the Bell Tolls once and asked Robert what the ending was. Robert had said, it tolls for thee, and Llewellyn had talked about something else. Literature wasn't exactly his line anyway.

His greatest worry on the Path had been getting lost. He'd imagined himself wandering around Northern Spain asking the way in his approximation of the language, but the Path was obvious, and when it wasn't there were these little yellow arrows pointing the way everywhere. And as he was to discover there were plenty of albergues too, just about every town, or even village had one. You could stop anywhere, meet new people, the next day overtake ones you'd met before, stop, start, go again, stay wherever you liked. It made him feel happy. He was free but looked after, a kind of Llewellyn heaven. It was like being at art school again, go where you want, do what you like, and there was always a bed at the end of the day. In his younger days that had been a matter of a simple faith, but now it was good organisation he supposed, or making money out of pilgrims? This was a question he spent a lot of time on as he walked. He and Robert - the economically challenged as Cindy called them - often expressed a high degree of concern and anger, as the dead broke often do, about the commercial world that frequently threatened to envelope them. In fact, as Cindy could clearly see, it entirely ignored them, which didn't prevent Llewellyn examining the question whenever he had the chance. Like now. Should he go into the Hotel Burguette for breakfast or would they overcharge him? He had a brief imaginary conversation with Robert. Robert was dubious. Llewellyn looked up at the place and thought he'd leave it to Hemingway and buy some bread in a supermercado.

Before he moved on he wondered about getting his sketch book out. He looked up at the hotel. It was white and some stone, had walls, a roof, an old door, been painted up recently, nothing that inspired him. At the back of his mind there'd been the idea that he'd sketch the camino as he walked it. Was that why he'd come, or was it just an excuse to stop painting in Swansea? Along with his questions about Hemingway, and the commercial or altruistic purpose of the Path, it was just another unresolved problem in his mind. Was he a painter or not? Funnily enough he felt he was just starting to get good when he left. Maybe that's why he left. If, as an artist, he was getting to where he wanted to be, he might not like it when he arrived, or he might just about get there and not arrive, or he might take a wrong turning and miss his way altogether. All a bit like the Path really. He stubbed his cigarette out and heaved his pack up. He adjusted his straw hat - he was very pleased he'd bought it, it made him feel like Van

Gogh - and went on his way, turning right where the yellow arrow told him to.

* * * *

Around ten o'clock Ingrid passed Peter. She saw him ahead with his straight back and regular stride and decided she'd include him in her plans for the day. She didn't know why she did this, in the same way as she didn't know why she did many things, especially in regard to men, although not only them. She behaved in the same way with her mother for example. Her invitations were meant but unconsidered and often unconsciously indicated the possibility of a relationship, long or short, casual or not, that she inevitably didn't want. She had no doubt that, whether she meant to or not, she definitely began these things, although her offer was usually so oblique that she could easily deny it. It was just something she did, that's all.

"Here's your water. You left it in the albergue," she said as she handed Peter the bottle. "Eva and me, we are staying at a privado in Zubiri, I'll check you a place." She didn't wait for an answer and walked on, her fast pace made to look merely jaunty with her hands tucked into her straps.

The rhythm of her walk was the speed of her thought and she rapidly decided she didn't want to dwell on reasons for being good to Peter, or even her reasons for being on the Path in the first place, which was something else that was going to have to surface sooner or later. She wanted to think about Siri. She was going to call her and wanted to work out what to say. She was slowly working her way through her feelings at her daughter going to stay with her father behind her back. She'd kept her away from him for years, so when he'd gone north to Malmo she thought she'd never see him again, and hoped Siri would forget him like she wanted her to. The anger began to rise again. And now Siri was with him, now, this second. They were probably having breakfast together as she walked. Maybe she wasn't clear why she was on the Path but something for sure, she hadn't come all the way to Spain, to see the life she organised so well fall to pieces behind her. Everything was correct and in its place. She'd left food, money, how to do everything, and if anything went wrong, all the phone numbers Siri needed. The girl was nearly twenty, what could happen? Couldn't a mother have some time of her own? She walked faster as her anger grew and filled her. As soon as her back was turned! Siri must have planned it, called him made the arrangement while she was still at home organising all the things her daughter needed when she was away. She walked even faster. Siri must have called him while she was out buying food! Food that Siri never intended to eat! She'd check the phone when she got back. She'd find out. The more she thought about it, the worse it was. She'd done everything to keep him out. Now that bastard had come back to her life! How had he done it? Written to Siri? He'd tried it before and she'd burnt the letters. Maybe he'd written to Siri at the university? The thought stopped her. Maybe he'd been writing to her for years? Maybe Siri had even been seeing him, meeting him in Stockholm, even Copenhagen! She felt sick. She couldn't believe it. Her own daughter. Didn't she know what kind of man he was? How many times had she told her? He was violent, he had anger running through his blood! You couldn't trust him to take the dog for a walk without him going for other women. Siri, I told you about that secretary at the print shop! There was the other one at the school. Don't you understand what he is?

She heard laughter ahead of her. She was on the side of a wooded valley and could see a river running below her. There was an old bridge over it and two Korean girls were sitting on the parapet eating pears. She wondered if they'd seen her talking to herself. If she was going to go crazy like this, the least she could do was keep it to herself. She smiled and nodded as she passed the girls. Something about them calmed her. She stopped on the other side of the bridge and looked it up in her guide. It was the Puente de la Rabia, built in the eleventh century. Apparently the remains of Santa Quiteria lay under the central pillar rising from the middle of the river, and if you led your dog three times round

70

it you would cure the animal of rabies. It seemed to her that you'd also drown it. She giggled and walked quickly away. OK, she would call Siri and tell her to be careful, that's all. What else could she do? Nothing. So if you can't do anything, don't do it. It was Siri's life and she could do what she liked with it. As far as she was concerned Siri was on her own. And so was she.

* * * *

Eva was at least an hour behind Ingrid. She was determined to look around as she walked. Study the Path, where it led, what lay alongside. The old friend who'd recommended her to the camino had told her that too many people don't even notice the beauty they pass through, don't even stop to look at the churches; these people, she'd said, are too full of their own thoughts and problems to see what's in front of their eyes; they are so fixed and determined to get to Santiago that they miss the way, the Path itself - and that's why they came isn't it, to walk, to stop the mind for a while? This was Eva's solution to the throbbing pain at the back of her head and the tension in her neck. She would go slowly, reach out to what she passed and try to breathe it in. Santiago could wait, the moment now was what she'd live for.

She'd visited the Iglesia de San Bartolome in Espinal, said a prayer at the same plaque to the virgin in Alto de Mezquiritz that had delayed Paul, and later had knelt for fifteen minutes in the hard wooden pews of the thirteenth century church of Saint Peter in Gerrendiain praying for understanding of what she'd seen half an hour before.

She'd stopped and stood under the beech trees that Paul and Harry had passed earlier. She'd known that Ingrid would make arrangements for the night, so she could relax. She looked up. It was late morning and the sun was almost at its highest. The light shone through the boughs of the trees casting motes on the carpet of dead, wet leaves at her feet. Up to her left, two smaller trees made a knotted and gnarled V shape with their intertwined and twisted branches. The sun seemed to be focussing its light into this aperture and just for a second she saw something that stopped her heart. It was the Virgin. She didn't move. The shape was unmistakable, a woman made of light, the curve of her cowl, the fall of her robe, the uplifted, beseeching tilt of her head, the hands clasped together, the form glistening and haloed by the sun as it danced bright through the foliage. Eva dropped to her knees, looked down and then up again. The shape was gone. The vision, if that's what it was, had lasted no more than a couple of seconds. She dropped back onto her haunches. The weight of the pack on her back nearly toppled her over. She stared up at the trees. A cloud had passed over the sun and there was nothing to be seen but a tangle of branches silhouetted against the grey.

She knelt like this, sitting back on her heels, for a long time, not noticing the strain of the pack on her shoulders. Her friend had been right, everything she needed was here. She remembered that as a child she'd gone with her mother to an early morning mass in the cathedral In the south of France where they'd been living. The congregation was small, and made to seem even smaller by the airy vastness of the church built not so many years before as a replacement for the old, which had been gutted by shell fire in the second world war. The walls were white and there was a line of four narrow stained glass windows high to her right. The design of the windows was geometric and brightly coloured. The light shone through them and just for a second the ten year old Eva had been convinced she'd seen a lady dance down through the dust-filled beams to a statue of the Virgin at the altar. The image had seemed so clear, she'd gasped. When she'd told her mother about it later, her mother had laughed in delight, then hugged her and said she'd had a vision of Our Lady! Her father had said it must have been a trick of the light. Eva had believed him. Her mother was always too full of visions and living spirits, devils (mainly devils), ghosts, poltergeists, ethereal Saints and all sorts of other mystical nonsense, as her father called it.

But now in the beech wood, she'd seen it again. Another trick of the light? She got to her feet and with a last look up at the trees, their tops now moving slowly in a faint breeze, she continued on the trail. The ache had gone from her neck and she felt a lightness in her step. Maybe her mother had been right! Perhaps it was a sign an answer to her question. She asked it again in the ancient church in Gerrendiain but received no confirmation. Perhaps she didn't need any. Perhaps all she needed was faith! For the rest of the day she ignored her old friend's advice and thought only of her childhood and the thousands of Sundays, Holy Days, Saint's Days and early mornings that she'd attended mass and seen nothing more. Until today.

* * * *

As Peter came down the hill on the last few kilometres into Zubiri he saw Oskar sitting on a fallen tree trunk eating a huge hunk of black bread.

"Ha, Peter. Sit. You want black bread?" He held out the piece he had been eating. "I have two kilos."

"Two kilos?" Peter only carried ten in total.

"Why not?"

Peter laughed, "No thanks, I'll wait for Zubiri. I've got an apple."

"Fruit make you shit." Oskar laughed with him and bit off a large, dark chunk of bread. "Carry only what you like, nothing else. My philosophy. We take too much. Most we don't want."

Peter nodded. He'd been considering dumping several unwanted items from his bag, but wasn't thinking of replacing them with black bread.

"You must ask the feet," Oskar went on. "They tell you, stop. They tell you, go." He looked down at his enormous boots. "They say take a rest. So I do. Only three K to Zubiri."

"If I hadn't seen you I'd have kept going."

"Sometime a big mistake."

They sat in silence. A bird sang, then stopped. No sound.

"Listen," said Oskar. "You hear? Nothing."

But there was something, almost inaudible, a low hum.

Peter said, "What is it?"

"The earth," said Oskar. "Can't shut up." He made a face as if frightening a child. "Because it's alive!"

Peter smiled and listened again. Nothing. Can there be nothing? The hum was felt more than heard. Maybe it was the merging of a million tiny sounds made by as many tiny creatures, or the individually imperceptible movements of countless blades of grass and their roots; or dead leaves, those as yet unfallen, the branches they fell from, and the air that passed through them, all together creating silence. There was certainly nothing moving, all was perfectly still.

"Alive," said Oskar again. Then, "To hell with listening to vegetables. We go to Zubiri." He got up. "The earth can crik."

"Creak," said Peter.

They walked down the hill together. It was then that Oskar told him about his past and his plans for the pharmaceutical industry. "And some time I tell you how it fits with Maria."

"What?"

"Last night. Same thing. Not good I do it alone. All of us do it and she gets food. Verstehen sie?"

The track became very steep. Peter slipped, nearly fell, and Oskar caught his arm to steady him, then he tramped on down, never stopping speaking. Peter had the feeling that he was being in some way looked after, talked down the trail. It made him feel slightly vulnerable and a little uneasy because of it. For most of his life it had been him pushing and encouraging those he commanded. Now it was the other way round and he didn't like it.

* * * *

Zubiri was bland and grey, a small town built along the main road; it's most memorable feature being the adjacent magnesite extraction facility, something Oskar said he would like to look at later. "For professional reasons, you don't have to come!" He laughed and crossed the road to the municipal albergue.

Peter went to the privado having arranged to meet Ingrid and

Eva there. It was the opposite of the one in Roncesvalles. It was new, small and had two rooms with half a dozen bunks in each. It even had a washing machine and a microwave, which two women were sitting in front of, watching a bowl of rice slowly revolve inside. Peter listened to them talking as he had his credenciale stamped. One of the women was from somewhere in the Far East, the other probably Eastern European. They were laughing, but he had the sense that they didn't know each other very well. Probably another of the immediate and temporary friendships that formed along the camino, he thought. When people want to know themselves better, or to find the answer to questions about themselves, intimacy comes quickly.

Ingrid came into the reception from the bunkroom. "It cost seven euros," she said. "I reserve you a bed. Did you see Eva?" Peter hadn't. "I hope she didn't go to the municipal. Only four euros. It get more cheap in Spain."

"Oskar went there," said Peter.

Ingrid shrugged as if it meant nothing to her, and went back to the bunkroom. Peter followed. The place was filling up with different pilgrims to those he'd met the night before. He wondered where they'd all come from. He'd seen several bicycles leaning on the wall outside belonging to a group of Spanish men who were doing the camino on wheels. A couple had passed him, and for a second he'd envied their speed, but decided, all in all, the only real way to do the Path was to walk it. He parked his bag in the huge cupboard provided with every bunk and walked the ten yards to the local supermarket.

The Koreans were there already with several others he hadn't met. He learnt later that if you want to find a Korean go to the local supermercado. Most of them were travelling on a very tight budget and never ate in restaurants, preferring to cook for themselves in the albergues. They made him smile. They had descended on the shop en masse and were picking up every item on display, examining it, having a laugh, and then putting it back. The air was full of the sound of their high tuneful voices. Their natural camaraderie intrigued Peter. He couldn't imagine a group of English cooking for one another having only just met. It would take most of them a week to say hello. He bought some bread and ham for the walk the next day and left the Koreans to it, though not before he had been greeted joyously by Chan. "You see Soon-ok? She got bad feet." Then he laughed.

That night he ate with Ingrid and Eva in a vast and empty local restaurant. They were joined by the three Swedes that Peter had seen in Roncesvalles the night before. They were all in their sixties; a married couple and a woman friend - Peter was sure that she'd been the one in the tight black knickers who'd bent over in front of him in the albergue. She showed no sign of recognising him, which wasn't surprising considering the part of her anatomy that had been directed towards him.

Eva was very quiet. She was drawing herself into the warmth of her experience in the trees earlier that day. Ingrid also was introverted and didn't seem at all inclined to engage with her Scandinavian neighbours. She sat red faced and pouting in what seemed to be some kind of angry sulk, and ignored Peter entirely. Half way through the meal she went out to make a phone call. Probably her daughter again, thought Peter. It was left to him to do the talking. He didn't mind. He felt energised. The Swedish man, Olaf, had been a construction engineer, his wife, a sculptor. By the end of the evening he felt he knew them well. From Oskar's pharmaceuticals, to Olaf's bridge building, and to the sensuality of his wife's description of working with clay - all in one day. Peter was amazed. I've been with these people a couple of hours, he thought, and already I know more about them than officers in the mess I've been drinking with for years.

PAMPLONA

Having had a cigarette outside the Hotel Burguette where Hemingway had signed the piano, Llewellyn felt a vague affection for the writer whose books he'd never read, and was wandering around the Plaza de Toros where he'd heard there was a statue of the American. He'd walked twelve miles into the city that day and couldn't believe that it had felt so easy. He even felt quite jaunty and wanted a glass of wine and a roll-up to celebrate. Hemingway forgotten, he ambled away from the bullring towards the centre, and the first person he saw as he walked into the Plaza del Castillo was the young German boy. He was casually wandering under the colonnades surrounding the huge square, skirting the bar tables and looking into the shop windows. He disappeared through the crowd and down a side street as Llewellyn crossed towards him. The next person he saw was his father. He was walking with the same energy that had attracted Llewellyn from the first time that he'd seen him on the mountain road up from Roncesvalles.

"Have you seen a boy?" he asked Llewellyn.

"Your son?"

"You think I would have a son like Willi? I am not so stupid."

"Who is he then?"

"Have you seen him, please?"

Llewellyn pointed to the side street, "About two minutes ago."

"Thank you. I am Heinrich by the way." He offered his hand.

"Llewellyn."

Heinrich went after the boy. The third person Llewellyn was to see turned out to be who his friend Robert later described as his nemesis, and then changed his mind. "Maybe you inspired him? Or was it the other way round? Difficult to say isn't it?"

At the moment this man whose name was Werner Schmidt was hidden from Llewellyn's view by the antics of a crazy impromptu band. There were about twenty of them capering and prancing around two drummers as they processed around the square in a loose mob. All young men, they wore green felt hats resembling the narrow brimmed trilbies worn in the Alps usually with a feather tucked into the headband. These were their only uniform. They were all drunk and playing a variety of brass horns, bugles and trumpets in what Llewellyn took to be a traditional Spanish style - although he wasn't too sure that they were all playing the same tune. A couple of them lunged at anyone foolish enough to get too close, like Llewellyn, and whipped off their green hats asking loudly for donations and cheering when they received any. Several tourists felt too embarrassed to refuse. Llewellyn took a step back and offered only his most disarming smile. He didn't have any money to spare and there was something about their aggression he didn't like. He knew anyway that the collection was going to be drunk in the next bar, and whilst he didn't begrudge anyone a drink, he couldn't afford a round for the band.

They didn't seem to notice his reticence, doubts, or lack of a coin and passed on. Then he was surprised to see following them, the three Italian actors who had been performing their version of the crucifixion outside the bar in Roncavalles. They were wearing old orange and red baggy clothes; the tallest wore a pilot's helmet and played the ukulele, the shortest sported a battered straw hat and was spitting into a flute, and the woman, bareheaded, was beating the time on a tambourine. They were playing a different tune to the green hats, and were much better too. If they'd passed a hat, which they didn't, Llewellyn would have dropped a euro into it. They were mimicking the other band seemingly entirely for their own enjoyment. The flute player gave Llewellyn a smile and a nod as they passed.

It was then that he saw Werner Schmidt. He was sitting on the ground leaning on his backpack propped against a pillar of the colonnade. He was thin and muscular, had white blond hair, tightly curled, and piercing small blue eyes. Even half-lying down it was obvious that he was tall. Leaning on the pillar next to him was a long knotty pilgrim's staff which he'd obviously cut down from a tree, making Llewellyn's shop-bought version look amateurish. He wore high leather boots and even at this distance gave off an undeniable air of danger. The way he lay sprawled, seemed to invite a challenge he would be happy to meet. Sitting next to him was a younger man with long hair and a miniature guitar. The whole world suddenly seems to be made up of musicians, thought Llewellyn. He could see immediately that they were smoking a joint.

He began to walk towards them, not to share the dope, although it would have been welcome after a long day's walk; it was something about the man that drew him on. As he got closer he caught his eye and immediately knew what it was. The man was full of a cold fury. Most people on noticing such a look would have walked the other way, but for Llewellyn fury meant energy, and energy meant life. He kept walking. Maybe it was because the rage was the hard-focussed opposite to his own confused centre that he was attracted to it. He also knew that although it might temporarily threaten it always ultimately passed him by. In his experience the angry were more likely to confide in him than attack. Robert had said, it was the female in him.

He stood over the two of them and said, "Buon Camino."

"You don't have to stand. Sit." The man said. "I am Werner. This is Fabian. Sit."

Llewellyn sat as Fabian stubbed out the joint on the paving stone.

"Sorry," he said, "It's finished." He had a French accent though it was difficult to tell because he also had a heavy cold. Unlike Werner he was short and heavy with a round, sad, innocent face and a much readier smile. Llewellyn immediately thought he was more likeable and less interesting than his companion.

"Are you German?" Llewellyn asked Werner.

"I am from Wien. Vienna." Werner didn't look at him as he spoke.

Llewellyn introduced himself and offered his hand.

Werner ignored it. "That bloody band is crazy," he said staring at the green hats. "All day this banging. It gets on my nerves."

Llewellyn didn't know quite what to say to him. It was often like this with Werner. He made statements, not conversation. And as Llewellyn was to discover the band wasn't the only thing that Werner was to describe as crazy. According to him almost everything was. They sat in silence for a while. Llewellyn had the feeling that the joint they'd just finished wasn't the first. There were quite a few pilgrims wandering around the square. Llewellyn felt a kinship with them; they'd all walked the sixty or so kilometres from St Jean too.

Julia suddenly appeared, "Hi guys. How you doing Llewellyn?"

Oskar had introduced them in Roncesvalles and he was quite flattered that the lovely Australian had remembered his name. Werner asked her to sit down. She took a step back. It was a very clear rejection. There was something inviolable about Julia, always joyous, always alone. And she didn't want to be with them. Werner noticed it too. His eyes clouded as he turned away.

"You going to the municipal?" asked Julia.

"Everybody is," Fabian was looking up at her with undisguised interest. "I am Fabian." He held out his hand.

She took it but kept her distance. "You got a cold?"

"Don't worry. No-one catch it."

"Don't come near me."

"If you sit down I play you my guitar."

"Could be tempted but I've got to go and buy my dinner. See you later." And she was gone.

"Maybe I sing anyway," said Fabian and he plucked at the guitar.

"Go to the municipal. That's where she is," said Werner.

"Non," said Fabian. "I walk again. I like to walk in the sunset."

"Slow down. What is to hurry?" said Werner. It was the first of many times that Llewellyn was to hear him say it. "Anyway, you like her. I can see it."

"OK, I go to the albergue." Fabian grinned. He got up and

80

walked across the square. Llewellyn wasn't sure if it was to get away from Werner or go after Julia.

"He wastes his time," said Werner.

"Everyone tries," said Llewellyn."

"Do you?"

"No." Llewellyn watched as Julia disappeared into the growing darkness followed by Fabian. He knew he didn't have a hope.

"I think it's time you and me took some drink," said Werner.

They found a small bar round the corner. Werner hadn't seemed particular and Llewellyn as usual didn't mind where he went. He asked for a vino tinto and Werner bought a bottle. They went through to the back and sat at a table facing the door. The lighting was low. The bar itself, closer to the street, was brighter. They drank and watched as men and women came in, leant against the bar, took a coffee or a beer, had a chat to the barman, or read a newspaper, and went out again. They both drank quickly.

Werner poured his second glass and said, "Everybody is insane. You look in their heads and there is what they don't admit. Everybody. No-one is different." He nodded towards the bar. "They all have total universe in here," he tapped his head. "Every man, every woman. Millions of universe on the street pass by and knocking each other. Everybody smiles and no-one understand anything, because inside is secret. Each universe secret. Look in your head. You want to tell me what you're thinking? Everything? All the time? Every second?"

Llewellyn didn't. Ninety-nine percent of his conscious mind was a hopeless jumble and he'd only be left with a helpless grin if anyone should be able to peer in. In fact the remaining one percent wasn't too clear either. He emptied his glass and poured another. He thought maybe it wasn't too wise to be sitting in the back of a dark bar getting pissed with this obviously mad Austrian, but in a way he didn't quite understand, there was something comforting about it. People like Werner were troubled and perhaps ultimately unknowable. Like he was perhaps, which is why he liked them. And as for this infinite number of universes colliding on any street. Well, he couldn't agree more.

"You open it," Werner tapped his head again, "You find trouble."

At that moment two pilgrims with heavy packs passed by on the street, came back, looked into the bar and came in. They ordered a beer.

"You see them on the Path. You think, nice people, very friendly, give you a drink, give you food. Open their heads you see, crazy. Even more on the Path. Path makes it all come up. You hide it, still there. You smile, still there. What you see on top just a picture. We agree on ten things so we can live. Don't kill, you know, don't steal, love mother, be friends," he counted them off on his fingers and then seemed to get bored with his own list. "Under it scheisse. Under it, pain. Under it, why they come on the Path." He stopped and drank. "I know. I walk for three months."

"Three months?" Llewellyn was amazed. "From St Jean?"

"From Wien."

"How far is that?

"Three months."

Werner went up to the bar and ordered another bottle. He didn't ask Llewellyn for any money, which Llewellyn wasn't unhappy about. "Don't you think there's some good things in these universes?" he asked when Werner got back.

"Ja. Many," the Austrian poured. "Problem to know which one good, which one not so good. So we go crazy because we don't know the answer." He drank.

"Oh," said Llewellyn. He drank too and waited.

"So I tell you. I was architect," said Werner. "Sure, look. I look like an architect?" He put on his hat, an old brown trilby like Harrison Ford in Raiders of the Lost Ark. The front brim snapped down over his nose emphasised his eyes, which glittered and were frightening. He took hold of his pilgrim staff which was leaning against the wall by the table and stood, tall, angular, his head thrust forward as if peering into some distant horizon. Llewellyn hadn't realised how good looking he was.

"I look like an architect?"

Llewellyn laughed, "No."

Werner laughed too and sat again. "I design kindergarten in Stockholm. It's good. Go and see it. And a church in Warsawa, Catolic church. Beautiful." He stopped for a second looking down at the table. "I work for Foster once. You know him?"

Llewellyn had vaguely heard of him and nodded.

"I was in London. It's a bloody good place. Maybe I got married, but I didn't. I go home. In Vienna I was big architect. Famous." He spat the word contemptuously then leant forward on the table. "Listen, I had three big works. All paid. Maybe I was very rich. Biggest architect in Austria." He listed again on his fingers, "Another school. For three thousand student. A building for the city government, the best design I have done. And a house for a rich man, design like Courbousier, you know him? You don't know anything. Three commission. I work, I work, no women, no wine," he lifted his glass. "Work twenty hours a day. Thirty people in my office." He drank, then spat a piece of tobacco out of his mouth. "Four months ago, comes one day. No money for the school. Cancel. No money for the office. Cancel. The rich man calls me. He go to live in America. One day. Everything gone. All the plan was finished. One day, you understand? Five hours, from everything to nothing. From biggest to nothing. How can you believe this? I tell thirty people go home. Seven o'clock I go home." He looked at Llewellyn. He still had the hat on, his eyes burned. "What happened? God tell me something?" Llewellyn could see it was a real question. "God tell me, Werner you are wrong? How should I know? Eight o'clock I pick up a bag and walk out the door."

"And you've been walking ever since?"

"I wanted to kill. I wanted to kill anyone. I kill my mother. Anyone."

He picked up the empty bottle and went to the bar. Llewellyn watched him as he paid for more wine, his head bent forward looking at the barman with an unwavering stare, and had no doubt that Werner had told him the truth. And that he was capable of doing what he said. Werner came back and filled their glasses, standing over the table.

"You still want to kill someone?"

"Not so much." Werner smiled. "Don't worry."

"What happened to the thirty people?"

"I walk. I don't care."

"What will you do when you get to Santiago?"

"I don't know." He sat down again and drank. He didn't seem inclined to continue.

"Where'd you get your staff?"

"I cut it from a bloody tree."

"I wish I had."

"Why don't you?"

"No, I'm going to keep this one. I got used to it, see? I'm going to decorate it."

"You an artist?

Llewellyn laughed. "Depends what you mean."

"Answer the question." Werner glared at him.

"I'll show you." Llewellyn took an iPod from his top pocket. "I photographed them, see?" He fiddled with the iPod and scrolled up the first picture. He showed it to Werner. It was a seascape with a fishing smack hardly visible in the spray and foam.

"You do this?"

Llewellyn smiled and took a drag on his cigarette. Werner scrolled on through the photographs, studying them intently.

"Why did you bring them with you?"

"I don't know."

"You are brilliant," said Werner. "You are like Turner. Don't tell me you don't know him."

Llewellyn laughed, "Oh I know him."

"I mean it," Werner was very serious, "These are Turner."

Llewellyn was flattered. "Too small for you to say."

"I'm going to call you Turner."

"Lew will do."

Werner pointed at him with the iPod. "Why do you bring these with you. It's important."

"Is it?" Llewellyn suddenly felt a little frightened and didn't know why.

"Because you think you are Turner and you are too scared to admit it."

Now Llewellyn knew why he'd met Werner. He smiled to himself. He always got it right, didn't he? They finished the bottle and Werner bought two more, never once asking Llewellyn for money. It was nearly one on the morning before they left the bar, long past the hope of any albergue. They hefted their packs and stumbled, laughing most of the way, a half mile to a park where they lay down and slept, side by side. The next day they were back on the Path, walking together.

PART TWO

SAN JUAN DE ORTEGA

There are memorials all along the path, some professionally constructed, others little more than simple wooden crosses erected to the memory of a pilgrim. They are all attended to in one way or another as pilgrims pass them by; most have flowers, wilting or dead, some plastic, attached to them, or stuck into pots or jars at their foot; many have photographs of the deceased or of close relatives; nearly all have messages pinned to them by friends or by others of the same nationality as the dead. The memorials are pushed back into hedges, stand proudly in front of walls, or look out from the top of a small rise or hill. They are an occasional distraction on the walk. Most pilgrims stop to look, many say a small prayer, and there are often short services said and blessings given by a local priest in exchange for a small donation to the nearest church.

The one Julia stopped by was just west of St Juan de Ortega, eleven days into the walk, around two hundred and fifty kilometres from St Jean de Pied Port, and not long before Burgos the second major city on the Path. This memorial was one of the simpler kind, in front of a stone wall under an oak tree. It was a wooden cross about four feet high with the usual messages pinned all over it, some tied with string, others stuffed in cracks and a few older ones attached with a rotting red ribbon. At first she thought it was German, then looking more carefully at the name, Van Hoogen, she decided it was Dutch.

It was hot and the oak offered shade so she dumped her pack

and picked up a brittle, curled paper from the grass at the foot of the memorial. Rain had washed away most of the message. She read, Bernice, we'll always remember...then at the bottom something about friends from Queensland. Queensland? She read a few more messages, even found an old, hardly recognisable photograph and put it all together. Bernice Van Hoogen, an Australian from Melbourne (where Julia came from) had died in the hospital in Burgos two years ago. She was seventy-three and had walked the path three times.

Maybe she came here to die, Julia thought. She knelt in front of the cross and looked at it. She didn't pray. Praying wasn't the kind of thing Julia did, she just looked. As a kid, she'd sat by the graves in the churchyard next to her house trying to imagine who was buried in them. Sometimes she spent hours there fantasising about the dead rising and visiting her. It didn't frighten her at all, she thought they were her friends. She took a banana out of her pack and tried to imagine Bernice Van Hoogen while she ate it, but couldn't. Maybe she was too old for that kind of thing now. She turned as she heard the sound of a guitar coming from further back down the track. She thought, 'oh no,' as Fabian came under the tree.

"I will sing."

"No, don't"

Fabian hadn't exactly been following her - at least he said he wasn't - but had certainly always been around since they'd met in the square in Pamplona, showing up whenever she happened to be alone. He began to sing John Lennon's Julia.

"I wish you wouldn't do that, Fabian."

"I can't help it."

"When are you going to do something about that cold?"

He didn't answer, continued singing.

She said, "I'm finishing this banana, then I'm going."

He stopped playing, "It's OK, I stop."

"Everything's OK, Fabian. Just look at this beautiful day."

Fabian lay back on his pack on the ground near her. He sneezed. She moved away.

"I told you. No-one take it. I wish they would. I get it from that Frenchman with the tent. You see him? "

"Yeah, I saw him. I gave him ten euros," said Julia. "You want some bread?" She felt in her pack.

"Non merci." Fabian closed his eyes and let the sun play on his face. He hadn't shaved for a couple of months but his beard was not a success, just made his round face look fluffy. He'd found another dealer in Logrono and wondered about making a spliff, but didn't know how Julia would take it.

"I go to India," he said.

"After Santiago?"

"Non. I go already. I get these." He plucked at his orange cotton trousers. "I was in Ashram for seven weeks. I meditate."

"Yeah?" Julia turned, interested.

He tried to tell her about it but his words couldn't match the experience. It had shifted something in him. He'd been a marketing manager for a sanitary-ware company in Nancy. He'd done it for three years since leaving university but was too bored to make something of it. "Who want to work with pisspot?" he told her. He'd decided to travel for a year and had gone to India with a friend. They'd parted company and he'd gone to the Ashram more because he didn't know what to do than for any spiritual reason. They'd taught him to meditate and every morning he'd got up at four to practise it. At first he'd found it impossible, the sheer physical pain in his legs as he sat immobile was almost unbearable, but there was an almost self-flagellating stubbornness tucked away inside of him that kept him there. "I don't know what it was," he said. "I have good parents, good house but something...something was like a mountain in me which I don't like." He stopped as he thought about what he was trying to describe. "My guru said it was the pain of being." He grinned, then shrugged. After three weeks of practice the time had begun to pass more quickly. His teacher smiled at him. He began to notice that there were sessions when he lost himself and wondered if he'd fallen asleep which was something he'd done frequently at the beginning, but after a while he knew he wasn't sleeping. He knew because there was part of his mind that was watching himself. He could see his anxieties rise in purple clouds and dissipate as they passed through him and then being gently exhaled on his breath. What began as pain ended in air. By the sixth week all sorts of feelings were rising up and disappearing and he very slowly began to understand how to master them, not in any sense of repressing them or using them, but in being able to watch them, watch himself allowing them to go. It was as though he was caressing the kernel of his being with his breath, which had become something live, active, powerful, and as the air touched, so these faint clouds would form and rise like puffs of dust and disappear. "I meditate two hours," he said. "Phew." He wiped his brow, "Blow my mind." By the seventh week he realised that this slow dissolution of self would take years if not a lifetime, because not only was there the past, the heart of what he was, there were also the day to day irritations (and joys) that seemed to take him two steps back for every one forward. He decided to leave. He only had three weeks left before his visa ran out anyway and he wanted to go to the South. His teacher told him to practise. It's not the end but the way, she'd said. And he'd understood her. One thing was for sure, he was never going back to the sanitary-ware. He'd returned to Nancy, given up his flat, sold or dispersed his possessions and then begun the camino by walking out of his front door. He intended to get to Santiago and then walk back. He had the vague idea that he wanted to leave home and return with a gift. He knew what the gift was too. "C'est moi," he said.

Julia smiled.

He didn't know if he could achieve it. His doubts were evident in the packet of weed sitting in the left hand pouch of his pack. And now there was this girl too, stirring up all sorts of feelings he thought he'd left behind. My days are too full, he thought. How can I ever be out of them?

"I am Poland."

It was a voice they didn't recognise. Then a laugh they would have known anywhere. They looked round and saw Oskar coming up the trail with the muscular Pole Peter had seen in the albergue. His name was Stanislav.

"No! I am Polish!" Oskar laughed again as they came under the tree. "I teach him English. He is worse than me. He is nonexistent!"

Fabian had spent an evening with Oskar three nights ago in a bar in Najera, and the big Austrian, full of beer, with no Spanish and the local's English, not to say German, as distant as London or Berlin, had managed to entertain them all for two hours on the subjects of alcohol and the benefit of becoming another person in your head. He'd been hilarious. Now it was Stan the Man who was receiving his full attention.

"Polish," Oskar repeated. "This is Fabian."

"I am France."

"No!"

"I am Australia." Julia laughed.

"Do not encourage him. He's an intelligent man. He knows!"

"I am Korea!" Chan was coming up the path towards them.

"Oh no, I give it up for the birds."

Chan dropped his pack and looked up to the sun, "Catch the rays." He started to take his shirt off.

"I am Germany. I surrender!" Oskar laughed loudly and sat down.

Stanislav dropped his pack and took off his T shirt revealing his well developed torso. They all lay in the sun for a while, then Fabian began strumming his guitar, an old Beatles tune. Stanislav sat up and began to sing. He was word perfect in English, even as far as a faint Liverpool accent. Oskar turned, Julia raised her head, Fabian stopped playing, Stanislav continued singing. His voice was pure and his enunciation exact.

That's gorgeous Stan," said Julia. "Do you know what any of it means?"

Stanislav stopped singing and grinned. "Beatles." He began to sing Sergeant Pepper's Lonely Hearts Club Band. Fabian picked up the tune on the guitar and they all joined in the chorus.

"You're amazing, Stan."

"Beatles, very good."

"Got another ten K's to do today, fellahs." Julia picked up her pack.

Fabian strummed Lennon's Julia again. Stanislav started to sing it.

"You're a cheeky chappie, Fabian." Julia went down the path.

"I am in love with her," said Fabian watching her go.

"You want tuna?" said Chan.

Fabian got up. "I cannot eat. I will follow her behind, but my guitar will be silent because she instruct me."

"His guitar gently whips!" said Oskar.

Stanislav began to sing it.

BURGOS

The city seemed thunderous after the peace of the past days. The soft became hard, earth gave way to stone, distant silence to hard-faced bustle, and vineyard to neon and traffic light. Rising above it all were the Gothic towers of the great Catedral of Santa Maria sitting comfortably in the medieval streets that Peter walked trying to get his bearings again in urban rather than rural, with a sightline now of metres, not miles. By accident he stumbled across the municipal albergue and checked in. It was four euros. Ingrid had been right, they were cheaper in Spain. There had even been one where you could stay for as much as you could afford. Some gave nothing, Peter, ten.

He'd found his stride now. He felt as if the Path was welcoming him. The weather had been good, sunny but not too hot, much of the countryside glorious, and the days easier. The walk was friendly, there was no denying that. Everyone he passed had a Buon Camino and often more; some news about the next albergue, a story about the last, a confusing sign ahead, or a good bar. It sometimes seemed that information flashed up and down the trail faster than it could be spoken. The Spanish were helpful. Occasionally he'd got lost and asked the way, and he'd never spoken to anyone who hadn't known it. Twice he'd inadvertently taken the wrong way only to hear a shout behind him and turned to see an arm pointing the right direction. This wasn't to say there wasn't occasionally some hostility towards them. An Austrian hospitalero in a privado had little patience and seen them only as tourists she could exploit. She'd thrown his clothes out of the drier onto the floor claiming his time was up. Peter had picked his clothes up and said nothing. He thought later that this indicated quite a change in his usually more assertive demeanour. He'd looked at the old woman, fat and grumpy as she was, and thought he'd rather be him than her.

He'd walked with Ingrid and Eva for about a week and then lost them for three days. Up until then it had been the same pattern. Ingrid would surge ahead overtaking anyone in her path and find them beds in the next albergue. She covered the ground ruthlessly, her body hunched slightly forward, her feet punching out the same strong rhythm up hill and down, her mind's eye fixed on Santiago. Her determination to put Siri out of her mind was holding only insofar as she'd resisted the desire to call her, but certainly hadn't stopped her thinking about what she was now convinced was her daughter's duplicity. This made her angry which made her walk faster. Maybe Siri and all of it was why she was on the path in the first place. She had to admit she'd felt bad about it for years. She didn't want Ingmar to see Siri, but then maybe it was too bad for a girl not to see her father and so she felt guilty, but she was still in too much of a rage about him to to have him in her life at all - and he would be if he saw Siri. And she had to admit also that his shadow fell on her, or someone's shadow did, or some man's shadow anyway, and always had, and it made her life too dark and she wanted some light, please. She walked even faster. For God's sake give me some light, For God's sake...she spoke it in the rhythm of her steps. She didn't know why she went so fast. Maybe she always had a desperation to please, to be liked, and to run away maybe, to find some light maybe, to be liked, to be liked, she was picking up the rhythm. She didn't mind that. What was wrong with wanting to be liked? And finding a bed for Eva was good. And now for Peter too. OK, so what? She didn't want to think about why she was doing that. Always to look after people. It's good. What's wrong with it? Nothing. Sometimes she felt that she was like a little girl. A little girl who looked after them all like her dolls. Last week, or some days ago she told to Peter and Eva that she said to a hospitalero he must reserve places, her family were coming! Peter had looked worried. Where am I in this family? he'd said. Nowhere, she'd said, it was a lie, what do you think? To get us a bed. If she was going to do it, she'd do it, so don't worry about it. He laughed. Eva didn't. Eva never laughed too much anymore. She'd got so serious about something. Maybe soon she'd say what it was.

Eva would always come in last. She would often stop for an hour or so, sitting by a fence or in a field trying to breathe in the sweep of the countryside and eliminate all the thoughts that would rise in her mind that would disturb the peace of her being just here and nowhere else. She knew it was important to be only where she was. She would look sometimes at trees for minutes at a time, wondering about what she'd seen in the beech wood on the third day, and perhaps willing it to reappear, but she even tried to put that out of her thoughts too. The Virgin would come only in her own time, there was nothing she could do about it and she was a fool to even think she could. She would wait, quietly, knowing that she wouldn't be disappointed. She walked slowly, her boots squelching in the mud. God is there, always, right now. He is just outside the vision of your eye, just above what you can hear. You can welcome Him in any second you want to, He always comes, and maybe He shows himself or gives a sign, or maybe not. You are nothing in this except the desire to be with Him. The desire to be with Him. This was Eva's path. She knew it now. She was there to ask the question that had been with her for months, but first she had to purify; to become nothing more than God's conduit for the energy to flow through her from the sky to the earth. And only then would she know her answer.

Peter rarely stopped for longer than twenty minutes at first but was slowly forcing himself to slow down and sometimes took longer breaks especially if someone he knew was sitting by the path. He'd once spent nearly an hour listening to Chan describe in detail the plot of Mission Impossible. The film had obviously affected him deeply. It's another reality, he'd said, as he'd looked around the huge roughly turned field they were sitting by. For a second Peter had the uneasy feeling that Chan was seeing more than he was. Maybe the harsh brown earth peppered by the white of crushed rock was actually a cover for the other world in Chan's mind and any minute it would peel back to reveal gigantic steel armatures peopled by aliens. Don't believe what you see, said Chan as he got up. It's all Mission Impossible! He'd laughed as he's wandered away, his bandy legs sticking down out of his baggy shorts.

Maybe it was because of listening to Chan, or maybe because of another extended break later the same day when he was a couple of hours outside Belorado and into the hills covered in oak and pine. It was a glorious day, the sunlight dappled the path, it was silent apart from the soft crunch of his own footsteps. He'd stopped and sat dreamily looking across a valley for so long that he hadn't reached the albergue in San Juan that Ingrid had designated as their target for that day. By four o'clock he'd had enough anyway. He'd done thirteen miles and stopped at a privado in Epinosa with a bar and a terrace still bright in the late afternoon. He'd decided he'd catch them the next day and have a beer while he watched the sunset. He spent the evening with the Koreans and a German woman showing her twelve year old daughter the Path for a few days.

The next day he realised he had no idea where Ingrid and Eva would be that night. He hadn't taken their phone numbers and there was no way of finding out. All he knew was they were somewhere ahead of him on the path. It took him three days to find them. It made him realise the intricate nature of what seemed to be a simple, single trail. Someone could be a few miles ahead, stop for the night, be overtaken, start out, overtake in turn, speed ahead, stop again unexpectedly and although you may often be only a few hundred metres apart you'd never see them again. He wondered how many men, women, colleagues, friends, enemies had travelled close to him in the track of his life and he hadn't known it. Even if he stopped to let one catch up, the one ahead would have moved on. This was one of the lessons of the Path. Ingrid had passed along it and so had Eva; so had probably millions of others over the years, often never connecting but always closer to one another than they imagined. What did that signify? The ancient trail trod by all men, each with their peculiar and unique plans but all moving in the same direction. We lived with the idea that we could plan ahead and organise our relationships with one another, but nothing could ever be predicted, there was always the slightest shift, another movement, an unforeseen obstacle, even a loose thought that would change everything and you'd miss your target by a mile, or even an inch, it didn't matter, the result was the same, the direction had changed, the momentum had shifted, the chance had gone. Once he'd met Ingrid and Eva again he discovered he'd overtaken them at one point and Ingrid had in turn passed him. How could she have known about a young Korean's enthusiasm for a film, or the subtle dissolution of Peter's resolve as he sat dreamily staring at a hillside? And come to that how could she have known that Peter's desire to be with them was slowly waning - when he didn't realise it himself? It was probably why he'd let them go. He needed a rest. Sometimes Eva's introspection and reluctance to participate in even the most trivial conversation could be wearing. But it was Ingrid he was really avoiding. She was usually polite but cool and the distance she was putting between them indicated to him only one thing, which was paradoxically, that the tension drawing them together was increasing. The fact that she was denying it was defining it. And maybe her attempt at withdrawal was precipitating his own? Perhaps they'd both realised that this kind of sexual attraction was little more than the habit that had become ingrained over the years, and one they both wanted to break? Perhaps she, like him, was trying to leave these old ways behind and just beginning to perceive in the vacuum created by their absence, the new and strange country they were both walking in - which had nothing to do with Spain. It was unnerving him and maybe her too. That, he realised, was why he'd let her go. To give him time to allow all this to be thought through before he met her again.

At least he'd finally got his pack right. It was becoming more basic by the day. His only luxury, if you could call it that was his History of Philosophy, still unread, but there as some kind of reminder of what he was trying to think about. As for the rest it had come down to one spare shirt and T shirt, another pair of trousers, socks and underwear, trainers, a sleeping roll, washing kit, Compeed, a guidebook, torch and sunglasses, plus some lightweight weather gear. That was it, down to nine kilos, his life on his back. Not only was the effort of the walk revealing his fitness to him, his diminishing material possessions were giving him no place to hide his thoughts. There was his body, these few things, a path and others on it, the sum of Peter Donald.

He took a last glance up at the Catedral, promising to himself a visit later, and went through into the bunkroom of the albergue. Maybe Ingrid and Eva would show up, maybe not. He noticed that the big Pole, Stan the Man, as Llewellyn called him, was already there. Peter took a bunk at the back of the room away from him as he had a reputation for snoring.

* * * *

The long walk in through the outskirts of the city was arduous and boring. As soon as Llewellyn spotted what he considered to be the real signs of civilisation - a street that had several bars - he decided to take a fag break and sit outside one of them. He'd wait for Werner. He ordered a beer and watched the traffic. He liked being with Werner. He didn't mind his aggression, or his absolute control of any circumstance in which they were together. Llewellyn could see he was trying to work something out like he was, and they'd begun a conversation; not about anything in particular; just the slow articulated drip of the day passing. Often it was funny, usually inconsequential, but they were slowly circling and scraping something away in an atmosphere they both understood would be receptive to whatever final intimacy they revealed.

Werner had been intrigued to hear about the priest on the camino, and been happy when Llewellyn introduced them. He said that he was going to ask Paul to hear his confession. He'd said it in such a way as to make Llewellyn think that whatever it was he had to confess, needed to be. He'd made a joke about it, but

Werner made it clear that he'd never reveal anything until a priest had given him absolution. Almost certainly something to do with Werner's sudden departure from Vienna, thought Llewellyn. He'd said he'd wanted to kill. Maybe he had - both desired and fulfilled the desire. Llewellyn didn't feel in the least perturbed by this thought. Even if it was true, it merely seemed part of their talking, an expression of that deeper anguish that had to be seen, turned over, chipped at, diminished and ultimately dissolved. As Werner had said, every man and woman is a universe, most of it unknown, but the existence of its content sensed all the same. Maybe that's why he, Llewellyn, was on the Path, to discover his own universe. One thing was for sure, Werner wouldn't tolerate any bullshit.

He looked back down the road, then across it. He could see one of the many yellow arrows that marked their way to Santiago. If he ever painted anything again, one of the first things would be one of those bloody yellow pointers. Wouldn't be hard, would it? And then he'd like to have a go at the view he'd seen that morning. He'd come over the hill from Atapuerca and stopped dead. It was still early, the sun was rising behind him, and diagonal layers of light were piercing the still heavy cloud and illuminating Burgos nestling in a valley in the far distance. It was golden. Llewellyn's heart stopped. He knew it wasn't golden, it was just another big metropolis with a cathedral in it, but just for that moment it was the shining city, singing in the newborn sun. He could well have imagined some old pilgrim, starving and half-frozen, with a cloak, a piece of bread and two apples to his name, standing where he stood, hat on head, staff in hand, looking down on what he saw. It didn't matter about the trucks on the highway and the faint wash of industrial steam rising from the east of the city, the sun would have been the same, so would the valley and the cathedral spires. To that old fellow it would have meant the same as it did to Llewellyn, a far away explosion of light, all the power of man touched and blessed by the mighty hand of God, and in this old man's heart, as in Llewellyn's, there would have been, momentarily, an inexorable upsurge of intangible and glorious hope.

He'd taken pictures with his camera of course, but he knew he could never capture such beauty, let alone his own feelings, with mere digital technology; it needed paint, and his heart and soul at the tip of a brush. The desire to do it and the impossibility of achieving it brought tears to his eyes. He slowly descended into the valley and in the flat morning light suffered the same culture shock as Peter in the hard ruck and dusty rumpus of any concrete city. Back to reality he thought. But maybe not. Maybe the reality was what he'd seen up there on the hill. Him and the old fellow with the wide-brimmed hat and two apples to his name.

"You want some more beer?"

He looked up. Heinrich and the boy, Willi, were standing by the table.

"You want a coke?" Heinrich asked the boy, who nodded and sat down.

Heinrich went into the bar.

"How you doing?" asked Llewellyn. The boy shrugged. "Feet good?"

"Ja."

"Mine are bloody terrible."

The boy replied with a smirk. Behind it there was a contrived irony as though he knew better and everyone else needed to try harder. He turned away and looked up the road as if there was something important there that only he could perceive. Llewellyn could see it was an act, part of some elaborate defence system he'd constructed. He also had the feeling that the boy understood a lot more English than he was letting on.

He tried again, "Camino beautiful?"

"Ich weiss nicht," Willi turned away.

"But you understood, didn't you?"

Willi grinned, looked directly at Llewellyn, held the stare with his head slightly cocked to one side, and drummed the table with his fingers as Heinrich reappeared with the drinks. He put the coke in front of Willi. "Trinke."

Willi drank the coke in two fast gulps. Then he said something in German to Heinrich, who clearly objected. The boy argued.

Heinrich turned to Llewellyn and said, "He wants to go on his own to the albergue. He always does this. Then I lose him."

"It's only about a kilometre," said Llewellyn, not particularly helpfully. "There's an arrow over there." He pointed across the road.

Heinrich sighed and, again in German, issued what seemed to be a set of instructions. Willi got up without comment and headed off down the street.

"You said he wasn't your son," said Llewellyn.

"He has many problems," said Heinrich. "I must have been crazy." Heinrich's exasperation was quite amusing. There was no anger in it, only a comic irritation at his own foolishness.

"Why did you bring him?"

Heinrich blew out his cheeks, put his beer down and stared at Llewellyn with his startling green eyes, "Because, I am an idiot." He looked up the road at the departing figure of the boy; his huge rucksack looked bigger than he was. "His father in prison, his mother, drugs. I don't know how he even gets to fifteen."

"You're a social worker?"

Heinrich laughed, "I sell houses."

"An estate agent?" Llewellyn couldn't believe it.

"I try to help."

The boy had disappeared.

"One day he start something and then he finish it. Then maybe he don't think he is so useless, and stop being so stupid. You understand?"

Llewellyn understood too well. "You're a volunteer?"

Heinrich smiled, "Why not?" Then his face darkened, "But I don't like this. I want to go home to my wife."

"I wish someone had taken me on the Path," said Llewellyn.

Heinrich laughed and then looked down the road. The boy had disappeared "He will be a criminal. What else?" He finished his beer and looked up.

Werner had arrived.

* * * *

Rhoda and Deena were sitting in the albergue reception when Willi walked in. He'd gone straight there.

"Hiya, Willi," Deena said brightly. They'd met the boy and Heinrich a few days back in Ventosa where a hospitalero from the local albergue had told them all the eighth century tale of Roland defeating the Saracen giant Ferragut who was a descendant of Goliath. The battle had lasted days and taken place yards from where they were standing. Apparently the giant had told Roland himself that his weak point was his navel. The next day Roland had speared him there and killed him.

"Giants aren't exactly famous for their intelligence," Rhoda had remarked and winked at Willi who had stared impassively back. Now he stood in front of them looking vaguely around the albergue reception.

"Where's your Dad? Papa?" asked Deena.

"Leave it, Deena, just don't get involved." Rhoda was in a foul mood. She didn't want to be in another damn alberg, she wanted to be in a hotel. And now the hospitalero wasn't even there to stamp their credentials or whatever they called them. "Why don't we just find someplace else?"

"Because our bags are coming here, Ma."

"Who arranged that?"

"Hey Willi, you want some chocolate?" Deena fished a bar out of her bag.

"Danke." He took it, went out of the door and sat on the steps outside

"I didn't mean for him to take the whole thing," said Deena.

"What you get for poking your nose in."

"He seems so lonely."

"Why don't we go to a privado?"

"We're staying here." Deena put her foot down. As mistress of the budget she was going to have to. The past twelve days had been a mixture of walking, sight-seeing, (Usually a disaster; Rhoda being determinedly unimpressed by anything Spanish which, as

Deena put it, was a little limiting), taxis, (too many) albergues (not enough) and small hotels. Rhoda was doing as well as could be expected but the small hotel end of it was beginning to stretch their resources and Deena knew she had to draw a line.

"You don't get the snoring in the privado," said Rhoda.

"Yes, you do."

"But it ain't the same kind. It's low pitch and occasional. In these damn places you get all those Spanish guys on bicycles and they blow you out of bed."

"Ma, were, staying..."

"God, Deena, you can be a dictator when you want to."

"Are you kidding?"

They lapsed into silence. Deena didn't think the place looked too bad. It was some old school or college they'd converted. It had a wooden staircase and a terrace out back, where a group of pilgrims were lounging around in the sun waiting for their washing to dry. She could see a couple of Koreans. "There's that Soon-ok."

"Yeah, wish I was."

Deena figured her mother must be regressing. And if she was honest she'd prefer to be in a hotel too. She glanced outside expecting to see Willi on the step. He wasn't.

"He went into that shop on the other side of the square," said Rhoda, "he'll be back."

Deena glanced at her mother. She was leaning her head against the wall with her eyes closed. For a second Deena wondered what she'd look like when she was dead. Would her skin droop down in the same way? She caught herself, half shuddered and looked round out of the doors. Willi was coming out of the shop with something in his hand. He came quickly back in through the doors with a carton of orange juice in his hand. He thrust it towards Deena. "Orange?"

She nearly cried, "Thank you, Willi, thank you so much."

"Probably stole it," said Rhoda.

* * * *

When Llewellyn had introduced Werner to Paul two days before in Santa Domingo, Werner had clasped the priest's hand in both of his and said fervently, "I've been waiting to meet you, Father." Paul had seemed a little embarrassed. He never advertised his priesthood and certainly didn't look the part in his blue walking jacket and baseball cap. Llewellyn hadn't talked to a priest for years and thought Paul was definitely an improved version of the ones he'd known. He remembered, as a boy, the local priest in Swansea, an old Irishman called Father Horan who clipped kids round the ear if they misbehaved on the street, not caring whether they were Catholic or not - and most of them weren't. He stood his ground firmly as God's representative on earth. They may have mocked his faith behind his back, but never to his face; it wasn't just the collar and black coat, it was how he stood there in continuous and unbending judgement of your every move. That's what pissed Llewellyn off.

Paul wasn't like that at all. There was a gentle quality about him, something slightly vulnerable and confined, even a sense of humility about his own position. He also drank too much too (he was with Horan there), and could get angry and curse - as he'd done the night that night in Santa Domingo. He'd looked down at his dinner, "Isn't there anybody in this country who can cook a damn egg?"

Harry had laughed, Werner had offered to get the waiter to change it.

"No, no," said Paul, "It'll damn do. Only bring more crap anyhow."

Later in the evening he and Werner had sat together on a bench in a square outside the restaurant locked in a deep conversation, or praying, Llewellyn wasn't sure which. And now Werner was very happy to see Paul again in the bunkroom of the Burgos albergue and went quickly over to greet him and Harry. The two Americans had just come from the cathedral.

"One of the biggest in Spain," Harry had said as they'd sat in the pews looking up.

"Wow, oh just wow," said Paul. The vaulted ceiling seemed like a hundred yards up. There was a guide nearby telling a tour group about the great architects and master builders who'd embellished the cathedral over the centuries. Harry eavesdropped. Paul wasn't interested. He could smell the incense, feel the weight of the place, the hundreds of years of...what? Enlightenment? Hell that wasn't the word, it was all too dark for that. Liberation? Are you kidding? Comfort? Well, guess so. He wanted to add, oppression, but was too shocked to allow the thought and tried to concentrate on the guide. In the end he wasn't unhappy to be out in the air. They'd quickly found the albergue and met up with Llewellyn who he liked, and Werner, who worried him.

"Great to see you boys too," said Harry. Far as he was concerned they took a little of the load off. It wasn't that Paul was bad company. Sometimes he'd talk a lot, but Harry could still sense this damn disturbance in him, didn't know what the hell it was, and the walk wasn't helping either, if anything it was making it worse. Harry was pleased when the four of them agreed to meet for dinner after Paul had slept.

"Damn boots," said Paul, pulling them off.

"Shoulda left them outside anyway," said Harry.

"All these rules, worse than the navy."

"The navy?" asked Werner.

Harry said, "Don't get him started on that. I had it for three hours today."

"The hell you did."

"Some story about a captain and an angry young sailor, who kinda reminded me of you, Paul."

"OK, OK."

"Seemed like that young man was going to get mutinous to me."

"I was sweet like honey," said Paul as he lay back.

"What happened?"

"Life happened, Harry." Paul closed his eyes.

Werner and Llewellyn went over to a bar in the square for a drink before dinner.

* * * *

Rhoda was sitting on her bottom bunk by just after nine. They'd been to a big and busy restaurant on a side street. The place had been packed.

"They ain't pilgrims," said Rhoda eyeing the mainly Spanish crowd. "So how come they're eating pilgrim menus? Because they're not pilgrim menus that's why. They're tourist menus and they're not even tourists. They live in the city."

"Only eight euros, Ma."

Deena was pleased to see Peter, Ingrid and Eva sit down at a table next to theirs.

"Haven't seen you guys for a while," said Rhoda.

Peter had found Ingrid sunning herself on the albergue terrace. He wasn't sure how pleased she was that he was there. Eva had joined them and seemed even quieter than usual, so he was quite relieved to see Rhoda. At first anyway.

"Five countries, three husbands. All died on me except the last and I don't know where he is. (This was Deena's father, not that her presence in any way inhibited Rhoda.) First was the best. Had money, you see? Met him in Singapore..."

Then came the long descriptions, country by country; the funny stories, the disguised but still obvious racism, the honed asides, the barbed remarks about men in general. If Deena had a dollar for every time she'd heard this she'd be a very rich woman indeed - richer than the first husband, a Malay by the way, a fact that Rhoda didn't dwell on. The story was as practised as the deepest rut in a fifty year old track. Rhoda rode along in the carriage of her own history impervious to any comments as she passed by. Every house, every town, every city was relived until her audience capitulated to the sound of her voice, went quiet, then dumb, and probably deaf too. Rhoda's life was her script, transcribed in a tone that yielded to no-one. Occasionally like a weary, but once talented actor, she brought life to it in the telling, but word for word it remained fixed. Seventy-two years had become a half an hour at a dinner table, a deadly recital of the past occasionally interspersed with complaints about the present and a blank denial of what was to come. She concluded with the statement, that of all the places she'd lived in, Canada was the best, mainly because there she was husband free, the departure of Deena's father being described in detail.

Deena looked at the others. Eva wasn't interested, Ingrid's face had a fixed smile painted on, only Peter was listening with any sympathy. Deena put her hand out to touch her mother's shoulder. Rhoda didn't notice. She was in the middle of a joke about her second husband.

They all left the restaurant together. As they walked down the street towards the albergue, Ingrid walking ahead with Peter said, "It was three days we don't see you. I missed you."

"Sorry, I got lost," he said. What did she mean by 'missed?' Passed him or regretted his absence? Either way, he realised he'd been happy to see her again.

"Where are we going tomorrow?" he asked.

"You decide."

"I'll look in the guide."

"I'll give you my phone if we miss each other again," she smiled.

"That would be good." She dropped back to say something to Eva.

Peter thought, 'Miss each other again?' She was telling him she meant it geographically. He didn't believe her.

* * * *

Werner and Paul had spoken to the hospitalero and asked him for a private space they could use. Llewellyn had guessed it was for the famous confession. He wasn't curious. As Werner had said, God must be told first. But probably only after Werner'd had dinner and a couple of bottles of the tinto. Llewellyn unrolled his bag on his bed and thought that if he'd had that kind of booze in him, he'd confess anything - frequently did.

It was a medium sized bunkroom, about forty beds. He was

on a lower bunk, the other side of the aisle from Rhoda. Peter passed between them. Rhoda liked Peter. He'd listened to her story. She wished him good night as Deena came back from the washroom.

Llewellyn said sociably, "You see Stan the Man's in?"

"What?"

"I am Poland." Stanislav's phrase had been adopted all along the path.

"What about him?"

"Fasten your earplugs, could be a bumpy night." Stan's snoring was notorious.

"Oh no."

"And Fronc the Honk." The wine in Llewellyn was laying it on. "He's probably worse than Stan."

"You hear this Deena?"

"What do you want me to do about it?"

"Complain to the management."

"At five euros a night?"

"You should talk to that English guy, he's got class."

"Goodnight, Mother."

A few later minutes later Werner came in with Paul.

"And him," said Llewellyn of Paul, as he passed along the aisle. "Mount Vesuvius."

"You'd think being a holy man he'd have compassion," said Rhoda flat on her back inside her sleeping bag ready to sleep.

"Like a low rumble, you never know if it's going to erupt."

"Llewellyn, do you mind." The last thing Deena needed was for Rhoda to get wound up again.

"You want to smoke?" Werner had put his gear on the bed above Llewellyn.

"Not allowed in here."

"You want to smoke, then smoke."

"Not over me," said Rhoda.

"I'm going outside," said Werner, Rhoda being one of the few people he was wary of.

"How'd you get on?" asked Llewellyn.

"I'm clean," said Werner.

As he left the lights went out.

"Night, Ma."

"Night, hon."

Five minutes later Werner came back, stripped down to his underwear and climbed into the top bunk.

Someone moaned in their sleep. And then the first snore.

"Oh no," said Rhoda.

Llewellyn said conversationally, "Now, is that Stan the Man, Fronc the Honk, or the priest?"

"Do you ever stop?" said Rhoda.

"Difficult to say, isn't it?"

The snore steadily increased in volume, each eruption followed by a wet splutter. Then came a deep rumble.

"Now there's two of them," said Rhoda.

The snoring continued, slowly increasing in intensity. It seemed to be in concert. A snort, a splutter, then the bass.

"Can it get any worse?" said Rhoda lying on her back with her eyes wide open.

It did. After the fifth or sixth bass, a high pitched hooter of a snore pierced the darkness.

"Definitely Fronc the Honk," said Llewellyn.

It continued; snort, splutter, bass, then the hooter, all in perfect and sustained sequence.

"It's like a goddam symphony," said Rhoda.

"Put your earplugs in," said Deena.

"I got my earplugs in. I couldn't sleep in this if I was ten miles away with earplugs in!" I had enough!" She began to push her sleeping bag down.

"Ma!"

"Five euros!" They can pay me next time." Rhoda got out of bed.

Deena pulled her sleeping bag over her head as Rhoda disappeared into the bunks. She heard her mother give someone a sharp shove. Whoever it was woke with a startled explosive honk.

"Hank the Man, or whatever your damn name is."

"I think that's Stan she's got there," whispered Llewellyn.

"Have you any idea what you're doing?" said Rhoda loudly. "You're keeping around thirty people awake in here."

"No English. I am Poland."

"And I am Canada. Thirty people a night, my friend. Do you know how many people that is every night over the whole Path? Could be thousands. And those people have got to walk. You can't walk when you haven't slept, can you? You could trip over and damage yourself. You're a danger to humanity, you know that?"

The bass continued unabated, unaware of the threat he was posing to mankind. It suddenly stopped mid chord as Rhoda poked.

"Sorry Father, but I got to sleep."

There was still the hooter, with now an additional whine as an embellishment to the original score, but magically that stopped too, with the bass. It was as if a conductor had brought the first movement to a close. Rhoda came back to her bunk. There was quiet.

"That's better, thank you." She got back into her sleeping bag. "And you can stop hiding up there, Deena. An embarrassing mother's one thing, a damn concert of snoring's something else."

Deena pretended she hadn't heard. Rhoda turned over preparing to sleep. Five minutes later it began again; snort, splutter, bass, hooter.

"Bon camino, Rhoda," said Llewellyn.

CARRION DE LOS CONDES

The weather was getting colder. They were down from the hills now and coming onto the plain. The walking was easy. Much of it was along the senda, concrete paths built alongside the motorway. There was nothing dangerous about this, they were usually more than ten metres from the traffic, but it was noisy and boring. Peter supposed it was inevitable that the pilgrims over the ages would select the easiest path along valleys and through the hills, and inevitable too that the road builders would take the same route. He walked quickly. There was nothing much to see and few places where it was comfortable to stop and take a break.

He saw the Italian theatre group up ahead walking quickly, huddled against the wind, their instruments tucked away in bags or rucksacks. He passed them and they gave him a cheery buongiorno. He admired them. It can't have been easy playing every night for their food and bed. He knew they'd been forced to sleep out several times and hoped they wouldn't have to tonight. It was too cold.

He passed Julia too. She was alone. He'd never seen her walking with anyone else. In the evenings she'd be part of a group for a while and then float away and was usually in her sleeping bag by eight thirty. She didn't seem lonely and the space she created around herself was respected by everyone, including Fabian who seemed happy enough to bemoan his unrequited love from a distance. It was good to be in the same albergue as her. She would usually, like the Koreans, cook her own dinner and sit around the communal table chatting. She'd say little that was memorable, but you'd remember her. Eva had described her as a good spirit. 'You don't have to talk to her, she is just there,' she'd said.

Peter knew what she meant. Julia reminded him of a young squaddie he'd known in Basra. He was barely eighteen when he arrived and he was fiercely protected by the other men. There was something about him, something innocent. The squaddies saw him as their luck and he had to be protected at all costs. When he was killed by an IED four days before he was due to go home, morale plummeted. Any unit suffers badly at the death of one of their own, but usually will come back stronger, fiercer and more determined to make their point. But the grief they felt at losing the kid was beyond anything Peter had ever seen. Even the officer's mess was deeply affected. Peter had felt it as soon as he'd got down from his Land Rover on the day it happened. The whole base had a different quality. It was quieter than he'd ever known. There was no-one hanging around, no football games, and the mess was empty. It was as if the air had been sucked out of the place. 'Our luck's up, sir,' a corporal had told him when he'd asked him what was wrong. "They killed the kid." The corporal's face broke into grotesque tears. The young squaddie, who knew nothing about politics, had somehow represented for them the reason they were there. It took days for the officers to pull the men round, and they'd had to do it very gently too; any blunt command, or pull your socks up, would have been met with the kind of unspoken hostility and intransigence he'd only ever seen in the army. It was an older sergeant who'd sorted it out in the end. He'd got everyone, officers included into a briefing room, spoke barely two sentences about the kid and then burst into tears. He cried for a full minute in front of them and then said, 'You've never seen me do that before, have you? Now get on with it.'

Julia was like the kid he supposed. The spirit of the camino shone through her. She was sociable, but didn't socialise, alone but not lonely, young, but in her own way, ageless. He couldn't have said the kid was similar. Probably not. Like the rest of them he would have been idle, jumped when ordered and spent his leaves drunk as a sparrow under a spigot. But he'd been their luck.

Thinking of the army made him think of Gemma; thinking of her made him think of Sam. He hadn't seen him for more than eight years now. He'd wanted to call him, or write but had no idea where he was. He was pretty sure Gemma didn't know either. All the usual feelings swelled up fast; a disappointment so heavy it made him ache, a father's guilt tangible enough to have sliced with a knife, a sense of such uselessness that it stopped him in his tracks. He was under a bridge carrying a slip road onto the motorway. The pale grey concrete was covered in graffiti. He found himself looking around to see if Sam had scrawled any of it.

His mood was low as he walked into Carrion. The centre of the town was medieval with narrow streets winding through irregular plazas. Apparently there'd once been a dozen pilgrim's hospitals sited there, and El Cid himself had executed most of the ruling family for insulting his daughter. The buildings hung low over the narrow, twisted, streets, giving the town a dark and foreboding atmosphere.

He was heading for the parish albergue when he realised his phone was signalling a text. It was from Ingrid telling him to go to a hotel. She didn't say why. It took him half an hour to find the place. Sitting in a cafe opposite it was Oskar and the three Swedes he'd met in Zubiri. Oskar waved for him to come in for a drink. He pointed to the hotel and indicated he'd join them later.

There was a sign on the wall saying Hostal Peregrino, and a yellow arrow pointing to the side of the building. He went down a flight of steps and came to a glass door. He pushed it open and was faced by a long basement corridor with several doors opening off either side. Ingrid came out of one of them. Her hair was wet.

"It's here."

Peter went through the door into a small, dark room almost entirely taken up by a double bed and alongside it an unpulled down sofabed.

"Oskar told me the hotel had rooms for pilgrims. It's only seven euros." She shrugged. "I think maybe luxury for once."

Peter looked round. At least they had their own bathroom. It was tucked away in a corner of the room. He could see that Ingrid was uneasy.

"I'll take the sofabed. You and Eva can have the double."

"OK," she said.

"I'll have a shower." He dumped his pack. She wasn't looking at him but he could feel her awareness of everything he did. He took out his washbag and went to the bathroom. "Oskar's in the bar on the street if you want." He closed the door.

The fact that this was a hotel room changed everything. The truth was that their proximity to one another wouldn't be much more than that of an average bunkroom, but hotel meant another set of values, the one's they'd left back there in another life. The pilgrim inhabited a world where a lack of sexual or physical perception seemed to be the norm, at least on the face of it - he remembered his cynicism in Roncesvalles, but he'd come a long way from regarding the Swedish woman in the black knickers bending over in front of him as being provocative. Now he knew why Oskar was sitting drinking with the Swedes. He was sharing one of these rooms with them. It was either that, or pay for the whole room for yourself. Twenty-eight euros! Hardly two weeks ago he'd have regarded that as cheap for a hotel room, but in pilgrim world where you existed quite happily on a couple of sandwiches, a beer, and a bunkbed, it was ridiculous. So they all piled in together as though it was the most natural thing you could do. What was unnatural was having a whole room to yourself. Unheard of, even for what he assumed was a wealthy man like Oskar.

He walked under the shower in his shirt, socks and trousers. He took them off as the water streamed down and trampled them under foot. An old army trick. How to wash yourself and your clothes at the same time.

As he soaped himself he thought of Ingrid probably lying on a double bed hardly more than a few feet from him. Was her uneasiness the same as his? Were they both contemplating the same thing? Was it just a shared sexual awareness noted by a man and a woman who knew a thing or two back there in nonpilgrim world? Is that how she saw it? And what was this habit of sexuality anyway? Did it have anything to do with love? No. Certainly not as far as his feelings for Ingrid were concerned. He had no love for her. No more than he had for any of the women he'd had sex with. He felt the water hot on his head and massaged his scalp. Gemma? Had he loved his wife? He'd admired her, respected her, and at first had loved her in that needy, lustful, baby way. She was the obvious, she was like his mother, not his real mother, but the one he hadn't had, and would have liked to have had. Maybe he still hadn't grown up. What the hell did that mean? How did a man grow up? By knowing how to love? What was love? A desire to protect? Sure, he could feel that for Gemma. A desire to control? Not particularly. He'd been happy enough for Gemma to run whatever she wanted to. In fact, as he was away most of the time, she'd pretty well taken over all of the domestic organisation of their lives. He was content with that, or most of it, and what he hadn't been content with, he'd let go. He lived his life, she lived theirs. A desire to let go, to let her be what she was? Sure, that's what had happened anyway. Maybe she'd had a life of her own he didn't know about? If she'd had it wouldn't have worried him. He came back to the question. Did he love her? Yes, of course he did, in a way that wasn't necessary to admit either to himself, or to her, which didn't make her very happy, he knew that. So why didn't he admit it now, to himself? OK, I loved Gemma. Loved? He noted the past tense. But he did love her at the time? Yes. Sexually? Yes. As a human being, as a woman, as a person? Yes. Did he still love her after a few years? Yes. But in a different way. They were a couple, new baby, all that. Still love her then? Not spoken about. Drifting apart? Yes. Why? He wanted to look around, couldn't help it - he remembered an Italian girl, his first betrayal of their marriage. Why couldn't he help it? Other men looked around but didn't. (Or at least said they didn't, but he knew damn well that they thought about it - and so did women too, come to that - all the time.) Anyway why couldn't he be the same as them and leave it to his imagination? Well if you're thinking about it, you may as well do it. Anyway, foreign places, alcohol, these were, some of them were, beautiful women. Why not? Because it was a betrayal. Gemma didn't know. She did. He knew she did in the way that women always seemed to sense these things. But he hadn't stopped and she'd thrown him out. Did he know she was going to throw him out? Yes. Did he want her to throw him out? Ah? Yes. Why did he want to be thrown out? So he could...what? Come on, face it, so he could fuck other women without feeling guilty. Alright. Where did that leave him? Here, in a hotel room with Ingrid who he didn't love. And he would have laid a very large wager that the desire was reciprocal - and so was the absence of feeling.

All of this made him feel very isolated, and then sorry for himself, feelings he instantly rejected. Well, anyway, the fact that he was thinking these things was hopeful. Wasn't it? The devil you knew? You mean, me? The devil I am? The devil I now know? Well, perhaps if it was out in the open, perhaps it would change? Can you change? Can anyone change? He didn't know about that. Although he was surprised to realise that there was a part of him that hoped so. And a part that didn't. He thought of Ingrid again on the bed on the other side of the door and felt the first stirrings of an erection under the soap.

* * * *

Eva didn't show up. She'd texted Ingrid to say that she'd spent too long in a church and was staying in an Albergue back down the trail. Ingrid had stared at the text for a few seconds, read it to Peter, and then smiled brightly, "It's just you and me, then?" Peter's feelings travelled a fast spectrum from excitement to tension to unease and then back again.

They went over the road and ate with Oskar and the Swedes; Olaf, the retired engineer, his wife Anika, the sculptor; and her friend, Johanna, who'd been a teacher. They discussed the proposition that to learn to walk the Path was to learn how to live. Oskar, drunk, had laughed his great laugh and shouted, "I agree! On the Path, you see what I am. Walk fast, climb quick. I am more high than the average!"

Johanna, the ex-teacher (she with the black knickers) laughed with him, "Absolutely!" She clapped her hands.

Peter said. "You must be prepared, as well prepared as you can be." He was thinking of his own lack of preparation.

"Not too prepared," said Oskar. "Where is fun when you know everything what is going to happen?"

"You must walk within yourself," said Johanna."

"How can you be outside?" said Oskar.

Johanna slapped his hand.

"You have to be on the edge of your possibilities," said Peter. The wine was getting to him too.

"Always leave opportunity." Johanna filled her glass.

"But at your own pace," said Oskar. "You only go as quick as your feet can do it. Or you fall over!"

"Only carry what you need," said Ingrid. It was about her only contribution to the evening. She seemed slightly intimidated by the Swedes. Perhaps they drew her back into a Scandinavia she wanted to forget. Most of the time she sat silent and watchful in that strange half sulk of hers, slowly sipping her white wine while the rest tipped back the Rioja.

'Always see the now," said Johanna. "Not the future."

"No. The balance between," said Oskar.

"I don't think of any of it," said Anika, Olaf's wife. She was a short sturdy woman with the direct outspokenness of a child. "I think it is interesting how people move. I look at the body all the time. All different. Nothing the same."

"This is all nonsense," said Olaf, "Walking is walking, good exercise. You do it to get somewhere else."

"Ah," said Oskar. "But not too quick. Go too quick and blur is everything. Go too slow and it's dead. Look at me. Just right!"

"Absolutely!" Johanna laughed, then filled Oskar's glass for him. "Enjoy the moment." She raised her drink and they all toasted the Path.

Ingrid was the first to go back to the hotel. The Swedes followed not long after. Peter stayed with Oskar to finish the wine.

"Are you sleeping with them?" asked Peter of the Swedes.

"Not with them. In the same room!" Oskar laughed.

"Are you married?" Peter asked him.

"No. You?"

Peter hesitated, "No." He filled their glasses finishing the bottle.

"I am not a sexy, no, I am not a sexual person," said Oskar.

"Aren't you," said Peter. He wasn't sure how to react to this.

"Not for many years." Oskar looked up at Peter. "Maybe this is my downfall. Ha!" He laughed and tipped back his glass.

"Each to their own," said Peter, aware that all he was offering was reticence and its subsequent reliance on cliché, the Englishman's escape.

"This is me," said Oskar, then added gloomily, "But the own self you have is not always so happy."

"You can say that again," said Peter.

"You are not happy?"

Peter looked into his glass, "No."

"Why not?"

Oskar was making him feel uneasy. "I think we should sleep."

"Tell me. Why you not happy?"

"Because.' Peter didn't know what to say. "I'm not sure we have any right to be."

"I don't talk about rights. Why you not happy?"

Oskar was looking at him with interest but unfeelingly as a scientist might regard a rabbit he was about to dissect.

Peter said slowly, "I am not happy because there is something in me that prevents me being so."

"So happy is a natural state?"

"I suppose I've always thought so. But maybe I think that because I don't want to live the reverse."

"So what is the something that stop you being happy?"

"I don't know."

"Why don't we discover it?"

"You think we can?"

"Why not?" Oskar roared with laughter. "We can discover anything!"

* * * *

The room was dark. Peter could see the silhouette of Ingrid curled away from him in her sleeping bag on the double bed. She was lit by a faint yellow glow coming from the narrow basement window that ran along the top of the wall opposite the door. She'd pulled down the sofa bed for him to sleep on. He undressed as quietly as he could and slipped into his bag. He lay looking up at the shadows on the ceiling cast by what must have been a tree on the street outside. The dark shapes above him meandered slowly across the room and then back again.

"I hope you don't snore."

Peter smiled, "I thought you were asleep."

"I was waiting to see if you snored."

"If I do, wake me."

"Goodnight, Peter."

"Goodnight."

She curled further away from him and pulled her bag up over her shoulders. She was wondering if he'd start anything.

He stared up at the ceiling, wondering if he should. He felt some sort of obligation to at least hint at it. Why was that? He knew from experience that if he felt it, then she probably did too and if he mentioned it then she could say no and the faint tension he felt in the room would dissipate and they could sleep.

She turned.

He was right. She wanted him to say something.

She looked up at the shadows above her and wondered why he didn't say anything. Get it over with and then they could sleep.

"Are you awake," he said. For some reason he felt nervous.

118

Oh God, she thought, now it's started. She said, "Yes."

He said, "I'm sorry, I'm stopping you sleeping. It's the walking. It energises you."

"And the wine," she said.

She wants me to shut-up, he thought.

He's going to say, why don't I come onto your bed? This sofabed is so uncomfortable.

"Would you mind if I had a cigarette?"

"I didn't know you smoked."

"I don't. One of the Swedes gave me one."

"I want to sleep."

"Sorry."

They both lay with their eyes open.

She said, "Now, I can't sleep."

"Nor me."

So why don't you say it then, she thought. Say it and I promise I won't be cruel. I will say I am tired and this isn't the right moment.

I'm sure she wants me to say something.

Please do, then it will be over.

"I was in the army for a very long time," he said for no reason.

"How fascinating."

He laughed. "I'll shut up."

"What was it like?"

"That's what I ask myself. All those years and I don't know." He suddenly felt very sad and knew why he'd brought it up. He didn't know what any of it meant and wanted her to tell him. Why should she know?

"I don't know what I've done either," she said.

"Don't you?"

"I do so many things and I forget them. Where do they go?"

"Who does remember them?'

"Eva says, God remembers," she said. "He writes it all down. Every second. It's all in a big book. He's the only one that remembers everything. Everything you think too." She giggled.

"Oh no."

"Everything!"

They laughed, then stopped. The shadows moved and the uneasiness returned.

Does she want me to go closer? He sat up and leaned on his elbow.

Here it comes. She didn't move.

"I wore a uniform," he said. "They saluted me. I told them what to do. Someone else told me what to do. When I went home I didn't understand why it wasn't the same. Nobody knew who I was."

"You like to tell people what to do?"

"Perhaps I do."

"You like to tell women what to do?"

Is that an invitation?

I shouldn't have said that, she thought.

"Do you like to be told what to do?" he asked.

"No. I don't." The tone in her voice was cold.

"Of course not," he said, and lay on his back again.

"Are you married?"

He told her, thinking it strange that after two weeks the question had never been asked of him and now it had been asked twice in the space of an hour. He knew a little about her; the daughter, the ex-husband. Somehow these distant things weren't the stuff of the Path.

"Were you a good father?"

"Why do you ask that?"

"You look to me like a bad father."

Where had that come from? Is she challenging me?

He said, "My son's a heroin addict." He could be as blunt as her.

"I'm sorry."

"Sorry you asked?" He looked at her profile.

"I'm sorry he's an addict. Do you see him?"

"No."

"Do you want to?"

"Yes." He suddenly felt tearful. Must be the wine.

"The only thing I have is Siri. That's my daughter. Nothing else."

"No men?"

"Oh yes, I have three. There is Soren who loves me, there is my dentist I have sex with, and there is Johannes I sleep with every three months for twenty years."

He turned towards her. "Are you serious?"

"It's the truth."

He paused. "That's nothing," he said.

"How many?" she said.

"Lost count."

"Do you regret it?" she asked.

"No. You?"

"Not at all."

They laughed. She turned her head towards him. He thought she was looking at him but there was a shadow over her face, so he wasn't sure. He turned away, then she did. She giggled. The tension was gone.

"You can have a cigarette if you want to."

He did. She fell asleep. It was done. The shadows had stopped moving.

The next morning when he woke up she was gone. He went into the bathroom, brushed his teeth and looked up into the mirror. She was a reflection of himself, he thought. He knew it, she knew it. How many times in his life had he looked into that particular mirror? And why had doing so made him feel so nervous?

PART THREE

THE MESA

It seemed like the earth was flat. The Old Roman Road was stone, wide and straight as far as the eye could see. Either side were ugly, rough, brown fields dotted with white rock outcrops and the occasional windblown tree. Ahead, solitary and isolated, were pilgrims pushing against the ice cold wind; none of them were walking or talking together anymore. Each was hunched into his or her own thoughts, fifty metres apart as if the elements were separating them.

Llewellyn thought it looked like a painting, the aloneness of each figure emphasised by the vastness of the landscape, all moving slowly, inexorably along the same road, towards the same goal. Santiago? He doubted if many of them were even thinking about it. They were barely halfway there and it was still too distant for it to have become a distinct image, let alone an ambition that felt real or attainable. So what was the compulsion to put one sore foot in front of the other, to shift their aching bodies by willpower alone, metre by painful metre, over mud, rock and tarmac? Was it to get to the shining city like the one he'd seen looking down the hill into that valley? Maybe in their fantasy, but they knew as well as he did, that Burgos had turned out to be the same as any other big place; ordinary mayhem, dirt, noise, everything and nothing. So what were they walking towards? God? Some religious idea? He wasn't, that's for sure. All he could remember was a cold church and a sparse congregation muttering sheeplike responses to the hunched back of a lonely priest. And as for confession, he'd leave that to Werner. That wasn't the kind of faith he was looking for. He passed a woman sitting on a rock outcrop. She was chewing thoughtfully on a piece of bread and looking down at her feet. Maybe they were all just thinking about who they were? He found the idea faintly frightening. He didn't particularly want to know himself at all. No thanks. He'd started down that road with three fifty minute sessions of psychotherapy paid for by the National Health after it had been recommended by his GP concerned about his drinking. He'd thought it would have been a better idea to have the therapist's fee put behind the bar in the pub - he found it easier to talk there, and talk about everything too - the therapist might have been surprised at the intimate loquacity he brought to bear on any number of secret and difficult matters once he'd had a glass or two. Confessions, therapies, Christ, he knew what he had to do. Paint. The long line of pilgrims stretched ahead of him as far as the horizon and he began to mark out the perspective on an imaginary canvas. Werner had been going on and on about it.

"You have a bloody thing to do!" He'd shouted at him in the albergue the previous night.

'Werner, please..."

"Turner!"

Christ, if only he knew. Turner had lived in a brokendown, wet, dripping house with only his mad father for company. Is that what Werner was wishing on him? Is that what he was wishing on himself? Maybe the therapist could have told him.

His ears hurt from the cold in this bloody wind and he decided to tie his scarf round his hat and knot it under his chin. He felt like a gaucho on the Pampas, or more like some old charlady out of Dickens, maybe the one who'd swept the water from under Turner's feet in his sodden studio.

* * * *

Peter was cold too and his face ached from the wind. He could see a small village ahead. The guidebook had said there was a bar. Distances on the plain were deceiving and it took him longer to get there than he thought. The place was as barren and unwelcoming as this part of the path. The room was square and high-ceilinged, with bare, dingy walls that hadn't seen a coat of paint in years. A plain, high bar ran down one side facing half a dozen old wooden tables and chairs, and that was it. Soon-ok was the only other person in there. She'd taken her boots and socks off and was examining her feet. He ordered a coffee and bought a cellophane wrapped cake and a packet of nuts; all the bar had to offer. He sat and looked over to Soon-ok. Her heels were red raw and each had deep, dark, inch long wounds where blisters had formed and burst. He could see she was in trouble and offered her one of his last and precious translucent plasters.

"It's Compeed," he said. "The pilgrim's friend." He tried to explain it was like a second skin. "You never take it off, it slowly wears away giving your own skin the time to heal." He wasn't sure she'd understood anything he'd said, so he tried to put it on her heel himself. She'd immediately withdrawn her foot from his hand. A look of panic had crossed her face and then she'd smiled nervously.

"OK, you do it," he said. He gave her the plaster. "Very careful, you have to get it on straight. Flat."

He went back to his table. It seemed that no-one wanted him to touch them. He thought of Ingrid. He hadn't seen her or Eva for three days. If the past weeks were anything to go by, Ingrid would be ahead of him and Eva behind, but he doubted if that was the case. Ingrid would have just shifted them out of synch. One albergue before his, or one further on, and they'd be walking in a different pattern. He sipped his coffee and thought of his last night with her. It was the first time he'd ever been that frank about his sex life, even to himself. And what a portrait she'd offered of her own. Their honesty had obviated any need for the kind of sex they'd been contemplating. What would it have been for anyway? A distraction from their once unadmitted view of themselves? Once it had been spoken, it was there in front of them - distraction impossible. He told himself again, he didn't even care about her, for Christ's sake, hardly knew her - nevertheless he felt grateful to her; even some affection for another searcher looking in all the wrong places. But there was something else at the back of his mind. He'd sensed that although sex was the drive that had brought them together, neither of them had really wanted it at all. What he'd wanted was for her to tell him what all those years in the army were for, what his life meant? What a ridiculous question. And why had he asked her anyway? Because he thought she would know? Because he wanted her to share this strange and heavy weight he carried - the something he'd told Oskar that prevented him from being happy? Because he sensed that she carried it too? Maybe she did, maybe she did. He stared at the splintered top of the plywood table. He'd seen something that night, something he'd always known, something so blindingly obvious it would be hard not to know it, but sometimes things take time to come into focus and when they do, it's not so much a shock, as the slight, slowly overwhelming pain of the unarguable truth, a truth that had seemed to have been growing in him over the past three days of solitary on the mesa. He looked up and watched as Soon-ok carefully pulled her sock over the badly applied Compeed. That won't last long, he thought. About as long as the sexual Elastoplast he'd been using for years to patch up the nasty little wound his loneliness seeped through. That was the truth. No wonder all his relationships, if he could call them that, had been so temporary. No wonder he'd needed so many at the same time. None of them meant much more than filling an empty evening, or more to the point filling himself on an empty evening. Had he always been lonely? It was a question he didn't want to answer, although he could feel it now; a dull ache slowly pumping it's hollow, endless pain. Maybe Ingrid would know. He looked round the dump of a bar and felt wretched. He'd like to be in a warm bed with a nice woman, but that didn't seem like an option anymore.

Soon-ok slowly pulled her boot on. She heaved her rucksack onto her back and stepped gingerly to the door. She turned, smiled, half waved, and was gone. The bar was empty except for him and the owner who was hunched over a newspaper and smoking a cigarette. Peter split the cellophane around the cake and stuffed it into his mouth. It tasted sweet. Like Ingrid would have done. He scrunched the cellophane in his fist.

The door opened and Willi came in. He gave Peter his usual ironic look and stood in the middle of the room looking at the bar. Heinrich came next and ordered a coke for Willi, without asking him, and a beer for himself. He sat by Peter. Hardly thirty seconds had passed before the boy had drained the coke and was heading back to the door.

"Willi!"

The boy didn't answer and went out.

"He does it all the time," said Heinrich. "I stop, he walks. I walk, he stops. So now I don't get a good beer." He stood over the table drinking quickly.

"Will you go after him?"

Heinrich sat heavily, "I give up. I call my wife and say I'm getting the bus to Santiago and then the airport. She said I'll feel bad if I do it." He burped and wiped his mouth with the back of his hand. "He gets lost, he gets lost. What do I do?"

"Difficult," said Peter. He didn't feel like getting too involved with this.

"He wants me to be angry. It's all he knows. Then he zuckt mit den Schultern... makes his shoulders?" He looked at Peter.

"Shrugs?" Peter demonstrated.

"Ja. So, I don't get angry with him, he does it again. I do get angry, he does it again. You tell me." He blew his cheeks out. "What is the point of this? He is responsible for himself or he is not. Maybe I let him get lost and don't look." He drained the last of his beer. "But not now." He grinned. "I am too perfect. Adios."

He went to the door as Oskar came in.

"Ich habe einen Plan!" Oskar raised his forefinger.

"Ich habe Willi finden." Heinrich went out quickly.

"Don't he want to hear?" Oskar went to the bar and ordered a beer. While it was being poured he turned to Peter, "You have it for him, my plan. It's good!" He took the beer and sat opposite

Peter. "I am to build einer stadt, a city!"

"That's quite a plan." Peter smiled. Oskar's big face and irrepressible energy were always impossible to resist.

"Hey! You want to know how to change things inside? I show you."

"By building a city?"

"Why not? This will the great city ever made. Will be the perfekte stadt. Will be in it, everything! You. Me. Everybody! Everything you want. All food, drinking, cloths, house, auto, all this, communications. All psychological und physical need for you. Hospital, place for playing, music, kino. Anything you don't like, out. No prison."

"And where are you going to build this city?"

"Everywhere. I forgot. It's a virtual city. And this...this..." he looked up at the bar owner, again smoking and reading his paper, hoping he would be listening too. He wasn't. "There is a big house. You go inside is a big screen. You see all the city in front. You see you, like avatar, you understand? You see you self in perfect city. Perfekte Sie in perfekte Stadt! A city you know. Exact identity like own city! Where everything is good. You watch yourself move around. You are happy. You see, you are happy! You ask how I do that? How I get happy all of a quick? Because the city is paradise! You understand? And in paradise, what do you do? Nothing that make you don't happy!" He laughed. "Computers, I need more power. For a hundred thousand people to see himself. A hundred thousand perfect virtual replica." He thought about it, then looked at Peter. "You think I am crazy. Everyone does. Then I do it and everyone know I'm not crazy!"

"And what do you call this city?"

"Santiago!" He roared with laughter then leant forward, very serious, "I mean it, like city of hope, verstehen sie? We all hope. We all want. This change. You see?"

Peter did see. And did want. But didn't know what to say.

"Hi guys," Julia came in. She looked around. "No I don't think so." She left again.

"She knows," said Oskar.

LEON

Two nights later Peter arrived in Leon and decided not to stay.
He'd felt battered, blown and vulnerable on the plain, and had
hoped for kindness and warmth from the city but as he walked
through the outskirts, his isolation was somehow exacerbated
by the noise, traffic, shift, shove and avoidance of strangers. He
cheered himself with the thought that in a couple of days they'd
be in the hills again and decided to find somewhere to spend the
night on the other side of the city so as to get through it quicker
in the morning. As he left the centre he came into the Plaza
Isidoro with its Basilica Church of the same name. Tired, he sat
for a moment on a bench and looked up at it. Another church,
one of hundreds. He looked at his guide. It was eleventh century
and had a Puerta del Perdon, or the famous door of forgiveness.
Medieval pilgrims who were too sick to complete the journey
to Santiago could rest here and receive the same blessings they
would have done if they'd completed their camino. He looked
back up at the church again and decided he wanted to see this
door. He discovered it under a lintel of exquisitely carved stone.
It was closed, which in his present state seemed apt. Not that he
wanted to curtail the walk; just have a look at forgiveness and see
what it looked like.

He didn't go to the albergue, he didn't want to talk to anyone,
and walked into the first hotel he came to. The room was tiny
and cost him forty-five euros which in a pilgrim world he'd have
thought was monstrous, but in his present state he didn't care
about. He wanted to be alone.

He went out to eat in a cheap cafeteria and was horribly

cheated. The meal was undoubtedly the worst he'd had in Spain. The owner of the cafeteria, a grubby, cheap little shit, charged him almost by the sip for his wine, and then retired to a table at the back with a shrug of his mean shoulders and sat playing cards with an ancient, sagging woman, smeared with greasy make-up, who looked like his mother. As he chewed on the paper-thin, leathery steak he'd been served Peter could have punched the self-satisfied creep in the mouth. He practised his mantra. I'd rather be me than him. And as for the old man's frank and complacent extortion, that was his problem. For Peter it was only a few euros. He'd live with it. Welcome back to the non camino. A waitress came over to his table with a crème caramel in a plastic pot. She was also heavily made up. She gave him a red-lipped smile of grimy teeth. It was a very obvious invitation. She held his look as she carefully placed the sweet in front of him. What did she want? To be fucked for money? He dropped his fork onto the plate, left the money on the table and walked out leaving her regarding him with some bemusement. As he came out of the door he glanced back through the window. The owner of the place had turned to the waitress and was laughing.

Back in his room he lay back on one of the twin beds and looked at the ceiling. He felt as if he had lost something. Something that should have been there, definitely wasn't. He worried, almost searched in his rucksack, then laughed as he realised that what he was missing was noise. For the first time in weeks he was sleeping on his own. He stretched on the bed and revelled in the luxury of privacy. There was no-one undressing a few feet away from him, no problems about who to eat with, and there would be no snorers either.

He turned the TV on and flicked through the channels. Most of them were local news which he had no appetite for, and one international bulletin, for which he had even less - it was still a strange and forgotten world out there. He turned to a game of football, not something that usually interested him. His thoughts came and went as he stared at the screen. He saw in his mind the ingratiating smile of the waitress in the cafe, and felt a terrible pity for her, wanted to run back to the cafe and hug her. No he didn't, he remembered the owner's leer, he wanted to put a grenade through the door and watch the old bastard disintegrate. No he didn't want that either. He wanted peace. He missed the army and Len Clarkson, his sergeant and best mate. Officer's shouldn't have sergeants as best mates. He wondered why he did. He didn't know the answer to that. He thought about Sam, and pushed it away. It came back. He saw Sam as a teenager, grinning. It was like a photograph. Was his son now a photograph? He didn't know what to do with the question and it died. He thought about Oskar's idea of building ein perfekte stadt. He'd like to find it, find it inside him. A place in yourself from where you could continually adjust your own sense of self - a citadel that contained only the best judgements and the recipe for wellbeing. He knew he was nowhere near constructing such a place. The cold wind on the mesa had seemed to be blowing him anywhere but. It was halfway through the walk now; two hundred and fifty miles behind, the same in front. He felt he was filling up and then he thought he was emptying out, but had no real idea of what he was losing or what he was replacing it with. Would Oskar ever change anything? Could anything be changed? A month ago he'd have said, no. Now he didn't know. On the screen a goal was scored. He watched for a while. It did the trick. He watched the players celebrate. He didn't want to think about anything.

LA FABA

There are three possible routes from Villafranca del Bieres to O'Cebreiro. The first was the Ruta Carretera, the easiest, mostly along a senda which ran along the main road; the second, the Ruta Pradela which took you up into the hills on the right hand side of the valley as you travelled west, and the third was the Camino Dragonte, the loneliest, longest and most spectacular walk running high into the mountains on the left of the road. By the time you reached Herrerias all three routes had converged leaving only the nine kilometre climb through La Faba to O'Cebreiro at the top of the mountain; a climb that was as steep, but rougher than that up to Roncesvalles on the first day of the path.

Eva wanted the isolation of the Camino Dragonte. Although Ingrid was confident of her own stamina she was concerned about Eva's on this, the toughest of the three routes. All the guidebooks said it was difficult and unpredictable. It was twenty-eight kilometres even to Herrerias, it wasn't well way-marked, the track was narrow and steep, often overgrown and it was easy to get lost in the mists. But Eva had insisted. This was the way she wanted to go. She'd had a dream in the albergue in Villafranca the night before. She dreamt of a broken table in a dark forest. An old woman came to her and offered her bread for the hard road that lay ahead. She'd taken this as a sign that she must take the difficult path. She didn't tell Ingrid about the dream but simply she said she was going to take the Dragonte. There was no offer for Ingrid to join her. It was clear she'd go her own way whatever Ingrid did. It was too late for Ingrid to change the system now. Eva made the decision, Ingrid would go ahead and organise the night. This was how they did it. She said, OK.

As they came out of Villafranca they could see the mountain shrouded in mist up to their left. Ingrid looked at Eva to see if there was any change of heart. There wasn't, and Ingrid set off up the steep asphalt road. As Eva watched her friend's red pack disappear round a bend ahead she felt pleased to be on her own. She leant forward on her sticks and began the climb. The road became a path and then a track. It was becoming mistier as she ascended. After a while she realised she was walking through low cloud and the visibility came down to about five metres. She passed through a small village, hardly more than a collection of houses. It was so quiet she thought it might be abandoned. Then she heard a child shout through the mist and had the strangest thought that the cry was her own. She stopped, looked back and saw no-one. She walked on; the mist closed in a little more, and then became thinner. She felt a nervous excitement. Something was going to happen. Suddenly the mist cleared altogether and she was in bright sunshine. Below her she could see the cloud shield she'd come through; above was bright blue sky. Ahead she could see the peak of a mountain. It must be O'Cebreiro, she thought, nearly forty kilometres away. She was surrounded by chestnut trees. She felt exhilarated and knew she'd made the right decision; this path was her path. She felt a great lightness as she walked beneath the trees in the clear air.

The path became narrower and began to twist and turn through lower, prickly gorse. The mist began to close in on her again. She had a sense that there were dark trees above her, but then remembered there were no trees here, she was on a path through scrubland. It became even narrower, the vegetation brushing her legs. A couple of times she had to push it back with her sticks and force herself through. The track veered sharply left and then right. She began climbing again, the path so narrow now it was hardly a path at all. She could see maybe two metres ahead, then one, her boots were getting trapped in the gorse and she was having to step over it. She realised that she was no longer

132

on the path and was pushing through heavy, thick bush that was reaching up to her thighs, scraping her legs and scratching her skin through her trousers. The mist by now had cut her visibility to barely half a metre. Then she quite literally couldn't see her hand in front of her face. The gorse became taller and thicker. This was no path at all. She realised she had to go back. She turned. And screamed. Standing behind her was an old woman. Eva could hardly see her face but knew she was smiling. She looked as if she was raising her stick. Eva could just about see its shape through the mist. Then the woman turned away. Eva could see her small, hunched back as she pushed back up through the bush, and followed as best she could. She could feel thorns scraping the flesh of her legs and knew they were bleeding. Blood was running down the backs of her hands. She didn't care, she knew she had to follow the woman.

Suddenly the gorse had gone and she could see thick, wide-bladed grass at her feet. The mist lifted slightly. She seemed to be surrounded by fallen, dark stone walls. The woman had disappeared. Eva didn't mind. She knew she had just been a guide to bring her to this place. She remembered that she'd read that there was an abandoned monastery somewhere on this trail. She took a couple of steps forward and stumbled on a rock. It was part of a larger pile. She sat down on it and saw that a toppled stone had created a table under her left hand. She looked round at the broken walls. She knew that they were for her protection. She burst into tears.

She had no idea how long she sat there. It wasn't until the straps of her pack began to burn into her shoulders that she looked up. The mist was gone and the sun was glistening on the residue of damp on the tumbled stone. She slipped the pack from her shoulders and took out some bread. She ate it washed down with water from a plastic bottle. As she chewed she sat very still. She was perfectly, perfectly happy. She was so happy, she felt as if she didn't exist.

There was a sound. It hardly permeated her consciousness. It became louder, like a cry. She wondered if it was the child again. Perhaps she'd followed her on the trail from the village? She looked round and could see nothing except the walls, those beautiful old stone walls, wrapping softly round her, hiding her. She wanted to stay within them forever. The cry came again. She realised it was her name.

Ingrid was standing in front of her. "Where have you been?"

"Here," said Eva.

"It's four o'clock. I thought you were lost."

Eva smiled. They walked down the sharp descent into Herrerias together. It was tough going even for Ingrid, but Eva hardly noticed.

"We're not going to O'Cebreiro tonight," said Ingrid. "I'm too tired. We'll stay here."

Eva didn't care where they slept.

* * * *

Peter, although he didn't know it, was by now a day behind Ingrid and Eva. He took the Ruta Pradela out of Villafranca up the steep path into the hills on the right hand side of the valley. He'd left the albergue early as usual and the air was clear; some cloud but nowhere near as much as had enveloped Eva the day before. He climbed out of the town and stood on the side of the mountain in bright sun under a clear blue sky. The mist was settling into the valley below melting down into it like a soft white blanket pierced only by the steeples of the churches in Villafranca. There was no sound. He breathed in deeply trying to inhale the silence as if it was the purest of air. Nothing moved. He looked up at the chestnut trees, their boughs were still. A dead leaf dropped by his foot. He felt at peace for the first time since leaving the Mesa.

It wasn't the only time he'd experienced such an inner joy at the stillness of the path, but the feelings were getting deeper and longer. In the six days since leaving Leon he'd felt himself becoming more relaxed, more accepting of the way. He was still walking too fast probably; his mind fixed on what was ahead rather than allowing himself to dwell on what was around him, but he was getting better at it. Better at not thinking. Better at being nothing other than a vessel for all of this. He stopped and looked up at the trees. Another leaf fell in front of him. As far as he was concerned it could have been the only thing that moved in all of Spain.

He heard voices behind him, then laughter and a snatch of a song. He looked down the trail and saw the Italian actors coming up towards him. The taller one, Francesco, with the long lugubrious, deadpan face had darted into the trees as the shorter man waited with the woman. The deep reds and orange of their clothes seemed to melt into the autumnal show of the chestnut. Peter assumed that Francesco had gone to relieve himself but he reappeared with a bulging bag. He showed its contents to the other two. The woman, Pina, thin wiry, with cropped grey hair, danced up and down with glee. Marcello, who had waited with her on the path, saw Peter and waved his crumpled straw hat. They came up to him.

"We have found..." Pina began.

"Non, non, non!" Marcello interrupted her. He pointed ahead. "La Faba."

"You're not going to O'Cebreiro?" asked Peter.

"La Faba is better," said Pina.

Francesco looked solemnly at Peter as if it was the gravest decision he would ever have to make.

"Cinque camino." Pina held up five fingers. "Always La Faba."

"You've done it five times?" Peter was amazed, but then remembered he'd heard of a man who'd walked it for eight consecutive years. He looked up at the leaves blazing in the sunlight. Who could blame him?

The Italians went on ahead but he soon overtook them and was heading down into Herrerias where Ingrid and Eva had stayed the night before. He went through the town, over the bridge, and began the climb to La Faba.

* * * *

135

The Iglesia de Santiago, the Monastery San Francisco, Iglesia San Nicolas, Divina Pastora, Iglesia Collegiate, Convento San Jose, Convento Annunciate; these are the seven churches or chapels that Paul visited in Villafranca on his walk round the town. He stayed in each one long enough to say ten Hail Marys, then left to look for the next. If you'd asked him when he'd completed the circuit to describe a detail of each place of worship he wouldn't have been able to; he might have said dark, or stone, or incense, or high window, but nothing specific. What he was looking for wasn't out, it was in, and he didn't have any idea what the hell it was, just part of everything else that was churning around inside him.

He walked slowly back to the privado he was staying in with Harry, Werner and Llewellyn. They were a foursome now. Despite a few growing strains between them, they enjoyed each other's company, especially the boozy dinners every night. Villafranca was no exception and they took the pilgrim's menu at a big place facing onto the square. It was a good, easy, warm night and they laughed a lot. Paul smoked a couple of Llewellyn's cigarettes, drank too much and put the whole damn business that was weighing him down right out of his mind.

The next day it didn't take long for them to decide to take the Ruta Carretera, the easy way out of Villafranca. Much of it was on the senda by the main road. Llewellyn knew the climb was going to be difficult at the end whichever route they took, but if he could avoid as many hills as possible that was fine by him. His feet were sore and he was getting fed up of these upclines and downclines as he called them. But he was OK at the moment as he was walking along the senda curving along the valley floor. The four of them were in a long line with Paul and Harry behind him and Werner, slower as usual, back even further.

Paul and Harry were beginning to separate too. Paul had for days been telling Harry the story of his life. He wasn't sure why, but for whatever reason it was all coming out in bits and pieces; his early years in the navy, his academic career, the seminary. He'd been at his angriest when he related how and why he'd walked out of the psychology department at the university.

"Sexuality is one thing, Harry, but why do you have to flag it up? It was like a homosexual heaven in there. Few years ago, I'll give you that."

"Thirty years," said Harry.

"Personally I believe homosexuality is abhorrent. So do you. But I accept it."

"Can't say I notice it anymore."

"Back then it was the revolution. They didn't admit it but they were hiring guys because they were gay. They were positively encouraging it. I was about the only straight guy left. You know, listen to this, someone had knocked a hole in the wall of a toilet cubicle so you could put your dick through it and someone the other side would, you know? I saw the damn hole. I complained about it. They looked at me like I was a dinosaur. I tell you, you'd have noticed it in there."

"Couldn't take a shit without someone looking in on you?"

"That's right." Paul looked at Harry, never quite knowing if his friend was mocking him.

"How about Dorothea?" said Harry. "You never talk about her."

"She was my wife. She was a pretty woman, got educated; thought she was cleverer than she was, she took off, what's there to talk about?"

"With that guy who worked in the drive-in burger place out on the interstate."

"That's him."

"Used to poke hotdogs though a hole in the wall there."

"Are you taking me seriously?"

"Just more meat, Paul" Harry laughed. "How about Dorothea? Come on. You never say."

"Maybe I don't want to." Paul was quiet for a moment. There was just the tapping of his sticks on the concrete as he walked. "Our sex life wasn't too good that's for sure."

"Oh that was it."

"No it wasn't! It might have been. How do I know?"

"If you don't know, who does?"

"Sometimes, Harry, you really piss me off."

"Burger guy, Jeez," said Harry.

"What in hell's that got to do with anything?" Paul walked ahead.

Harry let him go. He'd have preferred to talk theology but kept getting the life story and then only half off it, with nothing about what he thought mattered which was Dorothea. He caught up with Llewellyn who'd been sitting on a crash barrier having a cigarette.

"Where's Werner?' Harry asked.

"Behind somewhere. Did you know he prays as he walks?"

"Bout the best thing you can do, Lew, you should try it."

"General Patton!"

Harry laughed. It was a running joke between them. Llewellyn thought Harry sounded like George C Scott in the film. They walked along together.

"I mention the pilgrim transaction?" asked Llewellyn. "I have this theory, see, about the relationship between the pilgrim and the Spanish."

"Established commercial arrangement, Lew."

"But when you go into it, it's more than that, see? What is a pilgrim?"

Harry went with it. "OK. He's essentially a good guy."

"And intelligent too, from all walks of life, right? Some of them quite rich. But now the waiters..."

"You're not going on about waiters again?"

"And the shopkeepers, hospitaleros, all of them. They're not as well paid as the pilgrims, are they? So in normal life they're subservient aren't they?"

"They do a job, Lew."

"But it's a serving job, isn't it? However... " Llewellyn was getting into lawyer mode, "...on the camino the pilgrims all have this idea that they are somehow holy, and part of that is to be humiliated, isn't it?"

"Not in my book."

"You know what I mean, General. To be accepting of other people, and God's word and all that."

"Sure." Harry was coming and going with this theory.

"So the waiters serve people who are richer than them but who are pretending to be subservient because they're pilgrims."

"What? You lost me there."

"It's the pilgrim transaction, see? The waiters can be as rude as they like and charge what they like, and no-one will tell them to stop because they're all trying to be holy."

"I'll tell you something, Lew, the Spanish idea of commerce you could shove up a horse's ass. The damn shops are never open, at least not when you want them to be. You go at eight in the morning, they're closed. Go back in the afternoon, they're closed. Go at half past eight in the evening, they're open. Who wants to buy a shirt at that time? That's when you want to be wearing it, having dinner with your wife."

"It's because of the siesta, Harry."

"Sure, you don't work when it's hot. Except it rains all the time. Where's the sense in that? You told Werner about this pilgrim transaction?"

"He thinks it's shit too."

"He prays, see Lew. You should try it."

They walked on, came off the senda and went up into the hills again. It was a long day.

Paul thought the last ten kilometres from Herrerias up to La Faba were hell, absolute hell. It was a six feet wide, rocky, twisting track winding up the mountain side so steep you could have touched the ground in front of you with your hand sometimes. Kilometre after kilometre and no let up. His back felt like there was a red hot iron running up his spine, and his legs beneath were like dead weight; he could hardly lift them as he inched his way up. The weight round his gut wasn't getting any less; because of the amount he was eating and drinking, he guessed, to keep the carbs high. Maybe the fatigue was accumulating over the days and for a man of his age he'd just walked too far; nearly six hundred K with another two hundred to go. The hell he was going to the top to O'Cebreiro tonight, he was stopping at the next albergue they came to, he didn't care what anyone said.

There was no alternative, his body wouldn't go any further. Truth is, he was getting sick and tired of the whole damn thing. And Harry wasn't helping. All that shit about Dorothea. What in hell was she to do with anything?

* * * *

Peter reached the albergue in La Faba late in the afternoon. The village was tiny, hardly more than a street of a dozen houses running along the side of the mountain on the way up to O' Cebreiro. The albergue was surrounded by trees. Next to it was an old church which had been recently renovated. Between the two was a pretty garden built round a life sized bronze statue of a pilgrim. It was quiet, there was a dull, still air and a sense of peace. As Peter walked in it was beginning to rain. The albergue was run by two German women who were friendly but distant, giving the impression that their minds were on other, holier things. Maybe they've been in the mountains too long, thought Peter. The bunkroom was light and airy. Some of the bunks were blocked off by benches. It was getting towards November and the number of pilgrims on the path was decreasing, which meant he had a wide selection of beds. He dropped his bag on one in the corner and sat down.

He felt good, as if he was getting stronger and didn't need people so much. But he could feel something else was coming to the surface. He knew enough now not to force it. He looked through the wooden uprights of the bunks in the room. The low light of the sun was streaming through them. For a second they reminded him of the coloured poles stuck into his school playing field. He remembered a rugby practice when he'd dodged and weaved through them. He'd slammed his shoulder into the heavy bag strung at the end of the run. He'd fallen backwards and sat on the grass in tears. He'd hit the bag awkwardly and broken his collarbone.

"Get up, Dandy Kim," the teacher had said. "What do you think this is? Soccer?"

He stared at the bunks and the thought that had been on the edge of his mind all day finally emerged. It was nothing new. He known it for years, maybe all his life, and he'd repressed it because it was deep and rotten. It was that he was a fraud. And he'd always been a fraud. He thought, fuck I don't need this, but there was nothing he could do to stop it. When he'd first trod the path he'd thought it led to Santiago, but he was only now beginning to understand that the real journey was into himself. He looked down at his hands. He knew he had to finally admit that he'd spent his life pretending to be something he wasn't. He'd won a scholarship to a minor public school and it had all gone wrong from there. He hadn't even wanted to sit the exam. A teacher at his primary school had put his father up to it, and Peter had been told to sit at a desk in what had seemed to him to be a very grand and frightening hall with a huge clock set high in the wall over a dark wood stage at the end. He couldn't remember what he'd written, but it must have been good enough. They offered him a place and he exchanged his grubby jeans and torn bomber for a stiff, dark brown blazer with gold piping round the lapels and a school cap with a huge and embarrassing bright yellow crest on the front. He was called by his surname and taught Latin, he was made to stand in the quadrangle for hours as a punishment, and he never kicked a round ball again - football was for the oiks. And he'd changed how he spoke. His own accent was banished; he became a posh boy. What else could he have done? He clasped his hands tight in his own defence. They mocked him anyway and if he'd answered back in broad Brummie they'd have slaughtered him, debagged him probably, leaving him standing in his underpants, as was the custom, in a field in full view of every dormitory window. He was tough enough, he could fight them, but not all of them, and anyway it wasn't the physical drubbing he couldn't stand, it was the humiliation. The humiliation again. Was this where his dread began? The humiliation of being the different one? He wasn't strong enough to face it then, or since. He was amazed at how quickly he'd modulated his vowels. It took him only a few days and by the end of the week he sounded like everybody else. He could even shift, mid-sentence, from posh to Brum and back again. Returning to Edgbaston it was hard to tell he'd been away. Even his table manners switched back and forth; from a delicate knowledge of the appropriate cutlery, to a careless and aggressive stabbing with a fork; from a polite excuse me, to a quick grab; from a sip to a slurp. I must have been an actor, he thought. Or schizophrenic.

Slowly the working class boy became the young gent. His father had left his mother and gone to live alone in suburban vagueness. He'd become distant in unshared sickness, and finally passed away - the term was accurate, he drifted off, almost unnoticed. Peter hadn't known he'd died for three days, hardly knew he'd been ill. For years his father became little more than a misty notion in his mind, only achieving brief substance with the arrival of a Christmas card written in an almost illegible hand. His mother had started drinking not long after her abandonment, and his only, usually successfully repressed, memories of her were dominated by images of unstoppable tears, as full and wet as he'd ever known - and he'd known a few - rolling down a face pudgy with self-pity and bitterness as she sat at the kitchen table, a glass of brandy in her hand. His home visits were seldom. He'd left the remnants of family to his brother. His absences began early, barely a year or two after starting his new school. He preferred the invitations from his schoolmates to spend his summers swishing around their country piles. He forgot Edgbaston and became the boy from...? Where? Nowhere. Christ. He leant back on the wall behind the open bunkbed, pleased that no-one else was in the room as his past tumbled unbidden into his mind.

He went to a university with connections to the school, and quickly ran out of cash; his lifestyle at the time being more silver than brass. A chum told him the army were offering to pay an undergraduate's way if he joined up, and anyway what was wrong with being an officer of the Queen? He applied to and was accepted for Sandhurst; the grimy streets of Birmingham became a hazy memory. His mother, still doting but by now rarely sober, became an embarrassment and was exchanged in his mind for something better; a little fantasy he created of an early life that wasn't unlike that lived by his school friends; a dream that once in place, he left untouched, never offered, embroidered or probed. His parents became rested in his memory as shadowy, ill-defined figures in no particular place and no distinguishing features. When asked by another officer what his father had done, he easily substituted factory for industry, so his fellow cadets assumed he came from the nouveau riche, not the best background one could have, but acceptable. He'd done well, not that well, captain after an acceptable number of years. It was enough. The officer's mess, terrified at anything resembling introspection, never asked personal questions, too nervous of being on the receiving end. The only person who'd ever sensed the truth was Len Clarkson. Peter never told him of his background but he knew Clarkson knew. Knew that he should never have been a captain in the class-ridden British Army, that he should have been a sergeant like Clarkson was. And as he stared at the empty bunks he could see why Clarkson in his bizarre, foul mouthed way had become his closest friend. They both came from the same place. He leaned forward again and slowly untied his boots. If Clarkson knew then so did everyone else, all those boys in the school, the other cadets, his fellow officers, his commanders, they all knew. Knew he was a fraud. Probably pointed and smirked behind his back. His closely guarded secret was no secret at all. He was Peter the Fraud. He felt hollow. For a second he could hear his life laughing at him; boys, cadets, officers, commanders - women. Women? Did they know too? Is that why they loved him? Poor little chap, struggling to be something he's not?

He thought of the last time he'd seen his father, three years before his death. The old man, grey with loneliness, had looked at him with a kind of sad disgust. What a traitor you are, he seemed to say. And then his mother, her bile turned to vomit and erupting, too quick to catch, as she ran across the kitchen to the sink. He'd banished them both from his mind. He'd cut himself away from the root. Not my fault, not my fault. Yes it is. Not my fault. Where was he now? He didn't know. Who was he now?

Well that was the fucking question. He stared down at the laces in his hands for a long time.

Julia walked in. "Hallo, Peter," she said.

"Hullo, Julia."

"You alright?"

"No, I'm not."

She sat on the bottom bunk opposite him, put her elbows on her knees and leant forward. "So what are we going to eat for dinner? What do you think?"

"Julia..."

"We got to eat."

* * * *

The only bar in the village looked dismal and dark so everybody descended on the local shop to buy something to cook for dinner. Llewellyn went with Werner to get what they could for themselves and the two Americans. Werner bought four bottles of wine and insisted that Llewellyn bought another two. "You think I'm going to drink and other people don't," he said. "I never do that. I must share."

"There'll be about ten people!" said Llewellyn whose stash was rapidly diminishing. He already doubted if he had enough to get home. But he bought the two bottles. There was something about Werner's angry insistence that unnerved him. You didn't want to fight with Werner. Llewellyn was already on the defensive about the Austrian's continual demand that he should paint. It seemed a personal insult to Werner that Llewellyn wasn't using the talent that God had given him. He'd even taken Llewellyn's sketchbook out of his rucksack in a picnic area near Leon, thrown it on the ground and stamped on it. 'That's what you do with what you've been given!'

Llewellyn couldn't work it out. Werner's anger was real enough. Maybe he was missing his own art - architecture - and punishing Llewellyn for its absence. Llewellyn put this to Werner as gently as he could, but he only flew into another rage, tore a page from the book, ripped it in half and threw the pieces in the air. 'I will never design another thing. I'm telling you. Nothing!'

But the worst had come three days before and it was nothing to do with art. It involved a taxi. Llewellyn had felt ill in Astorga, a town that had housed over twenty pilgrim hospitals in medieval times, not that they were much use to him. He'd begun retching at the beginning of the evening, had terrible diarrhoea all night and puked again the next morning. He could hardly stand, let alone walk. Werner had no sympathy and ignored him. Julia had talked to the hospitalero at the albergue and found him a doctor. On walking unsteadily down the street to keep his appointment he'd seen Werner striding away with his pack and sticks obviously continuing the camino without him, and not saying goodbye either.

The doctor had given him something to calm his stomach and told him to rest for the day. The hospitalero had been kind enough to let him spend the rest of the morning on his bunk even though the albergue was closed. By the afternoon he'd felt better and decided to walk the twenty or so kilometres to Rabanal where the others would be spending the night. Within a hundred metres he knew it would be impossible. His pack felt so heavy he thought someone must have put a rock in it, and his legs didn't feel strong enough to carry his own frame let alone a pack with a rock in it. If he stayed in Astorga he'd be a day behind and never catch them up, which meant he'd walk the rest of the path on his own and he couldn't face that, so the only alternative was a taxi.

He arrived at the albergue in Rabanal a half an hour after Werner. He had it in mind to pretend that he'd walked. If he hadn't it was like he'd broken the convention; to complete the path you had to walk all the way to Santiago, every inch. Ultimately he knew he couldn't cheat it because he couldn't cheat himself; he'd always know he'd taken a taxi part of the way. But not lying to himself was one thing, not lying to Werner quite another. He knew he'd never hear the end of it, so he told the taxi-driver to stop before the albergue. He'd walk the last few hundred metres and arrive as though he'd done the whole journey on foot. Unfortunately Werner had been sitting in a local bar across the road from where he'd got out of the taxi. As the car moved away he found himself holding his pack with one hand, his straw hat with the other, and staring straight into the mocking blue eyes of the Austrian.

At least the discovery of this latest inadequacy on Llewellyn's part had the benefit of deflecting Werner's venom from his painting. Now, according to Werner, he was not a true pilgrim, Llewellyn didn't know why he put up with it and at least in part he hadn't. He'd made sure that the next few evenings were spent with Paul and Harry and the days walking far enough ahead of Werner to prevent any more criticism.

But it was always there like a dog waiting to bite. As they came out of the shop, Julia came in. She bought two bananas and an apple. I'd prefer to be walking with her, thought Llewellyn.

* * * *

Werner and Llewellyn were the first into the kitchen. There was a huge table in the centre surrounded by old wooden chairs and benches. Around the walls was rudimentary cooking equipment including a battered oven, hotplate, fridge and a microwave that had seen better days. In the assortment of cupboards above was a variety of old and chipped crockery. Taped to the walls were notices in several languages asking pilgrims to leave the room as clean as they found it.

Llewellyn put the wine on the table next to the plastic bag of food they'd bought. Werner immediately began to uncork a bottle as Peter came in with another, and bread and cheese. "Not many options in the shop," he said.

"You got wine, what else you need?" said Werner.

Peter laughed. He'd seen the Austrian but they'd never spoken until now. Llewellyn introduced them. Werner stared keenly into Peter's eyes as they shook hands, then gave him a glass of wine and abruptly told Llewellyn to show him the photographs of his paintings on his iPod. "I am saying he is a genius!"

Llewellyn not unwillingly took out the iPod and Peter sat down to scroll through the photographs.

"Turner," said Werner. "Eat with us if you want."

Paul came in with Harry who said hello to Peter.

Paul went straight to the bag of food. "What you got, Lew?" He took out a packet of sliced chorizo. "Don't the Spanish ever eat anything that's not full of fat?"

"Didn't get any bratwurst, did yer?" asked Harry.

"General Patton!" Llewellyn laughed.

"Know what I'd like? A big plate of buffalo wings!"

"Can of ravioli," said Paul taking it out of the bag.

"That'll do it," said Harry.

"I have some cheese," said Peter.

"God I could do with a big fat burger," said Harry.

"What about the paintings?" Werner asked Peter.

"Extraordinary."

"You think? Really?" said Llewellyn, "thanks." He went and sat in the corner, pleased with himself.

"Give me a smoke," said Werner.

"Can you smoke in here?"

"Why not?" Werner took Llewellyn's tobacco and rolled a cigarette. He said to Peter, "Come with us tomorrow to Fonfria."

"Where?" Peter checked his guide. "That's only twelve K."

"That's not far enough, Wern," said Harry. "We'll never get to Santiago."

"What's the hurry?"

"Some of us got a plane to catch."

"Werner doesn't want to get to Santiago," said Llewellyn from the corner. "Doesn't want to stop walking. That so Wern?" Llewellyn had meant it in a friendly enough way, though perhaps there was an edge to it. But it was a mistake.

"I don't take taxis to Rabanal," said Werner. Harry and Paul looked round. It was the first they'd heard about taxis. They thought that Lew had walked on his bad stomach. Paul had even complimented him on his guts and Harry had laughed at what he thought was a joke. They looked at Llewellyn.

"Sorry," said Llewellyn deeply embarrassed. "I'd been up all night."

"You told us..." Paul began.

"I didn't want to admit it. Christ." Llewellyn turned away.

"Like you don't want to admit anything." Werner leant back in his chair with his back to Llewellyn.

"He can do what he wants," said Harry.

"You take a taxi, you don't do the path," said Werner. He turned to Llewellyn. "Why don't you take a bus to Santiago?"

Llewellyn looked out of the window at the rain that was now falling heavily.

"How in hell am I going to heat this ravioli?" said Harry. "Where do they keep the pans?" He began to look through the cupboards.

"How far will you be walking the day after Fonfria?" asked Peter.

"How should I know?" said Werner. "I am not a tourist. I'm a pilgrim. I don't plan."

"Those old pilgrims planned, Wern," said Paul sitting with a glass of wine. "They were going a thousand miles and back. You know this was all forest then? Imagine hacking your way through that. Why do you think there were so many hospitals along the way? A lot of them were falling down with disease. And then there were the hustlers and robbers. Hell they planned. They planned for years. Trip of a lifetime."

"And they didn't have no shoes neither," said Harry.

"I don't plan, I walk," said Werner lighting his cigarette.

"We're treading the sacred path," said Harry. "Still can't find a damn pan. This too big?" He held up a huge pasta pot.

"You could boil a sack of potatoes in that," said Paul.

"You want to do it?" said Harry, continuing his search.

Werner tossed the tobacco back to Llewellyn and said to Peter, "Come with us tomorrow anyway."

Peter wasn't sure why he was being invited. Llewellyn had the feeling that it was for his benefit. Maybe he wasn't good enough for Werner anymore. A part of him was relieved, but he felt a slight panic all the same. Maybe he was getting addicted to Werner's criticism. It had happened before - all these violent types bullied him. Women as well. Maybe that's why he hung around with them.

Julia came in to chop her fruit. Harry asked her where the pans were.

"Why don't you do it in the microwave?" she said.

"Why didn't you think of that?" Paul said to Harry.

"I ain't a great exponent of the culinary arts, Paul. Where's the can opener?"

Julia showed him. Werner, Paul and Peter sat drinking. Llewellyn smoked in the corner.

"The German women asked me to say a mass in the church," said Paul. "Around eight-thirty, if anyone's interested."

"I'll be there," said Werner.

"Koreans will come," said Paul.

"And you?" Werner turned to Llewellyn.

"I might."

"Why don't you make up your mind?"

"I'll think about it," Llewellyn said sharply.

"They got this thing they do here," said Paul. "It's their custom. They wash each other's feet."

"Yeah?" said Julia, excited by the thought.

"You don't have to do it, I guess. It's after the mass. The German woman wants to say a few words, and then..." Paul shrugged.

"Hell, Paul." Harry wasn't too keen on this idea.

"She's following her Christ, Harry."

"I'll do it," said Werner. "I'll wash feet."

"Me too," said Julia.

"You wash feet, Lew?" Werner smirked.

"Will you leave me alone?"

"It's all you want. Leave you alone," Werner laughed. "And you stay same as you are."

"Why are you bullying him?" Peter hadn't meant to say it. He hardly knew these people. There was a silence.

149

Werner said, "You're right. I am a bully. I apologise, Lew."

"It doesn't matter. I'm very happy. And I might even go to mass."

"You don't have to," said Peter. He still wasn't clear why he was pushing this. Because he didn't like Werner? Or was there something in himself that was coming out?

"He's right, you don't have to," said Paul.

"Don't know about washing feet?' Llewellyn laughed, feeling better now he had some support.

"You don't know about anything," said Werner quietly.

"Aren't we all on our own spiritual journey?" said Peter still prodding at something.

"What in hell does that mean?" said Paul suddenly turning on Peter. Everything about this damn walk was beginning to piss him off, but nothing more than all this damn, horseshit spirituality from a lot of people who'd never given it a seconds thought. "This is the Camino de Santiago! We're here walking towards the bones of an Apostle. That's the journey, for God's sake."

"That's your journey," said Peter quietly.

"What the hell else is there?" said Paul belligerently. "Don't give me all that new age crap, that Shirley MacLaine bullshit. What's the spirit if it's not in an Apostle of Christ?"

"The spirit?"

"What is it? Tell me!"

There was a silence, Paul had almost shouted.

"Well," said Peter. He was speaking of things he'd never thought that much about before, let alone debated, and come to that, entering territory that would have had him thrown out of the officer's mess. "In its broadest sense, I suppose, the spirit is anything that we sense outside of the material."

"What's that supposed to mean?" There was something about Paul's aggressive questioning that was pointing at his own doubt. And he knew it but couldn't stop it.

"Everyone has their own question," said Peter.

"The hell they do," said Paul.

"Paul," said Harry.

150

"No, Harry." Paul went to bang his hand on the table and stopped himself. "I've got to say this. I've been walking on this damn path for more than three weeks now, and sure everybody's got their own ideas," he said the word with contempt, "but where do they put them? There's a lot of religions around, I give you that, and I respect them, but you got to remember most of them been here for a thousand years and longer, so they're not some crackpot, pikinini bunch of half-assed thinking. Some very great people have been involved in this, including Jesus Christ, and whatever else prophet you want to talk about, and they have suffered, have suffered a lot, dammit! You think all that's for nothing? You think it doesn't matter that on this trail there have been probably millions of people dying? Why do you think they did it? Because they read a book about some pop-up guru? About some holistic, cure-all, temporary thing? No, they didn't! They did it, because they knew, like I know, that there is only one God!" Then he did bang his hand on the table. "And you worship Him. You worship Him because He is life itself!" He stopped and looked around. "Been wanting to say that. Didn't mean to insult anybody."

"Why should you worship?" said Peter.

"He said it!" shouted Werner. "It's life itself!" He turned to Llewellyn and said nastily, "And you're too scared to live it."

"Leave him alone," said Peter, his voice rising.

"It's alright, I can look after myself," said Llewellyn sitting back in his chair and rolling another cigarette. He noticed the paper was shaking.

"Peter's right. Leave him alone, Werner," said Paul quietly, looking away, trying to calm himself.

"I will," Werner turned his back on Llewellyn.

"And, if you don't mind..." said Peter.

"No, go on," said Paul.

"Don't we all worship in our own way?"

"Do we?" said Paul. "What way do you worship?" He glared at Peter who had no answer to give him. He was saved by a loud crack from inside the microwave.

"Oh no, your ravioli's exploded!" Julia opened the microwave door. The interior was covered in tomato sauce. "Why did you use a glass dish, Harry?"

"Huh?"

"He doesn't know anything," said Paul.

"That's why I got a wife, Paul."

"Get a plastic bag, I'll clean it up before the German woman comes back." Julia took a cloth and began wiping the ravioli and broken glass from the microwave.

"Now what are we going to eat?" said Paul.

He said it so plaintively that everybody laughed.

"I've got some salad," said Julia.

The door opened and the Italians came in with Fabian strumming his guitar behind them. Marcello held up in front of him the bulging bag Peter had seen Francesco come out of the woods with. Fabian brought the entrance to a climax with a couple of loud chords.

"Porcini!" announced Marcello. He pulled a six inch, thick-stemmed mushroom form the bag, "E pasta!" He produced a long packet of spaghetti from inside his trousers. "E il maestro!" He pointed at Francesco who took a slow bow.

"We invite you to eat with us," said Pina.

"Ain't poisonous, are they?" asked Harry.

"They're ceps," said Peter. "You get them in France."

"That explains everything," said Harry. He sat down, happy to be out of the cooking zone.

Marcello poured water into a pan and Francesco began to chop the porcini. Julia cleaned the microwave as Fabian played the guitar again. Peter looked up. Another Korean had come in and was standing by the door with a small plastic bag.

"Come in, honey, sit down," said Harry. "We're about to get, what they called?"

The woman, who was in her late thirties, sat at the end of the table between Peter and Werner.

"Hullo, I'm Peter."

"Hi, I'm Karen." She pronounced it Kah-ren. She had an American accent.

"Are you Korean?" asked Peter.

"From California. I'm Japanese."

"Werner." The Austrian smiled as he shook hands with her. "I study Japanese architecture one time."

Peter thought she had an edge of sophistication about her, a reserve which was missing in the more easy-going Koreans. Werner was watching her closely. Peter asked about her camino. She'd started out from St Jean the same time as he had done.

"Then why haven't we met?"

"Out of step, I guess." She smiled.

Werner began to talk to her about Tokyo. He was obviously interested in her, and Peter could see why. He sat back and let Werner have his moment. Karen was attentive as though she was observing the Austrian and coming to her own conclusions.

Llewellyn came over through the melee of Italians, guitar and cooking, and sat by Paul.

"You do your own thing, Lew," said Paul, patting him on the shoulder. "I mean going to mass and all that."

"I don't know what I'm doing," said Llewellyn.

"Listen I'll tell you something. May help." Paul put his glass down. "It's when I was in the seminary. Harry knows this, don't you, Harry?"

"It's good, this is good," Harry had sat down, leaving the microwave to Julia.

"I was a fifty year old man, going to be a priest, and suddenly I didn't know if I believed in God or not. Like you. I didn't know. So I go to my Father Confessor. He's a gruff old guy. It's at night, he's in his office working. I remember there was just a desk lamp on, you can imagine the scene. He has his back to me. I say, Father I got a problem, I don't know whether I got the faith any more. He didn't even turn round. He said, 'What do you want me to do about it?' Father, I said, this is serious. I don't know whether I can go on with all this. He still didn't turn round. He says one word. 'Pray' "

"That's right," said Harry.

"And then he goes back to his writing. I started again. He says, I already told you, now close the door. He left me standing

153

there, looking at his back. I went out. I thought, to hell with him, then shit, OK I'll do what he says." He stopped again, swallowed, glanced at Harry, who smiled and nodded. He went on. "So I prayed. I asked God what to do."

"That's right," said Harry again.

"God told me I was doing the right thing. It was the best advice I ever had, Lew. Pray." He poured himself another glass of wine.

"Pray," said Harry.

"Thanks, Paul."

"Think about it."

Julia had sat down and caught the end of the story. "I came on the path because my boyfriend packed me in."

"What was he, crazy?" Harry laughed.

"It's true, I should be there right now in a little house with a kid on the way. I just sat in my mum's and cried for two months until my dad said, will you stop that bloody noise and get out of here! That was the best advice I ever had. I went to Paris and came down on to the Path. You eat those grapes out of the field, you see those figs? I'm so excited every day!"

Harry gave her a hug. Peter looked around. The place was noisy. Pina was putting plates on the table, Llewellyn grinning and smoking, Werner talking intently to Karen, Francesco cooking with Marcello his shadow mimicking everything he did.

Chan came in and said, "Look!"

Soon-ok came in behind and did a little dance.

"She walk!"

After the meal, which was delicious - Marcello had been a slightly over the top, but still very funny waiter - Paul and Harry got up to go over to the church to prepare for the mass. The Koreans and Werner followed not long after with Julia and Fabian. Peter saw Pina go out but he was surprised to see that the other two Italians hadn't. They stayed to clean up the kitchen. Llewellyn went back to his corner and read a book he'd found on the kitchen shelves.

Peter was alone at the table with Karen. He turned to her and smiled.

154

She said, "I think I'll take an early night."

She went. Peter watched her closing the door, and wished she'd stayed. He raised his glass to Llewellyn. "Looks like you and me."

"As long as we don't talk about bloody religion." Llewellyn went back to his book.

"Is Werner always like that?"

"Don't worry about him. I don't."

* * * *

As the others went into the church for the mass, Maria passed the albergue on the pitch black trail fifty metres below. She was walking with a torch between her teeth to see where she was going. She'd just climbed the same stretch of steep, sharp, rocky path that had nearly defeated Paul a few hours earlier. She'd come from Villafranca too. It had taken her twelve hours even though she'd taken the easier road route. She'd had one rest for half an hour at midday and another for twenty minutes at five. Her fatigue had become an exhaustion so complete she now no longer had any real sense of her body. Her sticks went forward one at a time into the darkness and her feet followed. She didn't see where they landed and didn't know until after she'd stumbled that she was on uneven ground. She straightened, held herself for a moment, and then a stick would go forward again. She was hardly conscious of the climb anymore. Maybe the low visibility offered by the torch helped her. If she'd seen how steep it was she might have stopped. She didn't; one stick, one foot, one breath. She'd gone through the pain to the point where it was now just something else she carried.

She came up to the albergue and the church, where the others were congregating, but kept going and stood for a second on the road a hundred metres past. Either side of her were stone houses with their walls a damp black in the steady drizzling rain and their shutters closed. She'd stopped moving. She was too tired for thought. Her mind contained only one image. It was a word on a map in the guidebook, O'Cebreiro, the village on the top of the mountain. She would get there. One stick went forward, then a foot, and she began to go up the mountain path. She wanted to be out of this body, this body that weighed her down, this body that she had to carry every second of her life, this two hundred and fifty pounds that pulled her down to the earth and stuck her to it. She would carry it, ache with it, cry with it, until it fell away from her, leaving only her mind and her will. O'Cebreiro. If she'd had the faintest whisper of breath to spare she have tried to say the word loud enough to hear it. She didn't. Her mouth was held open, her lips pulled back from her teeth, catching the air, her only energy, the only power she could suck from this mountain that was trying to destroy her. She wouldn't let it. She would pull herself slowly, centimetre by centimetre, stick by stick, foot by foot, to the top. She prayed to her namesake, Maria, mother of Jesus. She'd prefer to die in her body than live in it. O'Cebreiro. The sticks clicked down, her body followed. O'Cebreiro. Above her in the darkness.

* * * *

After Paul had said the mass the German hospitalero gently told them about the history of the church they were sitting in and the tradition of washing the feet of fellow walkers. She asked them to form a circle of chairs in front of the altar, then she and another German woman bought in bowls of water and several towels. The others took their boots and socks off.

"God, you can smell the camino," said Harry.

Everyone laughed nervously. Fabian sat to one side gently strumming his guitar. Pina took the first bowl and Werner carefully placed the other one at Paul's feet.

"I'm sorry for what I say to Lew," he whispered.

"It's OK, Wern," said Paul. He looked down as Werner gently took his foot and lowered it into the bowl, slowly washed and then dried it.

Pina did Soon-ok's. As she washed each foot, she said, "May it feel the earth it walks on."

"Funee."

"She mean, you tickle," said Chan.

He and Paul took the bowls next.

"Do you think we ought to change the water here?"

"For God's sake, Harry," said Paul.

"There's infections in feet," said Harry.

They all laughed again and the hospitaleros obligingly changed the water. Chan washed Harry's feet. He took his time, although it was clear that Harry wanted to get it over with as quickly as possible.

"It's OK, Chan, that'll do."

Paul hadn't wanted to wash feet either, although he wasn't going to admit it. He was pleased that he was opposite Julia and washed her feet carefully and slowly, trying to get into the spirit of the thing, which he found difficult. The truth was, he felt embarrassed, and angry with himself because of it.

Soon-ok did Chan who probably enjoyed it more than anyone else.

Julia washed Werner's. She cried as she did it, "Sorry I can't help it." Then she washed Fabian's feet and cried again. Those who hadn't had their feet washed by her felt they'd missed something.

* * * *

Peter lay in his bunk in the darkened room. Julia had come in and whispered to him about the feet washing and her tears. "It wasn't because I was sad or anything," she'd said, "I cried because I was happy." Then she'd asked him if he was OK now. He said he was, and she went away to her own bunk. He was grateful for her concern. In her own way she seemed to care for everybody, and at the same time was untroubled by what she saw. It was as if she knew that all suffering was temporary and all she had to do was notice the turbulence for it to disperse. He wondered about her faith. It didn't seem to be connected to any known dogma, or thousand year old religion as Paul had said, it seemed entirely her own and existed somewhere between her unbending belief in the decency of the people around her and a sense of excitement in the natural world - an excitement at times that seemed to verge on ecstasy. She was was an ordinary Australian girl, hardly more than a teenager, how did she know such things?

He knew he had no faith in the way Paul described it and felt strongly that he never would. But there was something driving them all along this path and if it wasn't in some way connected to this nebulous idea of the spirit then, like Llewellyn, he couldn't work out what it was. For those who already believed and were held within an established faith it was simple, but the rest? Maybe it was just the exercise? A physical shock that somehow shifted you into another state of mind? He'd talked to a Scottish physiotherapist a few days before who'd told him that walking twenty-five K with a pack on your back is the equivalent of a half marathon a day. She'd listed the benefits to the body; stronger heart, bigger lungs, weight loss, he couldn't remember the rest. Could there be such a thing as just sheer corporeal contentment? He was quite happy to let his body reap its reward, but there seemed to be no way he could let his whirring mind close down, whatever the physical benefit.

He turned on his bunk. Karen, or Kah-ren, the Japanese American was sleeping on the other side of the room from him. She was so slight he could easily have imagined her sleeping bag was empty. There was something about her that intrigued him, but since Ingrid he didn't trust his feelings in that direction anymore. It had been quite a night.

He thought now that his judgement on his recollections earlier had been too harsh. He couldn't deny the fact of them but could see also that what he called his fraud was a pretence that had been more a reaction to the world around him than any great fault or weakness. He was a kid, what else could he have done? Anyway it had been largely successful. How many boys from where he came from had a successful army career? Not many. Perhaps any man who'd managed to disassociate himself from his past felt to some degree fraudulent. All change meant leaving something behind, didn't it? To remould yourself, to adapt, to play the game, to defend yourself. He began to feel better about it all. But there was still a nagging sense of loss. As if what he'd rejected was more valuable than what he'd gained. He suddenly saw very clearly that he'd seen Llewellyn's vulnerability as somehow his own and defended him as a surrogate for that abandoned kid he'd left on a Birmingham street. The image of himself almost made him sit up: mop of blond hair, patched jeans, bomber jacket, football at his feet, terraced row behind. Perhaps he hadn't left him behind after all, he was still there, in him, still with something to say, still wanting. An inexplicable surge of anger rose in him and swept across his school, the army, his father, Werner for Christ's sake, and swirled back around the kid, there on that unknown street, himself, Peter, innocent, waiting. Waiting for what? He wanted to cry. He thought of his father. The old man had tried to change his own life and had failed. He'd spent his last years alone, looking out of his window at a world he was no longer part of, trying to trace back to where it all went wrong. But at least he'd changed his son, got him to a good school, into the army. What had Peter done for his own son? He felt his heart sink. Sam again. Always there, silent, unmoving reproach. Just another boy waiting. He was staring into a deep hole. He screwed his eyes shut. Darkness. Karen came to mind. Thank God for that. Thinking about women was safer. Remove that, where was he? What else was there to think about anyway? He smiled and opened his eyes. He looked over towards her bunk again. She wasn't there. He turned, nor was Julia. Then he heard for the first time the sound of music from outside.

He got up and went out. The rain had stopped and the clouds had cleared revealing a clean, bright, starlit sky. Just about everybody else was still up and sitting around drinking on the veranda. The Italians had decided to give an impromptu performance of what they called the Miracle of Santa Domingo. Peter hadn't caught the beginning but he sat next to Karen and she explained it was the legend of the Cock and the Hen - apparently one of each had been kept in coop next to the cathedral in Santa Domingo for the past hundred years.

The story was about a medieval pilgrim couple and their son who'd had stayed at a tavern in Santa Domingo on their way to Santiago. The innkeeper's daughter, played with unexpected lasciviousness by Pina, had tried to seduce the young boy. Protecting his innocence, he'd turned her down. Francesco, at well over six feet, was an unlikely boy but his horrified delight at the girl's advances was hilarious. She, furious at this rejection, had the boy arrested on a spurious charge of theft. (The contrivances of this part of the plot were beyond Peter.) The boy was condemned to death and hanged. Saint Dominic on hearing of his plight intervened and brought the boy back to life again. The boy's parents, seeing this, rejoiced and rushed to tell the Town Mayor, and to petition him for a full pardon for their son. The Mayor had just sat down to his dinner of a roasted cock and hen when the parents gave him the news of their son's miraculous recovery. The Mayor scoffed at their story. He raised his knife to carve the birds on the plate before him and said, if your son's alive, then so is this cock and hen! Whereupon both birds stood up on the platter and the one crowed as the other clucked. Marcello, playing both the mayor and the birds, brought the whole thing to a frantic climax. They finished with a song and a low bow. Llewellyn who'd drunkenly and cheerfully accepted the part of the Saint himself was given an especially loud cheer. Peter clapped loudly. Karen's response was enthusiastic too. Werner stared ahead at the church as if he hadn't seen anything. They went back to the bunkhouse. Peter couldn't sleep. He'd begun by trying to think of miracles and then sunk into a half-waking dream in which he was the cock and Karen, the hen. Who was the mayor? That was obvious. Werner.

* * * *

The path curved up ahead of Maria in the darkness. La Faba was two kilometres behind her, the songs and laughter of the others unheard. She existed only on and within the torture of this path as she hauled her bulk up the mountain. Even her prayers had gone. Her mind contained only one word. O'Cebreiro. There was no body left. Just breath. Just will. One stick, one foot, one stick, O'Cebreiro, one foot, O'Cebreiro. It became a chant, a mantra, a rhythm, not even a word anymore, just a sound, the tap of a stick, the crunch of her foot, O'Cebreiro, O'breiro, O'breiro. There was nothing else, just the gasp of the bravest woman in the world, gulping for air, and a movement so slow it didn't seem like movement at all. One stick forward, a scrape as it met the rock. One foot, crunch as it came down on the stone. The other stick, scrape. A foot, crunch. A stick. A foot. A stick. A foot. A stick. A crunch. A stick. O'bro. O'bro. Oh. Oh, Oh. O. O... If she had to she'd walk through the mountain.

She didn't remember arriving. The hospitalero of the albergue said nothing when he saw her. He pulled the pack from her back and carried it ahead of her into the bunkroom. She sat on the bed and fell back. He lifted her feet for her. She slept immediately.

O'CEBREIRO

The small village perched on the top of one of the highest points of the camino had been the sight of another miracle of the camino. According to legend, at a mass in the local church, the communion bread and wine had turned into the actual body and blood of Christ in front of the eyes of a doubting celebrant. Apparently the statue of Santa Maria la Real overlooking the congregation had winked. Oskar laughed out loud as he read this. His views on miracles were as idiosyncratic as his views on everything else. It's all claptrap, he thought, but at least they illustrated man's desire to be something more than he thought he was - an aspiration Oskar was all in favour of.

On the same night that the others had stopped exhausted in La Faba, Oskar, six hours ahead of Maria, had strode a further nine kilometres up the mountain to O'Cebreiro at the top. At around the same time that Llewellyn and Werner were buying wine and ravioli in the local La Faba shop, Oskar was sitting at a table outside a bar sipping a beer and looking out over the peaks and valleys below reading about the miracle in his guide. And why shouldn't man want to be something else? He smiled again at the vision of the statue winking and thought, we don't need Jesus anymore, we have our will, imagination, and, if you don't mind, our sense of humour.

And anyway a version of transubstantiation, not to mention the virgin birth, was already happening. Take a cell, inject the DNA and already you had a cloned sheep, a dog, a cow, any number of perfect specimens. What would be tomorrow? It was inevitable for Oskar, that the next step would be to create ourselves. And why not a new Jesus Christ? Maybe the body and blood celebrated in the mass had merely been a precursor, a prediction even, of what would come. And God? He looked across at the spreading reds and oranges of the sunset seeping into one another as the light died behind the mountains. Maybe we become Him too? All of us together. Never dead. Eternally alive. He frowned, looking down into the valley and then arched his neck looking up at the sky. He'd never been more serious in his life.

His perfect virtual city was developing from its fantastic beginnings into something he felt he could make a reality. He'd decided he'd have to start smaller. Maybe a village of just a few hundred people as a prototype. Why not make a computer model of it? Why not extend that into some kind of active virtual habitation? Why not digitally photograph every resident and make virtual images of them? Perfect replicas. They could live in representations of their own houses, could work as they did, could take their leisure as they enjoyed it already. And they could see themselves doing it, living the lives they'd already created. All of this was technically possible. The virtual clones of the residents would have to be accurate enough to engage their imaginations and therefore they'd be expensive - but Oskar never let money worry him. Anyway there were plenty of internet sites where you could already live in fantasy worlds. Maybe he would use them as a model? The difference between them and his notion was that they were designer's creations, his was real; a real town and real people. He would need computer terminals in every home with a personal screen and console for every family member. He wanted, no more or less, than every inhabitant of the town to be able to live out their real lives in cyberspace.

He'd enjoyed the day's walk. The mountains didn't trouble him, he'd spent too many weekends on his own high above the ski slopes of Bavaria. As he'd breathed in the clean air and looked at O'Cebreiro high on the next ridge against a sparkling blue sky, he'd known that no computer could ever create such beauty, or the feelings it engendered. No science can create emotion; it could act on you, stimulate, inspire it, but couldn't actually be the feelings themselves. But that wasn't what he was trying to do at all. He was concerned with the conscious mind, with the observation of our lives and consequently with our judgement of them. Our feelings were part of that, but maybe if we could see them and their cause and effect, we could alter them.

He sipped his beer. Why was he thinking of doing all this? Because he wanted to understand how this observation of inter-reaction with others affected man's judgement, his view of himself, his way of being, and how it improved (or not) the world he lived in. In other words, what effect did it have on a person (and his society) if you afforded him this super superego and ultimate control? Would it make him or her more or less productive; personally, socially, intellectually and materially? Ha! He knew what he was getting at! Could he, by giving man absolute control over his own actions turn him into a god? The ultimate act of creation! He laughed his huge laugh and for a second or two it echoed across the valley.

* * * *

One of those who would certainly have liked more control over her life was at that moment sitting in a taxi with her mother as they drove up the mountain road to O'Cebreiro. Her mother could shift from accommodating to querulous, flexible to stubborn, and wildly generous to downright mean within the flick of an eye. Four days ago she'd decided she wanted to see more of the ancient history of this fine old European country, so they'd stopped in Puente de Orbigo and stood on the longest medieval bridge in Spain, a narrow, cobbled, multi-arched traverse across the River Orbigo with a low stone wall running either side.

"This is thirteenth century, Ma."

"How long ago is that?"

"Well I'd say it was around eight hundred years, wouldn't you?"

through her question about Peter. She should never have asked about him. She thought about him again as she lay on her bed in the hotel. There was yellow light from the street coming through the window. It reminded her of the room in the hotel basement they'd been in. She smiled as she remembered their mutual admission of promiscuity and vaguely missed him. Vaguely? She didn't understand her own feelings. Everything was so misty. She could see he knew who she was. But there had been too many men in her life like Peter, although maybe she'd like to see him again. Anyway it was Eva she really missed. She felt the prickle of self pity as she turned over to try and sleep.

There'd been a brief storm in the middle of the night and the thunder had woken her. She slept late and dressed quickly, intending to leave immediately, and had then sat on the bed looking out of the window at the roof of the railway station. She could see pilgrims arriving to begin the short camino, the last hundred kilometres to Santiago, the minimum you could do to get your accreditation. It was still early and they'd probably begin their walk that day. She watched dully as they tied their scallop shells to their packs and adjusted their sticks in the rain. She was neither happy nor unhappy. She thought that perhaps she was contemplating something but wasn't clear what it was. Eva had said, just sit there in the trees and allow things to come to you. Well maybe that's what she was doing. Letting it all reveal itself. She thought of Siri and her ex-husband again. Siri had probably stayed out half the night, slept all day and then tried to organise him and tell him how to run his life. Ingrid had to admit, she'd done much the same. Trying to contain him while being uncontainable herself. Maybe she was untouchable. Maybe she'd always been so. The thought made her feel sorry for herself. She watched as a train came in. A group of pilgrims with bright jackets and packs got down from the carriages. They were laughing and excited. She felt like shouting out a warning to them, it's not what you think! If you'd have asked her a few weeks ago why she was going to Spain she'd have answered with a shrug and said something about good exercise, but like everybody else who packed a rucksack and took that first step out of their front door she knew there was something else, something intangible, some question she needed to ask, and it was only now, barely more than a week from Santiago, that she'd discovered what it was that she needed to know: had she become in some way that she didn't mean to, unknowable? Was that why men came for her and left her? Was it because they couldn't see her, or because she wouldn't let them in? She knew now that she needed to find these things out, and as always, as far as men were concerned, she knew what she was going to do without saying it - even to herself. And she knew who she was going to do it with too.

FERRERIOS

Llewellyn came out of Saria into vertical, slashing rain, like rain from a film set; fantasy rain, Singing in the Rain, rain. It splashed, formed puddles and ran in torrents down the street. He took off his straw hat, squashed it into his pack and pulled his hood up. He'd taped plastic bags round his trousers in the vain hope they'd cover the parts of him his poncho wouldn't reach. There wasn't much he could do about the tears in the poncho itself, he'd just have to hope that his jacket beneath would keep out the rain; serve him right for buying a cheap plastic waterproof anyway. He was resigned to getting soaked. He would have liked to have found a warm, dry bar, but there was no hope of that, his stash was finding a few euros a night for a municipal albergue a bit of a strain. He was almost down there with Chan and his seven euros a day, but Chan didn't drink. Or smoke. And Werner as a source of both was a distant memory. He'd been walking on his own since the big conversation and feet washing in La Faba. He'd had enough of Werner, at least for now. The Austrian had been drinking heavily for some time and his moods were switching ever more violently. A couple of times he'd shut up completely, sat silently, locked in by dark thoughts and a hard face. Llewellyn hadn't known why he'd turned on him so viciously that night, but had seen it coming. Werner telling Paul and Harry about the taxi had really pissed him off. Now it was out; Llewellyn hadn't really done the camino. If he'd taken one taxi, how many more would he get into? Mind you, Paul and Harry had been great about it. He'd spent a night with them in Samos, because Harry had wanted to stay at the monastery. Paul hadn't particularly, which

173

Llewellyn had thought strange. Anyway they didn't mention it again.

He'd spent the previous night alone in the municipal in Saria. Well not exactly alone. Julia was there but said she hadn't felt well and gone to bed. He'd finally called his sister. Maybe it was because of the absence of Werner's heavy spirit, or Julia's smile, or probably because he hadn't drunk so much, that he finally tapped out Cindy's number on his mobile. She'd been furious at his sudden and unannounced departure from her house, then concerned for him, then furious again. Even hearing her shout at him made him feel happy. Finally he was doing something right.

He hadn't seen Julia when he'd left and gone out into the rain the next morning. He felt content as he plodded along under the dripping eucalyptus. He even started to whistle. Then he heard someone shout his name. He turned and saw Werner sitting under a half shelter in a picnic area. His first reaction was not delight. His second was that Werner could give him a smoke and buy him a drink if they walked together again. He smiled, didn't stop, just slowed a little so that Werner could catch up with him.

"I waited for you," said Werner.

"You didn't stay in the municipal last night."

"Why should I?" Werner didn't say where he'd stayed. The rain splashed down on the brim of his sodden hat. With his heavy dark poncho he looked like a cowboy, thought Llewellyn.

"I apologise," said Werner. "I have been a shit."

"Don't worry about it. It's me. Everyone does it."

"Shit on you?" Werner laughed.

"Got a smoke?" Llewellyn walked through a puddle. Now he knew his shoes weren't waterproof either.

* * * *

Peter was around four kilometres ahead of them in the bar of a hotel just outside Ferrerios. He'd come in out of the rain. He was pleasantly surprised to discover the bar was a large comfortable

a wood burning stove in the corner and several
es and chairs around it. He took off his wet jacket
users, sat down and ordered a beer and a sandwich.
Like Llewellyn he too felt what he could have described as a
contentment, although in his case it was more an absence or a
flatness of feeling. At least he wasn't unhappy. Maybe the rain
was washing it all away. He no longer felt lonely either. Perhaps
the continuous movement of the camino was calming him.

"Ha!"

The sound made him jump. He turned quickly. Oskar had
come in.

"The man I must talk to!"

He said it with such ferocity that Peter assumed there was
something wrong. "What is it?"

"My plan!" Oskar took off his jacket. "I told you perfect city.
Wrong. Perfect village? Wrong. For discovery I work with just
one small family." He didn't wait for any comment. "It goes like
this." He sat down. "One father, aged forty. One mother, same.
Two children. I find this family. In real house I give them four
computer terminals, one for each. Each terminal in separate
room. I make virtual house." He marked it in the air with his
huge hands. "Same as their real house. Everything. Bed. Cocina.
Everything in closet. Same, same. The works baby! Same cloths
they wear. The whole kittycapoodle! Ha! They see own house
on screen. All rooms. We make virtual representation of each
of them. They see themselves on screen in own virtual home.
Where is the waiter?" He looked around. "I want a beer." There
was no-one at the bar. He continued. "So. Imagine this. They
look at the screen. Early morning. They see themself asleep.
They tell themself, wake up. They do it at the terminal. Voice
recognition, computer obeys. They watch themself get out of
bed. They speak to the terminal, they see and hear themselves
speak the same words on the screen. Anyone in same room as
them in virtual house hears also. Husband next to wife. He say
something. She answers. He control everything he does from
terminal. And she too."

The waitress a plump woman with a white apron had come over. Oskar ordered a beer and made a joke in Spanish. She laughed and went to the bar.

He continued, "They see representation of each other on screen, but only if in the same virtual room. So father in bedroom only see wife in same room, don't see kids in other rooms. And they don't see each other at the terminals in real house either. You get me?" Peter nodded. "And so day start. In room of mother and father, they wake. Another room, kid wakes up. At the terminal they make all the decisions. They watch themselves, how they live."

The waitress brought the beer over.

"But you see all of them wherever they are?" said Peter.

"Me? Yes. In real house and virtual house. It is an experiment."

"You see how they think?"

"No. Only what they do and say."

"They go out of the house?"

"No. Not now. Too big."

"Why are you doing this?"

Oskar took a huge gulp of his beer. "Because if we see what we do. Maybe we understand more why we do it."

"What are you getting out of it?"

Oskar thought about it, "I want to see how it happens when a man can see himself living his own life. And maybe he can make himself anything he want."

"Another person?"

"Why not? But same body. He can't change what he is physical."

"They'll think it's just a game."

"At first. Ja."

Peter thought about it. "What do you want them to do?"

"Best they can do in everything." Oskar became very serious. "Because I belief that is what they will think at the terminal. How to be the best."

"How to be perfect?"

"Why not?"

"Are you trying to make us all into Gods, Oskar?"

176

"Ha! You guess!" He laughed.

"You're bloody crazy!"

"I do it, I tell you!" Oskar turned as he saw Stanislav pass in the rain outside. He shouted his name. The Pole didn't hear him. "I go walk with, I am Poland." He swallowed the rest of his beer in one huge gulp, got up and put his jacket back on.

"Feelings, Oskar? What do you do about their feelings?"

"They do it themselves. The best. Only the best!"

"No bad feelings?"

"We see them, we see the reasons for them, we eliminate them!" He laughed, "Maybe I show you how to be happy!"

He went to the door, opened it and stepped back as Karen came in. He turned and grinned at Peter then went out, his exit as fast as his entrance.

Peter passed the back of his hand theatrically over his brow. "Phew."

"Who was that?"

"You haven't met Oskar?"

"I've seen him around. Difficult to miss." She went to sit down at another table.

"Join me."

"I got to go to the bathroom. Excuse me." She put her jacket on a chair at his table. "Can you order me a cafe con leche?" She went out.

He nodded to the waitress and ordered for Karen. He realised he'd have to pay for Oskar's beer. He was happy to do it. He couldn't begin to work the German out. What was he talking about; a psychological experiment, a philosophical treatise, or another strand of his never-ending commercial strategy? He wasn't going to do all this, was he; try and create a world in which a man would decide for the best in all things? Would any man actually do that? If watched, he probably would; he'd be too ashamed to do anything else. Is that the only reason we do good; because of what others would think of us if we don't? He knew what Oskar would say; we do good because it is natural to us and it's the only way we can be happy. You want to be happy, do some good! No bad feelings! Only the best! Peter smiled as he imagined Oskar laughing. Learn how to do it in a virtual world and live it in the real one? Is that what he was saying?

"I love watching wood burn," Karen had come back. She sat opposite him.

"Me too."

They sat in silence. The waitress brought the coffee. Peter glanced at her. She sat very still, her black eyes and hair in stark contrast to her pale skin. He noticed how full her lips were, and then with something of a shock realised how beautiful she was. He looked away. He suddenly felt anxious and not sure what to say. She didn't help him. His beer was finished. Should he order another one?

"I met a woman in Saria who knew you," she said. "Her name was Ingrid."

"Ingrid?" he hadn't expected that. "She asked about me?"

"Just if I knew you. No message." Karen looked back into the fire.

Ingrid had asked about him? The thought made him uneasy. He wanted that part of his journey to be over, complete. He worried for a second that he was so adamant about it. He sipped his beer and glanced at Karen. She sat immobile, hardly seeming to breathe. The silence between them grew longer. He turned away and thought again about Oskar. His virtual world was beginning to feel like a refuge.

"Do you think happiness comes from doing good?" he asked.

"What?" She turned regarding him impassively.

"Ah, sorry, Oskar. He...?"

"Sure, I could go with that."

"Could you?"

"Why not? I was in Sweden last year. They don't mind paying high taxes."

"I'm sorry I don't see..."

She was patient, "They want a better society, so they give up individual wealth. They do good, and it makes them happy, I guess." She smiled.

"I could go with that too," he said.

"I've just given up a hundred and fifty-thousand a year," she said.

"For the same reasons as the Swedes?"

"No, for my own reasons."

She looked away again into the fire. Before he could ask her what she meant he saw Werner staring at him through the window.

"Oh no."

"What?"

"It's the Austrian."

"Is that a problem?" She turned as Werner came in with Llewellyn.

They both stood dripping in front of the fire. Werner handed Llewellyn a ten euro note. "Get me a cerveza and a coke" Llewellyn went to take his pack off. "Do that after." Llewellyn went to the bar still with his pack on.

"We were just talking about Sweden," said Karen.

Why's she telling him that, thought Peter.

Werner took his wet poncho off and threw it on a chair. It slid to the floor making a puddle. He didn't pick it up. "I design a kindergarten in Stockholm. Sweden's no good. Sixty-five percent tax."

"We were just saying..." said Peter.

"You can't live. Impossible. You pay for everyone else."

"Maybe we should think about things in a different way." Peter tried again.

Werner wasn't listening. "I don't like them telling me how to live." He pulled up a chair and sat down between them.

"Yes that's right," said Peter. "You're a pilgrim."

Werner heard that. "Don't be funny."

"And you want to keep all you earn?" said Peter.

"Why not?"

"You could buy a nice house," said Karen with a smile.

"You buy it. I design it for you."

"Didn't you say you'd given up being an architect?" she smiled.

She's obviously remembered everything he told her in La Faba, thought Peter.

"Maybe I change my mind." He turned to the bar. "Where's my beer?"

"It's coming," said Llewellyn. He ordered himself a large glass of red wine.

"Swedes are depressed. It's not good for me," said Werner.

"Because you are?" asked Karen.

Not for the first time, Peter was impressed by her directness.

Werner looked clearly back into her eyes and said, "If you have a question you ask, and you can't answer it, what do you do?"

"You tell me."

"You ignore it. Or you pretend you know some answer. Or you keep asking, don't get nowhere, and you sit on the bed and go mad. This is depression."

"Not being able to answer a question?"

"Why not? Every intelligent man is depressed."

"I don't agree with that," said Peter.

"You don't know what you're talking about," said Werner.

Before Peter could answer Llewellyn came over with the drinks. Werner poured half his coca cola into the beer.

"That's an interesting drink," said Karen.

Peter leant forward, "Intelligence is depression?"

"You don't get the answers." Werner shrugged, "So you go mad."

"What about intelligence is useful, or inspiring?"

"Until it can't answer the question." Werner grinned, "Then it go mad."

"And there's no arguing with your view?"

"No-one can argue with Werner," said Llewellyn.

"Why should I care?" said Werner with a smirk.

"Because you might learn something," said Peter.

Werner looked directly at him. There was no denying the hostility.

"I gotta go," said Karen standing up.

"Yes, maybe I should," said Peter. He was pleased he hadn't ordered another beer. He half raised himself from his chair.

"It's OK, I like to walk on my own," she said.

Peter lowered himself back into the chair.

"She meditates," said Werner.

"How did you know that?" Karen looked at him with some surprise.

Werner grinned, "I guess."

"Good guess." Karen regarded him for a second, then pulled her pack on.

"It's pouring," said Llewellyn looking out of the window.

Werner and Karen both said, 'good,' at the same time. They laughed.

"See you." She went.

Peter got up anyway.

"You don't have to go," said Werner.

"I've been sitting here too long."

"Let her go," said Werner looking up at him.

Peter looked down on him, his anger rising.

"Don't be angry," Werner laughed. "Anyway I want to tell you something. Sit down."

"What?"

"Please. I mean it."

Peter sat down.

"I already told Lew. Three months ago I want to kill someone."

"Was that the confession then, Wern?" said Llewellyn.

Werner turned sharply, "You keep your mouth shut. That is private!"

Llewellyn sipped his wine. Werner turned back to Peter and told him about his work crashing and having to leave Vienna. Peter couldn't work out why he was being told this. To stop him following Karen?

"So I want to know why this happened?" Werner finished.

"Sometimes it does," Peter shrugged.

"Three jobs, five hours?"

"Are you saying someone was sending you a message?"

"Yes."

"Who?"

"God."

"What was the message?"

"I am here to find out."

"Why are you asking me?"

"It's what I tell the Japanese. We all have our questions."

"And this is why you're depressed?"

Werner half nodded and looked away.

"I'm sorry, I can't help you," Peter stood again.

Werner remained staring into the fire. Peter put his jacket on. He had a few questions of his own, but he wasn't going to share them with Werner. And Llewellyn was getting on his nerves too, sitting there simpering into his drink.

"You can go and get the woman," said Werner. "I'm not interested."

Peter felt like punching him in the mouth. "I think that's fucking impertinent!"

"I knew I like you," Werner grinned.

"I think I'll go." Peter picked up his bag and went towards the door.

"Hey Peter," Werner raised his glass. "Buon Camino!"

* * * *

Oskar had caught up with Stanislav. They walked together through the rain on a narrow country road, matching stride for stride.

"I am Polish," said Oskar. Stanislav didn't reply. "Shame you don't speak no English. I tell you, I love you."

"I not gay," said Stanislav.

"Ha! You do speak English!"

Stanislav pointed to his head, "I think." He pointed to his mouth, "I close." He smiled.

They walked in silence. Oskar held his face up to the rain for a moment. He liked to feel the water on his skin.

"I am professor," said Stanislav. "Sociology."

"And you know Beatles."

"I know Beatles." Stanislav laughed and began to sing, "Here comes the sun..."

Oskar joined, "Little darling..."

They sang as they walked into Ferrerios.

VILAR DE DONAS

Eva hadn't known that Ingrid had slowed down so much and thought that she would be caught up at any moment. She had no doubt Ingrid was capable of it. She felt no guilt about abandoning her companion, a woman who'd undoubtedly become her friend. Ingrid would survive. The pain had returned to Eva's neck and she needed to be alone. Santiago was hardly three days away and she hardly had any time left to make her up her mind. To avoid Ingrid she'd stayed in small private pension paying a premium for a single room, because she didn't want the company of others disturbing her. She wanted Ingrid to get ahead of her and had gone so slowly that even Maria had overtaken her. She'd dawdled, sat in hidden picnic areas, eaten her sandwiches under dripping trees, the rain tapping on the leaves above her, pulling her jacket in against the cold, her face buried in her scarf. And she'd stood for an hour leaning against an old and rusting tractor down a track fifty metres off the camino, staring at the water running through the mud at her feet, waiting for the moment that Ingrid would pass her so she could follow undisturbed and let the rain wash the ache away.

At Calzada she'd decided to take a detour to Vilar de Donar. There was a fourteenth century church there built on the site of a former nunnery. She thought it unlikely that Ingrid would do the same and if she spent an hour or two her there it was inevitable that Ingrid would pass her. She turned right leaving the camino behind and walked along a quiet lane to the village. She saw the church immediately. She pushed at the heavy door and went in. It was dark, musty and cold. There were faded frescos and several stone effigies of men with great swords standing over ancient sarcophagi. There was someone sitting at the front in the shadows beneath a small statue of the Virgin Mary. The figure was too big to be Ingrid. She walked slowly down the aisle towards it.

Maria turned, "Hola."

Eva nodded and sat a few pews back from her. She looked up at the walls and saw she was surrounded by images of the ancient Knights of Santiago. This had been the seat of their power in the fourteenth century. From here they'd ridden out to rescue the pilgrims from the bands of robbers along the way. She imagined being rescued by a knight in armour on a big white horse; being swept up behind him, clinging desperately to his breastplate as he galloped her off to his castle and deposited her in a stone walled room with a huge warm log fire. And then locked the door and left her there.

Maria got up, genuflected in front of the altar, turned and walked up the aisle. She stopped at the end of Eva's pew and turned back to the statue of the virgin.

"Ella tiene mucho dolor," she said. And then slowly left the church.

Eva didn't reply or even move her head to look as Maria left. She knew the Virgin suffered much pain and was staring at the statue hoping for it to turn to her through the shadows. She wanted another sign. She looked at it for ten minutes, willing it to move. She glanced up at the stern, silent, knights carved in stone on the walls, wishing they'd smile. She heard a sound and turned quickly. Ingrid had come into the church.

"How did you know?"

"Llewellyn and the Austrian are in the bar in Calzada. You passed them." said Ingrid.

Eva hadn't seen them. She looked back up at the Virgin and mouthed as if to a confidante. "S'il vous plaît la faire aller."

Ingrid sat in a pew behind her, "I was looking for you."

"I didn't want to see you."

"Why not?"

Eva didn't answer.

"I look for you everywhere."

"Parce que vous êtes solitaire," Eva said it half under her breath.

"What?"

"Because you are lonely."

"No, it is because..."

"C'est la vérité!"

"Please speak English."

"It's the truth!"

"No. I am not lonely!" Ingrid set her face in almost childlike denial. She was feeling the harshness she'd always known was in Eva. Why did she always meet people like this? Because she wanted to look after them? She said, "Can't I be your friend?"

"Be a friend of yourself first."

"That's cruel."

"I am doing other things."

"What other things?"

"Please go, Ingrid."

"After everything I have done for...?"

Eva cut her off, "You do it for yourself."

"I walked fast so..."

"You like to walk fast."

"I found every night for us a place!" Ingrid was shouting now.

Eva turned furiously, "Silence! Ceci est la maison de Dieu!" Ingrid looked down. Eva didn't stop, "You walk too fast. You don't see anything. Why don't you like to be alone?"

"I will walk with someone else." Ingrid began to get up.

"You hide, Ingrid."

"Why? Why should I hide?"

"I don't know." Eva turned away and faced the altar again.

"I don't hide." Ingrid walked away back up the aisle.

"From yourself," said Eva,

Ingrid stopped and looked back down the church at the statue of the Virgin. "Jeg hader dig!"

Eva turned, "Quoi?"

"I hate her!"

As Ingrid walked out of the church a small flock of crows rose high in the air from the gravestones. She watched them until they were tiny black dots against a high grey sky, then walked slowly back down the lane to Calzada. She was pleased she'd seen Eva again. Now she knew she didn't want to walk with her. She'd known it in the hotel in Saria, known there was something else she needed to do, but she'd panicked when she'd seen Werner sitting in the bar. She hadn't known what to say to him, and then Llewellyn had told her about Eva and she'd come quickly down to the church. Maybe she'd wanted Eva to save her. Perhaps she should have told her the truth; it wasn't Eva she'd been looking for at all. It was the Austrian. She'd seen him on the camino and at first wondered and then knew, like she always knew these things. He was still in the bar with Llewellyn in Calzada when she came back from the church.

"Why don't you join us?" he said as she went in.

By the time they left she was already a little drunk. She looked at Werner walking slightly ahead of her and knew she was going to do what she'd decided in the hotel room.

PALAIS DE REA

Peter checked into the municipal. Despite the rain it had been a relatively easy day's walk. His waterproofs had held up and despite his fleece being a little damp under his jacket he'd felt fortunate. He'd seen an extraordinary array of raingear improvised by pilgrims along the way; plastic bags tied round heads and shoulders, or taped to legs, and mainly over boots and shoes. Everyone had seemed cheerful enough. He assumed that it was the fact that Santiago was only sixty kilometres away that was causing the rising sense of excitement he could feel amongst them all. He couldn't deny it, he felt much the same thing himself. Was it because he was coming to the end of the Path? After the hollowness he'd had lying on that bunk in La Faba, he still couldn't quite shake the thought that having gone through one door he needed to go through the next, but as to where it was, or what it would lead to, he didn't know. He wondered about Karen and her admission that she'd given up an obviously very well paid job in order to walk the Path. Who was she? What was her job? There was something about her that fascinated him. Was she replacing Ingrid in his mind? The thought came out of nowhere and puzzled him. He hardly knew Karen, had spent an evening with her, sat next to her in a hotel bar. Perhaps it was no more than there always needed to be a woman located at some point in his psychic firmament to root him. Root him to what? Something he needed? Something in his past? He started to walk faster. Maybe it was just the rain that had helped lighten his mood. Perhaps it was cleansing. As he stepped through it he became increasingly aware of a sense of contentment, of emptying

188

out, of the rhythm of his steps, of time passing lightly. One step was one second; a thousand steps, one kilometre. Time passed as he stepped. It became hypnotic. Time passing, time walking, time passing, nothing else. Ingrid then Karen, one step, then another. Karen wasn't like Ingrid. He knew Ingrid, seen her before, knew she was vulnerable, easy meat. Karen wasn't like that, Karen was harder, he could see that, she had knowledge of... of what? Of herself maybe, of her place in her world? He walked, the rain fell. Time passing. One step, one second. Karen had walked alone for nearly three weeks, maybe she didn't need anyone? The thought of her excited him, and at the same time made him nervous. Why nervous? He didn't know. Sex? Ingrid, yes. Karen, no. Why? He didn't know that either.

The rain had stopped. An hour had passed. He was in Palais de Rea outside the municipal albergue. He checked in and went through to the bunkroom. Karen was the first person he saw. He smiled, she smiled back, and thus continued the game of what did Karen think? He couldn't read her, never knew what was going through her mind, and even at the end of it all couldn't really have told you what he felt she thought of him. Maybe that was part of the fascination. She turned away and took her sleeping roll out of her pack. He asked her if she'd like to eat something later on and she said, sure why not? Then turned away again, took a towel from her pack and went and had a shower leaving him standing by a bunk wondering whether he should have asked.

A couple of hours later they went to a small restaurant not far from the albergue. Oskar was already there with Stanislav, Heinrich, Willi and several other Germans Peter didn't know. Another communal meal wasn't what Peter had in mind, but having walked in they couldn't do much else but join them. He introduced Karen.

Oskar pointed to Stanislav and said, "Attention. I am Poland speaks English." He gave Peter an outrageously theatrical wink and said, "Don't worry, I don't tell him our plan."

"Our plan? All yours Oskar."

"OK, I make fortune all by myself."

Ah so it was money that was at the root of Oskar's machinations. He'd said he'd been a financial director, perhaps he couldn't detach himself entirely from pecuniary motive. Though, oddly, in Oskar's case, Peter wondered if it might be the other way round? What if the creation of profit was actually disguising, consciously or unconsciously, his real purpose which was more philosophical or - he didn't want to use the word - spiritual? Peter watched him as he laughed, joked and prodded everyone at the table to reveal, if not themselves, then something hidden or surprising. He was remarkably perceptive, always attentive to the most minute detail and usually discovered something unforeseen; often to the person revealing it.

Oskar quickly found out that Karen was, or had been, a junior executive in the film industry, which gave him plenty of opportunity to make barbed jokes about Hollywood and movie stars. He also got out of her how much she'd hated the whole business. He didn't leave it there, he wanted to know - always in his hugely jocular manner - the cause of her antipathy. What is wrong with tinsel town! She avoided him, he persisted. Finally she said she didn't like the pretence, the superficial behaviour, the pathetic cutthroat ambition, the jealousy - was that enough?

Peter could see she didn't like being questioned in this way.

Oskar listened intently, never taking his eyes off her and said, "So what else?"

For the first time in his brief knowledge of her, Peter saw her lose her customary cool. She was quiet and looked down at her plate.

Oskar said, "Don't matter. You don't want to say, so don't say."

"It's the racism, I can't stand." She looked up at him.

"Ah," said Oskar, "Japan."

"Sure," said Karen, looking away for a second. Then she turned back and said with a degree of feeling that shocked Peter, "It's supposed to be a melting pot. Most of the time I think they can't stand me."

Oskar didn't miss a beat, "This change how you work?"

"No." she paused. "OK, yes. It makes me want to beat the shit out of them." She stared at Oskar as if he was one of them. "And what's the point of that? I'm not doing what I want anymore. I'm just playing their stupid games." She was very angry. "So I gave it up."

"You tell them why?" said Oskar.

"No. How can you say that? I told them I wanted a break. They didn't care. They were relieved. They didn't have to worry about me coming up behind them any more."

Oskar suddenly laughed and said to Peter, "They don't see themselves! They don't see what they do! So they lose. They lose Karen!" He smiled sincerely at her, "They lose what they need."

"Nice of you to say," she said. "Can we eat now?"

They did and Peter wondered if the conversation had been about Oskar's interest in Karen, or his interest in the profitability of Hollywood. Or more likely, he had to admit, his seeming all-consuming fascination with what we are, how we inter-react, and especially how we create? Or maybe he just had a controlling ego as massive as his frame? Peter still couldn't make him out. His confusion was increased when Heinrich, who he'd so admired for his altruistic intentions in walking the camino with Willi, went into some detail about the profit you could still make buying and selling property in a recession. Peter wondered if all Germans were like this, achieving an extraordinary balance between self and selflessness? Could these ideas coexist?

Heinrich said, "Why not? One third of my life, it's family; one third, business, and one third, I help other people so I feel good." He grinned. "But my wife says the third I give to her is always asleep!"

They ate. The boy gobbled enough for three. Peter thought that if he wasn't careful he'd put on weight despite the walking. He spent most of the time speaking in German to Oskar, who made him laugh. A couple of times Peter tried to talk to him but the boy didn't seem to be interested in him and turned back to Oskar. This made Peter angry, not with the kid, but with himself, and perhaps because he was a little jealous of Oskar's ease, energy and ability to achieve an immediate intimacy with, it seemed, almost everyone. He noticed that he was referring to the boy in his own mind as the kid, and the chain of thought led him back to the army squaddie murdered in Basra and inevitably to Sam. Shit. His good mood was dissipating. He looked down at his plate. He was getting very pissed off with these pilgrim menus too. Karen didn't help. She left as soon as she'd finished eating. She was still angry and barely said goodbye. The Italians came in. Peter could see it was going to be one of those evenings and decided to leave it until Santiago. He went out. The restaurant faced onto a small square. It had stopped raining and the night was clear. He decided to walk round the square and found Karen sitting on a bench. He sat down by her. She glanced at him but said nothing.

"What did you think of Oskar?" he said.

"I didn't like the interrogation."

"He's curious."

She was quiet for a second and then said, "That's the first time I've admitted the racism to anyone."

Peter waited. She didn't add anything. He told her about his walk through the rain and his sense of time passing with every footstep and how the rhythm of it had become compulsive, blocking everything else out. He didn't mention his thoughts about her. "In the end, it was just my breath," he said. "My footsteps and my breathing, it's all I was conscious of."

"That's meditation," she said. "You bring it up because I'm Japanese?" She looked at him. He hadn't, and said so. "People do," she said, "You know, Oriental means Buddhism, means meditation."

"Didn't Werner say...?"

"Yeah, he was right, I do meditate, but it doesn't mean all Japanese do."

"So he's not racist, but I am?"

"I'm sorry." She paused. "I have a worn disc in my back. It's not comfortable." She leaned forward on the bench and pushed her knuckle into her lower back. "I need an operation, I guess."

"It must be painful."

"It's why I meditate."

"It helps?"

Her reply was terse. "You observe the pain. It's there, but it's not. OK?"

"I'm sorry, I'll leave you." He could see she'd been affected by what had happened in the restaurant. Oskar obviously wasn't harmless.

"It's OK," she relented. "I meditated anyway. I spent some time in a Buddhist monastery. Six months." Peter was surprised at the length of time. She explained, "I left my job a year ago." She looked up at the clouds curling around the moon, "For some Buddhists everything's a meditation, eating, washing, everything. Walking."

"I'd like not to feel the weight of my pack."

"Throw something away," she smiled.

"I did."

"They say that it's your thoughts that are heavy, not what you carry. Stop thinking and you'll be lighter."

"How do I not think?"

"You already did it, didn't you?"

Peter thought of the contentment he'd found in just walking. Maybe she was right.

"Heavy thoughts, heavy load," she said.

"It's happened before too," he said. "Sometimes, especially in the early mornings, I stop, just stand there, turn around, there's no sound. Nothing at all. Is that what you mean?"

"How did you feel?"

"Joyous."

"How heavy was your pack?"

He smiled, "I didn't notice it."

"It's always beautiful," she said. She looked up at the moon again. "It's just we don't see it."

"What do you do with it?"

"Be part of it, I guess."

"Can you teach me to meditate?"

"There are plenty of teachers around."

"Is love the same thing?" he asked, and then wondered why he had. "A lightness, I mean?"

"In my experience, it's neurotic."

"Love?"

"Being in love. You always need something." She glanced at her watch. Her wrist seemed very thin. "It's nearly ten."

"We'll turn into pumpkins."

"Well, I'm no Cinderella. That's why I walked out on the ugly sisters."

"You mean, Oskar?"

"No, I meant Hollywood." She smiled at him. "OK?" She stood up and they walked back to the albergue. They saw the boy come out of the restaurant and start off in a different direction.

Peter shouted, "Willi, it's this way."

Willi turned round and walked into the albergue with them.

MATO-CASANOVA

Paul and Harry picked up their pace during the day. Harry could see that Paul just wanted to get the Path over with. He didn't blame him, they were all getting tired. They were no longer talking as they walked. Paul seemed to have run out of things to say and didn't seem inclined to listen to Harry's thoughts on the Spanish failure to commercially exploit the camino. Harry didn't push it, he could see he was walking with a troubled man.

That night they checked into a tiny albergue in Mato-Casanova and were sitting in a graffiti covered pilgrim's bar just down the road from it. The walls seemed to be a message board for the pilgrims. Everyone was covered, top to bottom, ceiling included, in some kind of exhortation, truism, dogma, philosophy, addresses, you name it.

They sat at a table near an old woodburner. Harry read one of the messages out, "'The unexamined life is not worth living.' You ask me, you can examine too much." He looked at Paul.

"Sure isn't easy," said Paul.

"What isn't?"

"Doesn't matter."

Harry read another, "'We've all come from the same place, but have been given different maps to get back,' What in hell does that mean?" And another, "'There is no sun without shadow and it's essential to know the light,' Crap. I know what I do at night. I go to sleep. You notice the dates? They're all this year. My God." He looked around the room, the graffiti was scrawled everywhere, yards of it, crowding them in. "How many pilgrims written all this? You listening to me?"

195

The TV was on showing a soap, loud, and there was also an old cassette playing Elvis, louder.

"You think he could turn one of those off, and the other one down?" said Paul.

Harry turned to the barman, a small, wiry, middle-aged man with his thick black hair combed high into an Elvis quiff. He was moving energetically behind the bar whistling along to the singer as he washed glasses. On Harry's request he immediately picked up a remote and the TV went off and the Elvis went down. He didn't stop whistling for a second and returned to washing the glasses.

"That guy's perpetual motion," said Harry. "You want to eat?"

"What about Wern and Lew?"

"It's a bar, isn't it? They'll find us."

"I'll have a wine," said Paul.

Harry shouted over their order. The waiter was pulling a cerveza for him before he'd finished, still whistling.

"You see this guy?" Harry laughed. Paul didn't turn to look. Harry leaned forward across the table, "I'm a little worried about Werner."

"He has some problems."

Harry knew that Paul had heard Werner's confession and didn't press the point.

"You gonna write your journal?" said Paul.

"Every day for..."

"Thirty years, I know."

"Never miss it. The unexamined life, what is it?" he turned to the wall. "Socrates, who's he?" He leant back in his chair, "Matter of fact I'm planning my lecture on the camino for the family. Got it down to three sections." He took his journal out of the top of his bag. It was a battered hard covered notebook. He opened it and read, "Section one, the start out. Two, the plain. Three, the mountains. I thought I'd do one of those power point things. Nine pictures for each section."

"Why nine?"

"Three sections, makes twenty-seven."

"What's so special about twenty-seven?"

"It's a round number."

"No, it's not."

"Are you just going to sit there, criticising?"

"How about Santiago?"

"What about it?"

"Which section's that in? It's not in the mountains, Harry."

"OK, four sections."

"Another nine photos?"

"Uh? Getting a bit long. Don't want to bore anybody."

"No, you don't want to do that, Harry." Paul began to unlace his boots. "What else do you write in that thing anyway?"

"What I do. My day. What I think."

The waiter put the drinks on the table, gave them a menu each and stood with his pad ready to take their dinner order, still whistling.

"Give us a minute," said Harry.

The waiter went back to the bar.

"What do you need a minute for?" asked Paul. "Same damn menu we've been eating for a month."

"What's the matter with you?"

"Anyone ever read your journal?"

"Nope."

"No-one?"

"Caught Martha sneaking round it once. I gave her my view on that."

"Read me some of it."

"I told you. No-one."

"Why you writing it?"

"Clear my mind."

"Read some."

"You may not like it."

"I'm in it?"

"Paul, we've been spending every damn day together."

"I swear I won't divulge anything."

"Why do you want to hear it."

"I just want to hear what an asshole you are, Harry."

"Fine words for a priest." Harry looked at him for a second and then opened the journal, "You may regret this."

"Yesterday. Read yesterday."

Harry flicked a few pages and read, "Hospital."

"Hospital?"

"It's where we stayed, Paul. Hospital de la Cross or whatever it was." He read. "'Eight in the morning. Called Martha. Had coffee in bar. Nice eucalyptus. Maybe get some for the Lake. Paul stopped talking.'"

"What?"

"You did," Harry read some more. "'Had another damn bocadillo. Need some good food. Could kill for a burger. Walked.'"

"Walked? You wrote that?"

"What else we do?"

"We've been walking every damn day!"

"So I write, walked, every damn day!"

"Harry, there's no point in that."

"It's a record."

"Stuck record if you ask me."

"You want me to read it or not?" He went back to the journal. "'Some other trees. Not eucalyptus. I liked them too.'"

"What were they called?"

"If I knew I'd write it."

"So what's the point, Harry. You're writing nothing!"

"What is the matter with you?"

"Carry on reading?

"OK, you asked for it." He read, "'Paul's been like a bear with a sore ass. Uncommunicative. Can't wait for this damn thing to be over.'"

"Can't wait for it to be over? That what you think?"

"I wrote it."

"Shit." Paul took a gulp of wine.

"So, you going to tell me?"

"Tell you what?"

"What's wrong, Paul?"

"They said this was going to be a spiritually enlightening experience, Harry."

"So?"

"All I got is bad feet and a back ache."

"That all you got to say?"

Paul looked down at the table, took another drink, then slid his boots off. "I think I'm losing my faith."

The waiter came up to the table again with his pad.

"Momento, please," said Harry. The waiter went away. "You're kidding me."

"It's slipping away from me."

"The hell it is."

"These people," Paul pointed to the walls. "You read it out. Anyone mention Saint James? They don't give a damn."

"That's their problem."

"It's how they think. I can't compete with that."

"Who's asking you to compete?"

"Maybe that guy Peter was right. Maybe the spirit doesn't have anything to do with the church anymore."

"Where do I start?" said Harry. He opened his journal again and flipped through the pages. He read, "Ferrerios. Alberg. Paul served mass in the dining room. Three people there. Gave a short homily on tolerance. Beautiful.'" He closed the journal. "That's what I wrote."

"Three people."

"Who cares how many people?"

"The church is corrupt."

"Come on..."

"I don't mean money, Harry. Just, everybody's in it for themselves, every damn which way. You know that. Bishop Rigson goes around..."

"I know he goes around..."

"Can't walk past a mirror."

"I thought you were a strong guy."

"I've never been strong, Harry."

"You've been strong enough for me."

"Like a bear with a sore ass. You said it."

"Pray. Take your own advice, Paul. Pray"

Paul was close to tears, "I have, Harry. Every damn night. God's not talking to me."

"He will. I promise you."

"Don't you have any doubts?"

"No."

"I envy you."

"Paul..."

"Hell, I envy you, Harry." He looked like he was going to burst into tears. The door opened and Fabian came in. He pulled himself up and said, "Hi, Fabian, come and join us."

Fabian looked round the walls, "Formidable!"

"Why don't you add something sensible?" Harry laughed.

"Maybe I will," Fabian went to the bar.

"Where's Julia?" asked Harry as he passed their table.

"She sleep already. Don't feel good. She say she got my cold." He turned to speak to the barman.

Harry said quietly to Paul, "You OK?"

"Sure, sure."

The door opened again and Werner came in with his long coat, wide-brimmed hat and staff like something out of a B movie. God he brings an energy with him, thought Paul, it's frightening. Llewellyn came next, followed by Ingrid. She was laughing. Werner went to the bar.

"Cerveza por favor, Coca Cola. Quick, quick."

"What's so funny, Ingrid?" asked Harry.

"Nothing," she giggled and sat down heavily.

"Vino tinto, vino blanco." said Werner. The whistling waiter didn't miss a beat. Werner turned to Llewellyn, "Give me a smoke."

Llewellyn handed over the tobacco as Fabian took a red felt-tip from the bar and went over to the wall looking for a space to write. Llewellyn sat down with Harry and Paul. He sat there grinning.

200

"You guys had a few?" asked Harry.

"I want to confess," said Llewellyn.

"You damn need to," Paul laughed.

"I live off Werner," said Llewellyn abruptly and unhappily.

"Come on, Lew..."

"It's true, I do."

"That's just bar talk," said Paul.

"No, I want to confess. I do." Llewellyn slumped, obviously very drunk.

"Lew, for Chrissakes." said Harry.

"Every penny I spent came from my brother-in-law," said Llewellyn.

"Thought you just said it was Werner," said Harry.

"My brother-in-law commissioned a picture from me, see? Of his daughter. My sister's kid. He gave me a thousand pounds. Decent man, my brother-in-law." He stopped as Werner put a glass of red wine in front of him. He took a drink. "I took off with the money and didn't paint the picture." He drank again. "That's my confession." He looked glumly at the table.

Werner gave Ingrid her drink and sat down, pouring his coke into his beer. "Du bist ein Idiot."

"I know."

"I can help you out, Lew," said Harry. "Few bucks."

"Thank you."

Llewellyn stared down into his drink. No-one knew what to say. Ingrid giggled again. The three of them had been walking together for two days now, most of it from bar to bar. Llewellyn knew he was going to lose Werner again. The Austrian always attacked him more viciously just before he went.

"Ingrid is to write a guidebook," said Werner. "What is it?"

"Flora and Fauna," said Ingrid. "On the Path."

Llewellyn spluttered into his glass. Harry could see he was too half-assed to know what he was doing.

"No-one knows it!" said Ingrid indignantly. "No-one sees. What we go by. The trees..."

"Handy for you, Harry," Paul smiled.

"...the flowers, everything! Why not? I think so. Why not?" She was flushed and speaking too quickly.

"It's a good idea," said Werner.

"Anyone going to eat?" asked Harry.

"I'm hungry." Llewellyn looked at Werner.

"You eat," said Werner. "I walk."

"It's night," said Paul."

"Ingrid? You walk with me?"

"I finish my wine," she said.

"OK," said Werner. He poured the rest of his coke into his beer.

"Leave the smokes will you?" said Llewellyn.

Werner tossed the pack to him, "You keep it, I buy more."

"What you writing, Fabian?" Harry asked.

Fabian stepped back from the wall and translated from the French, "When it begin is the right time. Who come are the right people. What happen is only thing that can happen."

"God's will. That's God's will. See, they're writing the same damn thing, Paul."

MELIDE

Werner and Ingrid walked out of the bar into the darkness. Paul had made an attempt to get them to eat first, hoping they'd stay in the albergue, but Werner hardly listened to him. They turned left onto the camino. Werner walked two metres ahead. Ingrid followed and didn't even bother to look for the yellow markers; this was one walk she didn't want to organise.

It was raining again. She stumbled on a kerb. That was unlike her, sure-footed Ingrid, must be the wine. She didn't care; she'd drink a crate, a barrel, all the vino in Spain, whatever it took. The cloud cleared for a second and Werner was illuminated by the light of the moon. She knew he was probably crazy, but maybe only madmen knew anything. He seemed to have no doubts. And that's what she needed, no doubts. He moved steadily through the light and shadow and she came after. They walked alongside a busy road for a while; oncoming headlights silhouetted his dramatic hat and his long coat flapping around his legs as he strode ahead of her. She knew where she was going. She'd been here before, but not so clearly, not with such intent. Usually it was blurred, fumbled, now it was bright and cold. This time she'd made up her own mind, not in so many words, what did words matter, the decision was made sitting on that bed in Saria, when she'd been failed and abandoned for the last time.

They came off the road and walked four kilometres on a path alongside fields and woodland in silence. As they came to the crest of a ridge Werner could see the lights of a town ahead. Melide. It will do, he thought. He felt he was on some kind of insane mission, moving towards an undeclared objective, like a bull in a corridor lurching from side to side, smashing against the walls. He'd tried to turn but the corridor was too narrow, the only way was forward wherever it would lead him. He knew he'd been gathering momentum over the past weeks; he'd tried to slow down, told himself, told everyone else to slow down, tried to hang onto Llewellyn and pull him back, but it was hopeless, the Welshman didn't understand. Alone now, all he could do was pick up more speed. Any doubts he'd had were falling away. He looked up, the brim of his trilby cut across the moon. He needed another drink. She'd come. She'd come anywhere with him. Their paths were converging, the collision was inevitable.

As they came into the town the streetlights lit them for what they were, frail, uncertain, a pair of drunks with packs on their backs, their faces pale yellow. He turned. Her face had no expression. He frowned. She was waiting for him to move again, so she could follow. He thought about saying something, tell her where they were going, but didn't. He turned away again and walked into the town. She watched the back of his heels, mesmerised for a moment by the steady rhythm of his walk. She saw his feet stop and place themselves half a metre apart. She looked up. He had turned towards a light. She saw his face in profile, a long nose, thin mouth and a delicate chin. She wanted to bite his chin. He was moving again up some steps.

She only half saw the entrance in the blurred light. The receptionist was distant. Ingrid later remembered her pitying eyes. But they were just a couple of pilgrims, what did she care? Ingrid was giggling again as she fumbled for her passport. Werner filled in a form. He seemed strong, capable of anything. Perhaps the receptionist had been intimidated by the hat. They went along a corridor. She waited as Werner unlocked the door. She let her pack fall onto a bed.

"Eat," he said.

And they were leaving again. Another empty restaurant with white tablecloths. She thought of the pretty Japanese girl the other night, her white teeth, like the tablecloths, and for a second Ingrid loved her so much her heart could break. Werner said something about pulpo. He kept saying pulpo, pulpo. They drank more wine. She watched it glisten in the light as he poured. Pulpo, pulpo. A white plate, something swimming in a red liquid and she understood, octopus. She saw him laugh at the pulpo on the end of a silver fork. He shook it and made it wriggle. Maybe it was alive. The red sauce dripped on his pink tongue and white teeth and mauve lips closing. He needed a shave. He had dark red wine, another bottle. Some sickly caramel that stuck in her mouth. He was talking, she couldn't hear his words, she was dreaming. Her wine sparkling, getting sour, like vinegar. She was laughing, eating bread, she didn't know why the bread or anything else.

He said, "All the priests in the world."

She laughed although she didn't understand him.

"Maybe I am a priest. You hear of the butafumeira? Swings...smoke... words... seven priests." He was laughing. She remembered he said it again, Seven priests." He was frowning. "Santiago."

She closed her eyes. He sat back and watched her. Another bottle. He was drinking a glass in a swallow. How many bottles today? Five, six, seven. He didn't know. It was time to go. He put the money down, waited for the change to come back and was very careful about the tip. His hat fell off as he counted it out. Blond white hair. He watched her stand. She nearly fell. A waiter helped her. Cold air, yellow light. Another bar. She sat, he stood. She watched his pelvis thrust, leaning himself on the bar from the front, as he pushed his head back and drank. His hat was gone again. It was on the table in front of her. His hair was curly, she noticed. She ran her fingers through it. He had dropped to her breast to pick up something. He stood up, she was still looking down at her breasts. She thought they looked good. A clunk. Another bottle on the table. She picked up her glass. Her nails were shining. She thought they looked good too. She drank tinto now with him. She had no idea how much she'd drank.

Then the corridor again. He was leaning against the door this time trying to unlock it. She put her head on his shoulder. It was bony and hard and her head slipped away. The door opened. She stood to face him in the box which seemed to be at a weird angle, the curtains weren't hanging right. She felt a bed against the back of her knees. He hit her across the face with the heel of his hand. She didn't feel it but her head swung and faced in a different direction. A door was open, she could see a washbasin. She heard him piss. Her head was down. She was sitting. He hit her again, same place across the side of her face. She saw his zip slide down. She took him in her mouth. He wasn't erect but she wanted it. It was like the suckly pulpo. She liked the shine on his prick's skin. She wanted to suck it all in. He was holding her head with one foot up on the bed. She unlaced the boot with him still in her mouth. She pulled his sock off. She fell back. He grabbed her and pulled her forward. His other boot was on the bed. She tried to unlace it. She couldn't. He grabbed her hair with one hand and unlaced the boot with the other. She pulled his sock off. His jeans were easier, then his shorts. She had to lift each foot to get them off. She stood up to push his jacket off and fell against him as she undid the buttons of his shirt. She kissed his chest. He grabbed her hair again and pulled her head back. She thought he was going to hit her again and closed her eyes. He didn't. He pushed his T shirt up and his face disappeared. She wanted it back. He took a pace back from her. He was white, naked. He leant forward and kissed her on the mouth. She felt his tongue. She sat suddenly on the bed and looked at the pillows. She wasn't clear where she was. He pushed her flat on the bed and pulled her legs round. He knelt between her legs, undid her belt and pulled her jeans down and then her pants. She lifted her buttocks to help him. He knelt above her, white, naked. His face was harsh. He came down towards her. She could smell the wine on his breath. She felt him fuck her. She felt I can take you, whatever you have to offer. She urged him on but didn't move herself. Come on then, come on then. I am Ingrid. I am the Virgin. Do what you want. You can't touch me.

Some time later, she opened her eyes and was surprised to see herself in a hotel room. The curtains were orange. Her legs were heavy, her neck hurt. She was propped against the headboard. She looked down. He was lying across the bed over her shins. He was white, naked, his buttocks caught in the light coming through a crack in the curtains, his head and shoulders were over the side of the bed. She pulled her legs out from under him and put a foot on the side of his thigh and slowly pushed him off the bed. He slid and bumped down onto the floor. She noticed she still had her boots on. And her jacket. She could see the brown of her vagina against the white of her thigh between the lowered top of her jeans and her pushed up top. She pulled her pants and jeans up and fastened them, slowly buckled her belt, then rolled onto her side and off the bed. She walked slowly to the bathroom and ran a tap. The cold water only seemed to touch the top layer of her skin making it cool but not the heat underneath. She went back into the bedroom, tripped on his foot, half fell and put her knee on the bed to save herself. She stood, still strong enough. Strong Ingrid. She picked up her pack and went to the door. As she opened it, she turned. The shaft of light from the corridor lit him lying on the floor, half curled round the foot of the bed. He was white, white skin, white hair, white heart. He snored. She went out. The first thing she saw outside the hotel was a yellow arrow. She turned back onto the Path.

* * * *

Llewellyn came into Melide about four hours after Ingrid had left it. It was ten o'clock. He found Werner drinking beer sitting outside a bar in a narrow street. He hesitated, then sat down. He didn't know if he wanted to talk to Werner, but he didn't want to walk on his own either. Werner took ten euros out of his pocket and put it on the table between them.

"Harry already lent me a hundred," said Llewellyn. "Five per cent interest. I don't think he was joking."

Werner said, "He's a good man."

Llewellyn bought himself a coffee and a croissant, and sat by Werner again. "Where's Ingrid?"

Werner pointed in the direction of the camino.

"You have a good night?"

"I don't know."

"Can't remember?"

Werner shrugged.

"Paul and Harry had a big conversation. They didn't get back to the albergue till half past eleven. I had to let them in."

"Don't talk to me," Werner sipped his beer, looking at the road.

"Ingrid's alright, is she?"

"Why do you ask?" Llewellyn didn't reply. "I don't know."

"Christ, Werner."

"I told you, I don't know!" Werner was getting angry. "She walked out of the hotel. She's alive."

"She's alive?"

"What do you think?" Werner looked at him and laughed, but Llewellyn could see it wasn't a real laugh, it was harsh. "You think I killed her?"

"I don't know. All this secret..."

"The confession? Forget it. Sometime I will tell you." He took another sip of beer. "I'm sorry. I apologise. Again I am shit. Hell is here. I am telling you. It is here."

"I don't know what you're talking about."

"I know. I apologise."

"It doesn't matter."

"It does matter!" Werner shouted and banged his glass down. A woman on the street turned and looked at him. He sat back in his chair and was quiet.

Llewellyn could see he was close to tears. "You want to walk?"

"Soon."

"I don't know how I'm going to get home," Llewellyn said.

"I pay you."

"I want to go by boat. I found out you can go from Santander. I don't want to fly anymore."

"Whatever it is, I pay you."

"Thanks Wern."

Llewellyn looked at him. He was staring ahead, not saying anything. The sun was coming out. In two days they'd be in Santiago.

* * * *

By the time they were back on the camino, Ingrid was fourteen kilometres ahead of them and coming out of Arzua. She was walking fast with her hood up to hide the bruises on her face. She'd seen the concern on the face of a woman who'd served her coffee in Ribadiso four kilometres back and been shocked to see herself in the toilet mirror. The left hand side of her face was swollen, her eye was already closing and coloured a deep red. She knew it would soon be purple and then black. She began to cry, threw water on her face and looked into the mirror again.

She didn't remember much of the night. She knew he'd hit her and penetrated her. Did he use a condom? She thought probably not. She remembered pushing him off the bed with her foot and how white his skin had been. All she could think was that he'd done what she wanted. She felt her anger rising through her. Her hands gripped the washbasin and she remembered splashing water on her face as she woke up. She drew back her lips and stared at her teeth. She clenched them, unclenched them, wanted to cry again, but didn't. She looked into her eyes, her left was blurred, but the right was bright blue and seemed to be smiling at her, for her, Ingrid, little Ingrid.

She walked fast, very fast, faster then she'd ever walked in front of Eva. She walked thirty-five kilometres that day, hardly noticed Arzua, and still arrived in Arca by two o'clock, her body, her rage exhausted. She checked into a pension and curled into bed. She'd sleep for sixteen hours. And then Santiago.

ARZUA

Arzua was more than twenty kilometres back on the trail from Arca where Ingrid was sleeping in striking distance of the city of Saint James. The first thing that Julia did on getting into the town was go to a farmacia. This bloody cold had got onto her chest. It was really heavy like she had indigestion all the time or something. Fabian was waiting as usual as she came out with a decongestant.

"I'm sorry," he said.

"If you'd stayed away like I asked you to, Fabe."

"No-one catch it. I wish they would," he repeated his sad joke.

"I'm going to the albergue. I'm going to take my medicine and I'm going to sleep, OK? Goodnight, Fabe."

She left him outside the farmacia and walked down towards the albergue. It was already dark. The walk had taken her eight hours and she hadn't slept too well the night before either. She was supposed to be enjoying herself, the last thing she needed was a cold, and definitely not one as heavy as this. She passed a pizza house. She could see Paul and Harry in there. Harry was talking a lot, prodding the air with his finger. She waved but they didn't notice her.

Harry and Paul came out of the pizza place an hour later. They walked for a minute and found themselves in a small triangular plaza bordered by shuttered, dark houses on two sides, and a derelict row of shops on the third. There was no-one around.

Harry pointed to the shops, "You could do a lot with that real estate."

"I'm going to sleep," said Paul.

"I know you think I'm an asshole."

"Harry, I'm going to sleep."

"Paul, God gave me everything I got."

I know."

"So how many times I got to say it, take your own advice."

"And how many times I got to tell you, Harry, I've prayed till my knees are sore, until my damn fingers got cramp. I'm all prayed out. It's empty, Harry. No-one's talking to me."

"OK, I'll pray for you."

"Thank you." Paul walked on down an alleyway at the side of the plaza, taking a shortcut back to the albergue.

Harry moved quickly, passed, then overtook Paul. He stood in front of him.

"Will you get out of my way?"

"Right here. I'm going to pray for you, right here."

"Please, Harry," Paul sighed.

Harry clasped his hands together and looked up at the narrow strip of sky visible between the houses looming high either side of them. "Dear God..."

"Harry..."

"Wait a minute. I'm praying. Dear God, please will you listen to me. I am a sinner, you know what I am, but you have seen it right to reward me with a fine wife, five daughters and two houses, one by the lake, so I figure, if no-one else does, you listen to me."

Paul lowered his head to hide his smile. "We're in an alleyway."

Harry went on, "I have before me a good friend of mine, someone I love and respect. Someone I thought was strong in his faith. He's a priest, God, one of your own. A fine man, except now, like Samson, he's lost his strength. I don't know why, God, he's just mislaid it, I guess."

"Harry, for God's sake."

"God, for his sake, I'm begging you." Harry dropped to his knees on the stone paving and lowered his head over his clasped hands. "There's a lot of sin in this world, God, and sometimes there don't seem to be a lot of faith." He looked up, "Kneel, Paul, kneel with me. Come on, Paul, kneel."

Paul knelt. The ground was hard. There was some garbage nearby which stank.

"God, my friend who is kneeling before you, is behaving like a ten cent fool. I'll be frank, he's behaving like an asshole. Not because he's always been, he's been your faithful servant and helped many people, including me. He's given me strength when I didn't have any, especially with Martha starting writing letters to that guy in Oregon. He wasn't an asshole then, God, he was a tower, a tower I could lean on. He didn't waver. He showed me the way to love and forgive, and as you know Martha tore up those letters. And now, God, I pray to you with all my heart, with everything I got, to see him, my friend Paul kneeling here in this trash, and give him back the faith he has put down and is too weak to pick up again. Please, please, God, help my friend." He crossed himself and got up. "You'll be OK, Paul, I promise you." He helped Paul to his feet.

"Thank you, Harry, you're a good man."

"Don't say nothing now, let God talk to you."

Paul nodded and they walked down the alley to the albergue.

* * * *

Julia had a great dream that night. She was walking up a mountain. The sun was shining and the trees either side were very green and their branches were waving gently in a cool breeze. It was like a picture out of a nursery book. She noticed to one side, the boy Darryl who'd dumped her. He was bending down looking into a hole of some kind as if he'd lost something. Julia felt sorry for him but was too happy to stop and kept on walking up the mountain. She could hear her Mum calling her from the bottom of the path, but she thought she'd go back down in a minute as it was just too beautiful up here, and she wanted to keep on going right to the top where Santiago was. She climbed for a while and noticed how easy it was to breath. That bloody old cold had finally gone. There were no trees on the summit. She looked out around her. The views were amazing. She could see the whole earth spread out before her. Down below was a valley and she started to fly. She didn't fly downwards as she usually did in her dreams. She flew straight up.

She woke up. Someone was snoring as usual. She smiled. Her chest was OK. Must have been cleared by the decongestant.

SANTA IRENE

Karen and Peter had stayed in the same albergue as Julia, but left earlier than her on the penultimate stage up to Arca. The sky was darkening and there was the occasional brush of rain on their coats. They'd begun to talk. He could feel her opening to him. Not too much but at least she seemed happy to walk with him. The camino was winding through more densely populated areas now. They were on side roads passing through small, quiet hamlets every couple of kilometres. Peter thought the landscape was not unlike Wales where he'd done most of his basic training. Galicia had a similar climate.

Karen was teaching him how to meditate, or at least explain the method. "You follow the breath," she said. "Feel it on the edge of your nostril and let all of your mind focus on it. Think of nothing else."

"Is that all?"

"Only takes about twenty years to perfect it." Karen was enjoying talking to him. He was attentive and receptive. Like everybody else she'd had many conversations on the camino - most of them inconsequential - but there was a warmth to this which she liked.

"There's another meditation," she said. "It's called loving kindness. You can do it too if you like." He nodded. "Think of someone you love. Don't tell me. Maybe in your family, someone very close to you, someone it's not difficult to love."

It's a sad truth that Peter was thrown by this. His parents were dead. He'd never really thought of his brother as someone he loved, but supposed he did. Gemma was still a problem and it was difficult to tell exactly what he felt about her anymore. Then of course, there was the one he was avoiding, Sam. His feelings in that direction were such a contradictory mix that he could hardly clear a space to know anything. This shocked him. How could he not admit, even to himself, that he loved his son? He did. Of course he did. The deepest love he'd ever felt. He looked down as he walked ashamed of his feelings, or inability to touch them.

"Think of this person," Karen went on, "Put him or her at the centre of your mind, concentrate, and let all your love for this person come up through you. Oh and I forgot to tell you, you got to relax first. Get in a comfortable place."

"You can't do it when you're walking?"

"No, that's a different kind of meditation, and there are probably too many distractions. Anyway imagine this person as the centre of a circle. Now he or she is entirely surrounded by your love. You feel nothing but good towards him or her, OK?"

He did. He put Sam there. He had an image of him as a kid running, panting, lunging, chest bursting, to win a relay race in his school sports day, and coming straight to him, his face beaming with pride, 'Dad, Dad!' The thought almost brought tears to his eyes. How could he have doubted that?

"Now think of someone else you love and include them in the circle."

Peter decided on his brother.

"And again allow your feelings, your love to come through you and go into them."

Her voice was soothing. He put his brother next to Sam in his mind and saw how they had both loved and needed him. And how he hadn't allowed it. How he'd let Gemma do all the loving for him. Even loving his own brother for him, let alone his son.

She said, "Now think of another person."

This is getting too difficult, he thought.

"All the time you're increasing the power of love that you're creating. Hold them in your mind, love them, love all of them."

He wanted to give up. He'd soon be into the army and the

idea of love permeating the stink, sweat and blasphemy of the barracks was impossible to contemplate.

"It might start getting difficult," said Karen as if reading his mind.

He thought he'd have to pretend and didn't want that. He said, "I'm not sure I can do this."

"Why not?"

"I don't think of my life in this way." It sounded lame, was lame, and he knew it.

"What else is there?"

"I don't know. What I do all day."

"What's that?"

"You're a hard taskmaster."

"Answer my question."

"Everything. Everything I am, everything I've done. That's all there is." He was sounding, and feeling, weaker by the second.

"What did you do it all for?"

How did he answer that? Because it seemed right at the time? Because he needed to earn a living? Because he needed to be the same as everybody else? He said, "I'm not entirely sure why I've ever done anything."

"About time you found out, isn't it?'

He laughed, but didn't feel like laughing.

"You want to carry on?" She didn't wait for his answer. "So find a third person to bring into the circle."

He decided on Gemma.

"And now a fourth."

He went back to the army. He thought of Clarkson carrying him home after a drunken night in Aldershot, pulling him away from a regimental dinner where he was about to make a fool of himself. He thought of a hundred other nights with Clarkson. Maybe he loved him? But how could he love a boozing, leathery, foul-mouthed, belligerent and heavy-booted army sergeant? Well, he did. Of course he did. The thought hit him like a punch in the gut. Love and Clarkson weren't words that you'd usually put in the same sentence but he loved the insane bastard to death. And that's why he'd been friends with him for years. And the others too. He suddenly realised he felt deeply sorry for all those repressed, buttoned-down, mealy-mouthed arseholes in the officer's mess, all of whom would probably give their lives for the arsehole standing next to them. Why? They called it camaraderie, loyalty, shoulder to shoulder, the badge, the queen, but the truth is they loved each other; and their embarrassment, their sheer inability to even think those words, let alone say them, somehow made them even more sad - and lovable. And he was one of them. He felt for a second an immense pride that prickled his eyes as he realised he was part of all that, he was included in that love, and it was probably the greatest love he'd ever known.

"You include them all in the circle," she said. "And keep going. You bring more and more people into it including those you haven't seen for a long time."

His thoughts went back to his parents again, his mother passed out on the kitchen table with her head in her arms and spittle running down her cheek, of trying to clean the vomit off her chest with a dishcloth; his father pushing him into that school. He loved them both, and especially her. Ingrid came immediately to mind and he made the connection. He was surprised at how much his feelings could merge and shift from one memory to another. Then he considered the boys at the school; the boys he hated, imitated, became friends with. He realised that they didn't know what they were doing any more than he did. They came in to the circle too as he walked slowly by Karen's side. He thought of the women he'd known, of Ingrid again, and looking into the bathroom mirror the morning after the last night he'd seen here and thinking how he and she were so similar.

"Even people you didn't like too much. Your love is flowing by now; try and include them in it, try not to see their faults, try and understand that they're like you, like all of us, they struggle, they don't get it, they lash out, they've hurt you, maybe they were hurting themselves. Now get the circle even bigger and include those you hardly know, see them in your mind. After a while you can see that your love is so big, so powerful, it can enfold

217

everyone. And you can..." she stopped and smiled. "You can get to place where you can feel their love being returned to you, and understand that all they are is love, and all you are is love. That's it. Nothing else."

Was this all that new age shit that Paul had been going on about? He expected her to laugh at the end of it.

She didn't laugh. She said, "That's a very old meditation. Monks have been practising it for hundreds of years to increase the amount of love in the world."

"Thank you," he said.

"You're welcome."

* * * *

Harry had left Paul behind. He figured there wasn't much more he could say. Now was the time to let God do his good work. Paul walked slowly, his sticks clipped the road. He noticed a cafe to his right but didn't want to go in though it looked nice by the river. He didn't need anything, so what was the point? Maybe that was the point, he didn't need anything,

He thought about Werner for a while. His confession had been disturbing. But why enter into it if you can't do anything about it. He could only watch as the man went crazier. Wern needed to stop drinking that was for sure, come to that, so did he. Shift this damn weight from his gut for one thing.

He sighed. There was a bird singing. Autumn leaves. They were falling heavier now. Apparently this country was Celtic, like the Irish and the Scots; they even had bagpipers. He didn't know why he was thinking these things. He let his mind wander. If he had it he'd give Lew some money. Damned Harry would have him sign over his shirt before he passed the bucks. Good guy though. That praying in the alley had touched him. He'd still got the shit on the knees of his pants. "God, this man is an asshole." Paul smiled as he remembered Harry's description of him. He'd bet his prayers got through though. They were entertaining if nothing else. He spoke aloud, "God, am I an asshole?" He looked up. God didn't seem to want to respond. He felt lonely. Lonelier than he'd ever been. So lonely he stopped until the feeling passed. Get used to it, Paul. It comes and it goes. Everything comes and it goes. Maybe that's what he'd miss most, a kind of constancy, like his faith was always a road under his feet. Miss most? Is that what he'd thought? Was he seriously thinking of giving up the priesthood? He walked on. There was still a road under him. If he gave it up maybe there'd just be a different road that's all. The arrow said turn left. He did and came into a wood. The dead leaves were covering the path. He kicked a few away as he walked.

"Papa!"

He stopped and looked to his right. A woman was sitting at a concrete picnic table set back under the trees.

"It's Eva. Do you remember me?"

"Sure. Nice to see you. Buon Camino." He continued to walk.

"I have been waiting for you."

He stopped again, "You have?"

"They told me you were in Arzua."

"You want to talk to me?"

She nodded and smiled. "Only for a minute."

One of the problems of being a priest was that you couldn't say no to things like this. Reluctantly he went under the trees, dropped his pack and sat on a concrete bench across the table from her. Everything was wet.

"Hell," he got up again.

She gave him her poncho to sit on.

"Aren't you wet?' he asked.

"I am sitting on a plastic," she said. There was a supermarket bag under her.

He sat down again, "How can I help?" The trees were dripping on him. He wasn't too comfortable.

"I have seen some things." He nodded. "I think I have seen the Virgin Mary in the trees. And there was an old woman who took me from the mist. She rescue me."

"So?"

"But she wasn't there."

Paul paused. "Tell me about the virgin you saw."

She told him about the first time; the light in the branches and then the old woman. "And there is a third time," she said. "It was the Virgin again, she come to me from the trees. It was very clear. She stood by me."

"You sure it wasn't someone walking through the wood?"

"No it was her. She had a robe. She touch me on the shoulder."

"A lot of people see things, Eva."

"These were real."

"Why are you telling me all this?"

"Because." She stopped and looked down. "For a long time I have been thinking of making a promise."

"What kind of promise?"

"To God."

"Uh-huh," he leant forward. "Come on, tell me."

"To a convent."

"You mean becoming a nun?"

"Oui."

"It's quite a step, Eva."

"I know."

"I remember you said, or someone said, you were a lawyer."

"Oui."

"Pretty rational people."

"I am," she said. Then, "I know you don't do it so quickly."

"Depends on the order, but there's usually around three years before you have to take your vows. You know this, I guess." She smiled. "So you came on the path to ask yourself the big question?" She nodded, very serious now. "And you were hoping to get an answer. You were looking for a sign. So you prayed and prayed and drove yourself half insane and you got yourself a sign. Three of them." He looked at her and waited.

"Non."

"Come on, Eva, you're an intelligent woman. Virgin in the trees. Not on my watch."

"I don't understand."

220

"It's a common enough phenomenon. People having visions before they make this kind of decision." He remembered the voice he'd heard in his car before entering the seminary and pushed the thought away. "You may say they are so desperate for an answer that they give themselves one."

"I do not imagine this."

"How do you know? You know how they research miracles? Boy do they research them. It's getting so they need empirical proof. You get me? Empirical proof for something..." he stopped, then said it, "For something that doesn't exist."

She was shocked. "You are a priest."

"Yeah, well we all doubt sometimes, Eva. There's not a man... It's part of what we are."

"I believe what I saw."

"You'll have to make your own decision, honey. Maybe you just got me at a bad time. Sorry, I can't help you." He got up.

"You think I am insane?"

"No. Just trying too hard, that's all. Sorry." He picked up his pack. "Don't mean to be hard on you." He went back to the path.

"I've waited for you," she said.

"And I came."

He walked on, leaving her under the trees.

* * * *

Rhoda and Deena had stayed in a pension in Arzua that night and were on the trail again to Arca. There had forty kilometres left to walk, a stopover in Arca and then Santiago the following day. Rhoda had gone quiet. It had begun with Oskar's detailed questioning of her past, egged on by Rhoda herself it has to be said. Parts of her life that she hadn't considered for thirty, forty, or even fifty years were coming to the surface of her mind bringing with them an assortment of feelings long suppressed. All she could do was keep her mouth shut or she might scream, or cry, or laugh.

How many memories can you damn have, she thought. Now

released they seemed to go on forever, each inspiring the next. "I must be goddam eternal," she'd said to Deena.

"Hope so, Ma.

"You don't mean it."

"Anyway you mean infinite."

"You think I could be dying, Deena?"

"You take your heart pills?"

"You'll be pleased to see me gone anyway."

"God, ma, how can you...?"

"OK, OK." Rhoda was quiet for a moment. "Damn strange Deena, must be this path. You know the other day I had this figure of a man come to my mind. A good looking guy in a sharp suit with a charming smile. I didn't know who he was. And then, know what? I remembered. It was my first husband. Eduardo! I'd forgotten he was like that when I met him. I'd forgotten how much I loved him, Deena."

"You've had quite a life, Ma."

"You betcha! That Oskar, you know, he drew it out of me. I never realised. Nothing else this damn walk has been worth doing just to know that." Ahead of them on a ridge was a small village. "What's that up there?"

"Must be Santa Irene."

"Why don't we stop for lunch?"

"Sure."

Deena didn't feel like listening to any more of it and they walked in silence for a while until they came to a water fountain on the edge of the village.

"Isn't that the boy?" Rhoda pointed to where Willi was leaning against the circular wall around the other side of the fountain, eating a bar of chocolate.

"Oh hi Willi," said Deena. The boy gave her one of his quizzical smiles.

"Hey, you see those cows back there?" Rhoda said to Willi, "What were they? Steers?"

Willi didn't know what she was talking about.

"Ma, a steer isn't a kind of cow, it's a young bull."

"Bull, my ass, they had milk tanks on 'em."

"I think you mean udders."

"Yeah, I'm always wrong," said Rhoda irritated. "And this damn pack, I had enough of it." She slipped it off and put it by the wall near where Willi was sitting.

"How you doing, Willi?" Deena asked, putting her own bag down.

"OK." Willi stuffed the rest of the chocolate bar in his mouth.

"See, he speaks English," said Rhoda sitting on the wall. "You understand, don't you son?"

"Ich verstehe."

"What?"

"He says he understands."

"What I tell you?" Rhoda leant towards the boy and said, "You do whatever the hell you want with your life. Don't let anyone live it for you. You hear me, and a damn fine life you can have too!"

Willi pulled himself up, "Ja, danke." He wandered off down the path.

"Why'd you say all that to him?" said Deena, not sure why she was feeling so angry. Had been in fact since the night with Oskar.

"Because it's what I believe!"

"Alright for some."

"What's got into you?"

Deena looked back down the trail. "Isn't that Julia?"

"If it is," said Rhoda, not turning, "It won't be long before we get that French guy playing his damn guitar."

Julia arrived and sat on the wall without taking her pack off. She was breathing quite heavily.

"You OK?" asked Deena.

"Yeah, thanks. I feel a bit chesty. It's these decongestants, I think."

"You sure you're alright?" Deena leant forward to look into her face. Julia seemed paler than usual."

"I'm OK, thanks."

"I don't want to go into a restaurant, Deena. I'm tired of these

223

damn restaurants." Rhoda leant forward to feel in her pack. "Isn't there one of those supermercados around here?"

"What do you want one of those for?"

"Get some ham and cheese. We'll eat it on the way." She was searching in one of the pockets of her pack. "Where's my small money purse?"

"You got your big one?"

"Yeah, I got that."

"Small one's only got coins in it."

"It was in this damn pocket and it's gone."

"It's there somewhere."

"It's gone, Deena." Rhoda looked up. "It's that damn boy. He took it."

"No, he didn't."

"It was here, Deena! Now it's gone. He was sitting next to my pack!"

"Ma..."

"Put your hand in, it was near the top. It's gone. You see anything, Julia?"

"No," said Julia. She closed her eyes.

"You sure you're alright?" asked Deena again.

"Yeah, thanks."

"I'm going after him," Rhoda had lifted her pack.

"No you are not."

"I am not having my money stolen, Deena!" She didn't wait. She hefted her pack on her back as she went off down the road after Willi.

"Oh dammit, dammit!" Deena picked up her pack. "Sorry, Julia."

"It's OK," Julia tried to smile, but there was a pain gripping her chest.

Deena went after her mother. Julia sat for a while. The discomfort eased and the sun came out again. It was getting hot. Her chest felt full and thick. She decided to take her pack off and lifted her arms. Her face creased in pain. She sat very still, hoping she would feel better. She tried to ease the pack off again, then suddenly slipped off the wall and fell forward onto her knees. She was breathing heavily and beginning to cry. She tried to undo her jacket pocket to take out her mobile phone but her hand was numb and her fingers kept slipping from the zip. She fell forward. Now she was on her side on the ground with one pack strap still over her shoulder pulling her down and trapping her left hand. She gasped as she felt another hard, shooting cramp across her chest and hugged herself with her with her right arm as she tried to free her left. The spasm became too much and she curled on the ground. She was breathing very fast. She tried again to get her mobile out of her jacket pocket. She managed the zip but then the phone fell out onto the ground. She picked it up with her right hand and pushed at the buttons with her thumb, then dropped the phone. Her chest felt like it was squeezing tight. She tried to shout, but it was just a hoarse whisper. She picked up the phone and dropped it again. She lay very still looking at it on the ground in front of her. For a second she saw the top of the mountain that she'd dreamt of and heard her mother's shout. She closed her eyes.

Fabian came to the fountain a couple of minutes later. By the time he got there, Julia was dead.

PART FOUR

ARCA DO PINO

Arca is three kilometres further on from Santa Irene. It's a satellite town of Santiago and runs along the main road into the city twenty kilometres ahead. It's often the last stop on the path before the final destination. Usually nights in Arca, at either the municipal or the privado, are spent high in the excited anticipation of the arrival in Santiago the next day. This time it was very different. The news of Julia's death travelled fast up and down the camino, from bar to cafe, to fountain, to albergue, to a brief, shocked conversation on the trail itself. It took only a few hours for everyone on these last sections of the journey to hear the terrible news. For those who had known her it was devastating.

After Fabian, Peter had been the first to find out. He'd been sitting in the cafe in Santa Irene barely two hundred yards up the road from the fountain where Julia had died. He was alone. Karen had decided she wanted to walk the day on her own. It's what the path is for, she'd said, and had left him earlier that morning. It was a sign of his growing strength that he'd accepted her departure with some degree of relief. As he'd walked with her he'd felt his attachment to her increasing; there was something about her sense of certainty that was attracting him, and inevitably it was her desire to be alone that made him want to be with her. He'd sensed an old set of feelings beginning to surface and had been sitting in the cafe with a beer trying to accept them as the temporary and meaningless infatuation he knew they were. He felt she was impenetrable, in more ways than one. Now maybe, and at last, it was time to be alone. As she was. He smiled to himself. She'd taught him that much at least.

He looked up and saw Rhoda go quickly by, followed almost immediately by Deena obviously trying to catch her up. As they'd passed it had grown suddenly dark. He'd looked up, a small cloud was obscuring the sun. He sat in silence waiting for yet another tortilla as the shadows grew longer. The barman didn't put the lights on. As he brought Peter's food over, Fabian came in fast.

"Telefon! Telefon!" he shouted. "Vite! Vite!" He turned to Peter, "Julia!" He pointed back along the camino.

Peter didn't need a second look at Fabian's face. He got up quickly and ran out of the cafe as the barman picked up the phone. Julia was lying by the fountain. An old woman was kneeling by her, holding her hand and shaking her.

"Get her pack off!" Peter half lifted the girl and the old woman helped him pull the rucksack away. He turned her flat on her back and put his ear to her mouth listening for breath. There wasn't any. He sat up and brought his clasped hands down hard on her chest. He did it three times, then another three. He put his mouth over Julia's and blew. There was no response. He felt a mounting desperation and told himself fiercely to calm down. He raised his hands again and brought them down on Julia's chest. Her body rocked under the impact. He went back to her mouth again and blew, emptying his lungs. Then hands raised high he thumped them down again so hard that the next day he'd have bruises, dark purple and useless, running from his wrists to his little fingers.

He shouted, "Come on, Julia! Open your eyes! Julia!" Again and again he pounded the sides of his fists onto her chest, pulled her chin down and blew into her mouth until his breath was exhausted. Fabian came running back as the body rolled as if Julia was alive. He shouted, "Julia!" Peter put his mouth over hers again and blew. He raised his hands. Fabian was shouting, "Non! Non!" Peter didn't know if the Frenchman wanted him to stop or whether he was howling his grief. The old woman had sat back with her hands covering her face, tears welling in her eyes.

227

"Come on, Julia, come on Julia!" Peter brought his hands down on Julia's chest for the last time and went back to her face to blow the last of his breath. He felt the cold of her lips on his. He raised his mouth from hers and looked into her unseeing eyes, his mouth inches from hers as if he was going to kiss her. He slowly sat back. There was no life in her, or at least none he could bring back. He was aware of Fabian and the old woman standing perfectly still. As silent and motionless as the dead girl lying on the stone paving beneath him. Her eyes were still open. He closed them gently and felt the brush of her eyelashes on his palm.

"Non. Ah non." Fabian sat heavily on the wall of the fountain.

After a while Peter said. "I'm very sorry, Fabian."

The Frenchman looked down with his mouth hanging open. This was something entirely beyond his capacity for thought. There was Julia lying there. There was no Julia lying there. After a while he said, "It's my cold."

"It's not your cold," said Peter. "Cold's don't do that."

The bar owner and the barman came running up; then a girl from the kitchen still in her apron; an old man walking with a stick came to them slowly, asking what was wrong, and then a young woman from the village; she was around Julia's age. Peter got unsteadily to his feet and stepped back. They all stood in a ragged, broken circle round the body. The bar owner put his jacket over Julia, but didn't cover her face. No-one wanted to believe she was dead. The ambulance came quickly, and then the Policia. The medics had the resuscitation equipment strapped neatly into the back of the ambulance. The police officer came quickly forward with his own taken from the back of his car. But everybody knew it was too late. They covered Julia with a blanket and put her carefully into the back of the ambulance. It drove away as two pilgrims came up to the fountain. Peter told them what had happened. He could see Heinrich coming up on the trail behind. He told him too. That's how the news began to spread through the gasps and tears of the peregrinos on the path.

228

* * * *

Rhoda could walk very fast when she wanted to; so fast Deena could hardly keep up with her. And she wasn't listening either, couldn't even be bothered to answer Deena's shouts. "Come back here, mother! How do you know it's him?"

Rhoda knew damn well the boy had taken it. They all knew the kind of place he came from. What were they doing anyway, bringing a kid like that on the camino? The camino was for decent people. The kid could face what he'd done. Like she had to. Like everyone did!

After about half an hour she was breathless and beginning to think that maybe she had passed the boy because he was hiding. And why should he hide? Because he's guilty, that's why! She came into a wood of eucalyptus. She could smell it before she saw it. Willi was sitting on a log a metre or so from the track shuffling his feet in the dead leaves. He saw Rhoda coming up. She was virtually past before she noticed him. She turned quickly. "You! Give me my purse back!"

Willi arched his eyebrows and said nothing.

Rhoda trampled through the leaves and stood in front of him. She shoved her hand out. "Give it back to me!"

Deena came up quickly behind her, "Ma, for God's sake, we don't know he has it."

Willi looked slowly from one woman to the other as if they were both mad.

"Look at him! He's laughing at us, Deena."

"Wait. Just wait." Deena smiled at Willi. "Have you seen a money purse?" Willi looked at her as if he didn't understand. "A purse? Like a little bag," Deena made the shape with her hands. "With money in it? Euros. In my mother's pack." She pointed to it.

"Ich nicht verstehe."

"What's he saying? He understands, Deena."

"Ma, please." Deena took her wallet out of her pouch. "Like this."

229

"That's a wallet," said Rhoda. She shouted at Willi. "Money purse? Money? You take?"

Willi looked at her for a second, then shrugged.

"I'll knock that damn grin off his face!"

"You will not."

"You're gonna have to search him. That's the only way. Empty his pack. And his pockets."

"No,"

"You're going to let him get away with it?"

Heinrich came up behind them, "What is happening?"

"What is happening, Heinrich, is that he stole my money purse. Back there at the fountain."

"In Santa Irene?"

"I don't know. Where was it, Deena?"

"You've come from Santa Irene?" said Heinrich.

"I just told you." Rhoda was losing patience again.

Heinrich looked at them for a second and then spoke to Willi in German. Willi answered, shaking his head and raising his hands. Heinrich nodded for him to go on up the path. The boy got up and went with a smirk at Rhoda.

"You just letting him go?"

"Do you know Julia?" said Heinrich.

* * * *

Ingrid was past Arca coming into Lavacolla ten kilometres from Santiago when she heard. She was sitting outside a bar, still trying to work out what had happened to her. She'd got drunk and gone with Werner on the dark road into Melides. He hadn't even bothered to take her clothes off. She felt sick. She touched her face. It was more swollen. She wondered if she was pregnant. If she was, she'd get an abortion. She thought about infection, but would face that if it came to it. She felt as angry as she'd ever been. Angry at all of them, every single one of the men who had done this to her. But she'd known what would happen. She'd watched him doing it and let him, willing him on, forcing

230

her into the place she couldn't touch. She'd dared her herself because she'd needed to see what she'd always known; that the night with Werner had been, like many others, a pursuit of a love she'd always wanted but could never give nor receive - and all the pretty plans in the world wouldn't change that. And Werner was the same, he couldn't love either, so couldn't be loved - and all his prayers and faith and worship wouldn't change that either. It was why he'd hit her. And it was why she'd let him do what he did. It was all they had.

Just for a second she felt like she was falling and gripped the edge of the table. She wanted to cry again. This was ground level, it was dark and hard, but at least she couldn't fall any further. She had no idea where all this would lead her. She sat for a while, still furious - although she wasn't clear who her rage was directed at any more. She sipped her coffee and stared at the ground. Her mind blanked. What next? She tried to make a decision and forced herself to think. She'd be in Santiago before the others. She knew that much. She'd spend a quiet night on her own. See no-one. Get a plane out tomorrow. That's what she wanted. To go now. Her Path was done.

"Ingrid?' It was Anika one of the three Swedes she'd met with Peter. "What's happened to your face?"

"Nothing. I fell." Ingrid hoped they'd go away.

"Have you heard this terrible thing?"

She wasn't quite sure why she'd done it, but she'd picked up her bag and walked back the same way she'd come. To Arca.

* * * *

The man who'd caused Ingrid so much distress was sitting in a bar waiting for Llewellyn to buy a pair of underpants. They were also heading towards Arca but from the other direction. They hadn't travelled far the previous day from the bar where they'd met up in Melides after Werner's night with Ingrid. They'd got as far as Arzua. Werner had paid for them both to stay in a pension and they'd spent the night continuing to drink. Even as the alcohol slowly diffused his guilt, Werner was frightened enough of what he'd done to not want to see Ingrid again. As the evening had worn on, and they'd moved from bar to bar, the openheartedness and easy friendliness of Llewellyn had to some extent salved his shame. The grinning and naive Welshman made no judgement of Werner, which is why Werner needed him so badly, and at the same time despised him. Werner preached forgiveness as fundamental to his faith, but at the same time hated to be the object of it, because it showed him what he was.

He hadn't told Llewellyn what had happened between him and Ingrid. Quite the reverse. He'd given the impression that they'd both had a good night and then he had revelled in Llewellyn's boyish envy.

"What was she like, you know?" Llewellyn had asked.

"Find out for yourself," Werner had grinned. "It's a free world."

"Some hopes," said Llewellyn.

They had been sitting in the last bar of the night and Werner was drunk enough to admit to himself that what had happened was a logical conclusion to everything he'd done since walking out of Wien. The perceived notion of the Path was that the rhythm of the walk, the sociability, the beauty of the landscape relaxed you to the point where you allowed trapped feelings to emerge. For Werner it had been the opposite, a tightening, a turning of the screw, an almost unbearable increase in the pressure until finally he'd cracked and released what he'd dreaded.

Llewellyn had gone to the bar and as he brought over their drinks, Werner felt the residue of his rage raise. It came to the back of his throat and for a moment he'd thought it would suffocate him. He got up quickly and went to the aseos where he tried to be sick. Nothing would come up. He returned to their table. Llewellyn smiled at him.

Werner rocked in his chair. For a second Llewellyn thought he was going to explode. Werner said, "I want to tell you about my confession."

"Are you alright?"

"No. Listen to me! I told you in Wien, three jobs go. Everything collapse." He was staring out of the door to the bar. The street outside was dark and empty. "I tell you eight o'clock at night I take my bag and walk out of Wien. It's a lie. It was eight o'clock but not the same night. It was one week later. The same night I lose the work I go home from my office and sit in my house." He stopped, took a sip of wine. "I look round my house and I see my life. I work for fifteen years, nothing only work. My girlfriend gone. I don't even see my mother. I don't care about nothing. Work, work. Because I want to be the biggest architect in Austria. All shit. I go to a ..." he mimed opening a door and taking something out.

"A cupboard?"

"I take a..." He mimed it again.

"A hammer?"

"And I break my table for drawing. It's in pieces on the floor. I go to my bathroom and I find pills for sleeping and other things. I sit on the floor in the middle of the pieces of my table and I eat all the pills." He stopped. His head was pounding.

"Go on." Llewellyn whispered.

"I was a dead man. My house was my father's house. Only one other person has a key. My brother. I don't like him, he don't like me. He come to my house only one time in five years. But..." he paused for a second and his eyes filled with tears. He wiped them away with the back of his hand. "That night my brother come. He don't know he is coming to Wien. It is for his work. So he decide to come and see me." Werner looked at Llewellyn, "This is two times in five years. He come in with the key, see me and he call the hospital. The doctor said, I had maybe one hour to live. I am in hospital for a week." He looked up at Llewellyn, his eyes burning, "You tell me, why my brother come this night. You tell me who told him to come."

"What are you saying?"

"I think it was a miracle." Werner picked up his drink and put it down. "So now I know I have to find out."

"Have you found out?"

"No." He flicked the wine glass and stared at it with a long stern face.

"Thanks for telling me," said Llewellyn. He reached a hand out to Werner.

Werner shrugged it away, "I don't need no sympathy."

He didn't say much after that. He sat and brooded. He didn't want the wine and he drank it. They went back to the pension and slept late. As they sat in a cafe the next morning Llewellyn realised he'd left his underpants in the bathroom. They were in such a state that he was embarrassed to go back and collect them. As he had only one other pair, which were in a similar state and on him, he'd decided to go and buy some more. He left Werner drinking coffee. The cafe was on the path. Within minutes of Llewellyn leaving, Chan had come in with Soon-ok. Chan told Werner about Julia as Soon-ok sat and cried. Llewellyn came back with a new pair of underpants. He took them out of a paper bag. "Look," he said, laughing, "Only ones they had. They've got Mickey Mouse on them."

"We have to go to Arca." said Werner.

* * * *

Paul and Harry were already in Arca when they heard. They'd checked into the privado but walked down to the municipal as soon as they'd been the given the news by a pair of middle-aged Spanish cyclists, who although they hadn't known Julia, were as shocked as they were.

Karen was already in the reception with Oskar and the Koreans. Stanislav sat to one side, his hands clasped in his lap. The albergue was old and obviously had been converted from some other public use. Maybe some old admin building, thought Harry, as they came in. He sat down opposite the others. "One hell of a blow," he said. "Who'd have believed it?"

"No-one," said Oskar.

Paul went over to the hospitalero sitting behind her desk. She was a dark, middle-aged woman who listened sympathetically as he spoke quietly to her. He went back to the others, "When everybody's here, I'd like to say a mass. Sometimes it's good for people to come together when this kind of thing happens."

"That's a good idea, Paul," said Harry.

"The lady says she had a room. Shall we say around eight?" he paused, then added, "If anyone's interested."

* * * *

Peter arrived at the Albergue an hour later. He felt numb. All he could see was Julia's face beneath his own as she lay dead on the ground. He went into the bunkroom. It was empty apart from Karen sitting on the side of her bed with her eyes closed. He put his pack on a bunk and turned towards her. She didn't move. Her face was pale, immobile. He stood and watched her, wanting to speak. She opened her eyes.

"I heard. I'm sorry you had to go through that, Peter."

"It wasn't very pleasant," he looked away. After a second he turned back. She had closed her eyes again. He thought she might be meditating.

"Karen?"

She opened her eyes again, looked him and waited.

"This is fucking awful."

"I hardly knew her."

"Nor did I." He paused, wanting to say something but didn't know what it was. She waited again. He wanted her to say something, but didn't know what that should be either. "I think I'll wash some clothes," he said.

"Sure."

He emptied his pack on his bed and began to pull his clothes out of it. He began to speak, not really knowing what he was saying. "I was in Iraq and a young soldier died. We called him the kid." He turned, she was looking at him, waiting again. He saw Julia on the ground beneath him. He could feel tears coming into his eyes. "I had this idea, you see..." He pushed the heels of his palms into his eye sockets. "I had it then. It was that nothing could be helped. Ah? I mean, that everything that happens, has nothing to do with us. Do you see?" He stopped. "So what do you do? I mean, how do you live if you have no control over anything?"

"If that's what you think, you should accept that's what it is."

"I don't know what I think."

"If you're talking about Julia, and you're saying there was no alternative to what happened to her, then she had no choice in the matter."

"It's terrifying isn't it?"

"Maybe it's not. Maybe it's good."

"To die like that? At her age. On her own?"

"We all die."

"Is that it?"

"I believe that as we decide ourselves so we decide our fate."

"We become what we are?"

"Some people call it karma."

"You mean she caused her own death?"

"I don't know anything about her."

"Anyone! Are you saying that any twenty-two year old can..?"

"I didn't know her, Peter." Her voice was hard.

He paused, "I don't agree with you, Karen."

"Then you tell me why it happened."

"I don't know."

"You had a tough time."

"I'd better do my washing." He gathered his clothes. He'd wanted her to speak and she had. He didn't want to hear her anymore from her. "Thanks for listening."

"You're welcome." She closed her eyes again.

He went quickly through the back of the room and into the lavanderia. The room was dark and cold with a bare concrete floor. He bundled the clothes into a washing machine and injected coins into the slot. There was nowhere to sit. He stood in front of the machine, legs apart, hands in pockets, watching through the round glass as his clothes slushed in the soapy water. He looked up at the window above him, a long, narrow slit high in the wall. The day had almost gone, the sky was a deep grey. He felt terrible; like an iron hand had grasped his gut. He closed his eyes. The kid won't come back. The kid's gone. And so was Julia. He knew what was coming next. And so was Sam. How much choice did his son have?

Oskar came in behind him with an armful of washing, "Why not?" he said.

"You want to put all this in your virtual room?" said Peter.

"It's a problem, I admit," said Oskar shovelling his clothes into a machine.

"A fucking problem? Is that what it is? Some programming fault?"

Oskar straightened, "You know we can find the soap?"

"It's over there," Peter nodded to a dispenser on the wall. "It's a euro." He felt in his pocket for the change."

"I have," said Oskar. He pushed the coin into the slot, then watched as the powder poured into a plastic cup. "Everyone get a genetic test when they are baby. And maybe we do something about it." He poured the powder into another machine and pushed the bundle of his clothes into it. "I have heart, Peter."

"I'm sorry."

Oskar touched his shoulder and went out.

* * * *

The room they'd been offered for the mass was some kind of utility room obviously used as an overflow sleeping space at the height of the walking season. The ceiling was low, the floor was dirty and there were old mattresses stacked against the walls. Paul came in carrying a foot square, black velvet bag.

Harry came after him, "God it smells."

"It's those mattresses," said Paul. "Give me a hand with this." He took one end of an old table with a badly chipped and scratched top. Harry took the other end.

"Sure you want to do this?" asked Harry.

"Leave it be, Harry. Get the table."

They carried it to one end of the room. Paul took a white cloth out of the bag and Harry helped him spread it on the table.

"I mean it," said Harry. "Listen to me, Paul. This is a mass. If you don't believe what you're doing…"

Paul lost his temper, "For Chrissake, Harry!" He banged a couple of small bottles down. "Did you get the wine?"

"Sure." Harry pulled a bottle out of his bag as the others came slowly into the room. Chan bought in a pile of chairs and Werner another. Someone turned on the neon. The room became very bright.

"Sit wherever you like," said Paul.

Ingrid came in and sat a couple of chairs along from Werner. She was no longer trying to hide the bruises on her face, or her half closed eye. She'd used the same excuse as she had with the Swedes. She fell. She didn't add to it. She was there because she wanted to pay her respects to Julia, that was all, she didn't want to talk about anything else. She was shocked to see Werner, hadn't thought she would, or Eva come to that, which she realised was stupid of her and she began to feel angry. She considered leaving, but sat in a chair across the room from Eva wishing she hadn't come.

Peter and Karen were next to each other. He was shocked when he saw Ingrid. He looked over at her, wanting to know if she was alright. She was holding her head away from them all, looking up at the corner of the ceiling as if inviting them to stare at her and at the same time indicating she didn't care if they did or not. Peter thought she seemed very isolated. He wanted to go over and sit by her, talk to her, put his arms round her, but she wasn't returning his look, and this being a gathering for Julia, it didn't seem appropriate to pick up his chair and cross the room to her. He glanced at Karen. She sat perfectly still, hands clasped on her lap, waiting for the meeting to begin. If she'd noticed Ingrid, she showed no sign of it.

Chan and Soon-ok took a mattress from the pile and sat on that. Fabian came in last. He sat apart from everyone else. They were all there except Heinrich and Willi.

It was the first time Paul had seen Ingrid's face. He had no doubt how it happened. He glanced at Werner who was staring at his feet.

238

"Well," he said. "This is a very sad day. I thought we might want to come together before Santiago and go our separate ways. I'm going to say a mass, you can stay for it if you want, but before I do, anyone who wants to say anything about Julia, you're welcome." He looked round the uneven circle of chairs. "Hell this is hard. She was twenty-three."

"Twenty-two," said Fabian quietly.

"Sorry, Fabian, twenty-two. We all have our thoughts about God, I'll leave those to you. It's too early to celebrate her life, so I'm not going to try. I can't tell you how sorry I am that this has happened on the Path. It's not what I had in mind."

There was a silence. Oskar took a camera out of his pocket and turned it on. "I have a picture of Julia. He passed the camera to Paul who looked at it and said, "Sweet kid," then gave it to Harry.

"Didn't someone say she was an angel?" said Harry. "I go with that."

He passed the camera to Fabian who couldn't speak. He shook his head and gave it to Soon-ok on the mattress. She whispered something to Chan sitting next to her.

"She says, good spirit, she will come back strong. Me too." He gave the camera to Maria, who said, "Ella tiene mucho dolor."

"What?" said Rhoda.

"She has pain," said Oskar.

Maria passed the camera to Eva who said, "God took her because that's what he wrote for her."

Ingrid suddenly shouted out from the other side of the circle, "So this is a God I don't want! That's shit, Eva!"

Maria raised her hand, "No, no."

At the same time Harry said, "Hey, Ingrid.'

"Let her speak," said Paul quietly.

"Jeez," Harry looked down.

"Ingrid," said Paul.

She held her head high, her face bruised and swollen, flat and red in the white light. She spat out the words, "What God let's her die? She was sick. Everyone has said it. Why don't we help her? We knew she was sick!"

A couple of people said, 'I didn't.'

"We have spirit in the head!" said Ingrid. She tapped her forehead as if they were all mad. "We don't see each other." She stared at Eva, "She need help and we don't give it to her!"

Out of the silence Fabian looked up, his face full of tears, "I agree. I should take her for a doctor."

"You can't blame yourself," said Harry.

"Last night in the albergue she had pain in the chest," said Fabian. "I said it was the cold. I say to her, why don't you come to the restaurant for a drink?" He covered his face with his hands.

Harry leant over and touched his shoulder then looked round the room for some support, "Come on, this isn't right."

Peter said, "She was a very young woman, none of us could have..."

"I don't know if it was God or not," Rhoda interrupted him. "Or what it was, but it wasn't us."

"We should have seen," said Ingrid quieter now.

"Nothing to do with us," said Werner leaning forward with his hands clasped. "The almighty God..."

Ingrid didn't let him finish. She pointed to her face. "This is nothing to do with you?"

Werner hung his head and said nothing.

"Did you do that?" asked Rhoda.

Werner seemed to contract into himself, "Yes, I did it."

"Well you should be ashamed."

Paul raised his hand. "We're here to talk about Julia."

There was a silence. Eva glanced over at Ingrid with pity in her eyes.

"Don't you look at me!" Ingrid got up and walked out of the room, slamming the door behind her.

There was a silence. Harry said, "Matter of interest, anyone talked to the girl's parents?"

"The police," said Peter. "They took her mobile phone."

Stanislav took the camera and crossed himself. He passed it on to Pina who was sitting with the other Italians.

"We loved her," said Pina.

She gave the camera to Llewellyn, who said, "It's a beautiful picture." He looked at it for a long time. "Can I take a copy, Oskar?"

Oskar nodded and Llewellyn offered the camera to Werner who shook his head.

Deena said, "I'm so damn shattered."

Peter said nothing when the camera came to him. He wanted to, but the weight of that moment by the fountain seemed too heavy to dislodge; he could feel it pushing down, hard and heavy, releasing feelings he didn't understand.

Karen said, "I didn't know her as well as you. She was very friendly to me. I knew she would help me if I needed it, but I felt she would never need my help. Or anyone's help. She was herself."

She gave the camera to Oskar who turned it off.

BACK TO SANTA IRENE

Heinrich finally arrived at the albergue in Arca as they were all preparing to set off for Santiago the next morning. Willi had gone missing again. This time it was serious. The boy had lagged behind Heinrich as usual and disappeared at four in the afternoon of the previous day in the three kilometres between Santa Irene and Arca after he'd been confronted by Rhoda. At first Heinrich had been confident that he would reappear as he usually did, but as the evening drew in he became more anxious. He'd asked around on the path and a couple of pilgrims had seen a boy with a pack looking lost in the woods off the trail. One had been sure that he'd been heading back away from Santiago. Probably looking for me, thought Heinrich, and there were no yellow arrows to help him go in the reverse direction. As the evening had become night Heinrich had become increasingly worried and had finally called the Guardia Civil. They insisted that he went ahead to Santiago to make a statement. He'd taken a taxi there, and they'd officially posted the boy missing. By that time it was midnight and Heinrich had checked into a hotel, having been told the police would look for the boy. The next morning Willi had still not been found and Heinrich had taken a taxi back to Arca, walked into the albergue and asked for help in the search. Several of them had already left for Santiago by the time he arrived.

"We think he's back near Santa Irene," he said. "It was the last place he was seen. Perhaps he slept in a field."

Paul had apologised and said it was impossible for him to backtrack, his feet couldn't take it. Harry had said, he'd go. He

242

had the feeling anyway that Paul wanted to make the last of the journey on his own.

Peter had volunteered as a searcher. He glanced over at Karen sitting opposite him in the reception area. She was tightening the straps on her pack. "I don't think I can be much help. Sorry."

Llewellyn hadn't wanted to go either. He told Werner on the street outside that he had something to do that couldn't wait.

"What's so important?" said Werner. "This boy is fourteen years."

"I don't think you should be telling anybody what to do," said Llewellyn. "And what I'm doing is my business. Alright?"

"OK, OK." said Werner. It was the first time he'd ever seen Llewellyn angry. "I think maybe you want to come with me, that's all."

"No, I don't." Llewellyn walked away, then stopped. "I'm sorry you're in such a mess, Werner, but there's nothing I can do." He dithered for a second, not knowing whether to go on or not, then said, "Look we'll have a drink in Santiago." He walked off down the street.

* * * *

Werner arrived back at Santa Irene first. He'd seen no sign of the boy and nor had anyone he'd asked. He sat on the wall of the fountain waiting for the others. He looked down at the paving stones at his feet as if there would be some sign as to the exact place where Julia had passed away. There wasn't. He tried to imagine her death and couldn't. He thought maybe he envied her. After his suicide bid and the days in the hospital bed he'd felt numb. His brother had saved him. He didn't understand how. He didn't believe the coincidence. He had no idea what was happening to him. He was hollowed out, a cardboard tube of torn paper. His work seemed a past fantasy, his constructions just clouds. And now he was seen on the camino as he had been in Vienna; brutal, sad, to be avoided, failed. He looked up the sky, it was grey. He glanced down at his watch then remembered he'd

243

lost it somewhere on that night with Ingrid. He wondered if he could have killed her. He thought so and it frightened him. He looked up, Peter was coming down a track through the fields. He hadn't found the boy either. He sat on the fountain wall a couple of metres from Werner. "He could be anywhere," he said.

"You don't have to talk to me," said the Austrian.

"Ingrid looked a mess, Werner."

"What do you want me to say?"

"I've seen a lot of violence."

"But not to women?"

"No." It wasn't true. Peter had seen plenty of attacks on females. Soldiers sometimes didn't discriminate. He turned to Werner, "Why?"

"You want to know? I think God abandon me."

Peter wasn't in the mood for that kind of bullshit. "Come on Werner."

Werner shrugged, "It's true. I had everything. He gave it to me, He took it away. I don't know why."

"Maybe he didn't give it to you. Maybe you made it yourself."

"We don't make nothing ourselves."

"And maybe you destroyed it yourself." Peter thought as he said it that he was beginning to sound like Karen.

Werner looked away. "She like you."

"Who does?" Peter thought for a second that he was talking about the American.

"Ingrid. She like you a lot. She told me."

"What else did she say?"

"You want to know?" Werner smirked.

"It's none of your fucking business anyway."

Peter looked away and they sat silently looking out over the fields.

After a while Werner said quietly, "We're both the same."

"No, we're not."

"Why don't you tell the truth?"

"The truth, Werner, is sometimes difficult." Peter wanted him to shut his mouth.

"You chase women all your life."

"Werner..."

"You think I don't see it? Me too, I do the same thing. Except when I work. Then I don't do it."

Peter stood up. "I don't think I need this now."

"You don't hit Ingrid, but you leave her."

"I don't know what she told you. I didn't leave her. We both decided...anyway I wasn't with her."

"Don't matter what you both decide. All your life you decide the same thing because that's what you are. If you don't run after them, you don't think you are a man. It's true! I know!" He pointed his finger. "You don't have a second in your life you don't think about chase women."

"We're looking for the boy, remember?"

"She die here!" Werner shouted and pointed angrily at the stones as if the death of Julia demanded they scour themselves for the truth.

"And I tried to save her!"

"You save yourself first!" Werner glared. "Always! You save yourself." He paused. "Me too. Except this time I want to destroy."

"Ingrid?"

"Maybe."

"Why?"

"So I can escape. So I can be back with God again."

"Christ."

"Ja. With Christ."

Peter realised he was shaking. He wanted to attack Werner, crack his head open against the wall. He shoved his hands deep into his pockets.

"You want to kill me. Do it. Maybe it's the only way we find the truth."

"Why don't you go to fucking hell?" Peter shouted, losing it.

"Maybe I will."

Peter turned away. He was relieved to see Harry plodding along a track across the fields towards them.

"Hey guys, you see anything?" Harry yelled from fifty yards away.

"No," said Peter.

"One hell of a day, huh?" Harry came up to them.

"Yes it is." Peter moved away from the fountain.

"We go to Santiago. Maybe he is there already," said Werner.

"Hope so," said Harry. "God this where she died?" He'd been as upset as anyone by the death of the girl, but knew these things happen. He didn't want to think about it. He sat on the wall and looked at the village up the road from the fountain. Another great investment opportunity. It was on the Path. Get a cafe selling some kind of sacred food, holy burgers, something like that. Invent a few miracles. This fountain where the girl died. Give her a name. The Angel of the Camino, how about that? He looked at the old pump behind the wall. Holy water? Sell it in bottles? Why not? Harry had no problem in making a profit from God. It was what God wanted, wasn't it? As for the boy. Who knew where he was? He'd done all the walking he was going to do. Hell, still had to get to back to Arca and then Santiago today.

They sat around until Heinrich came. "Thank you," he said, "We must let police do it now. We go to Santiago."

Chan came running up.

Heinrich turned, "They've found him?"

Chan looked round as if there might have been a police car behind him with Willi in the back. "No," he said. "I come help. Look." He'd been five kilometres towards Santiago the other side of Arca when he'd heard Willi was missing and had turned round to come and search. It meant he'd already walked nearly fifteen kilometres.

Harry said, "Chan, I'm going to buy you a very large beer when we get to Santiago."

They went back up the road. As they passed the cafe where Fabian had come running in to Peter with the news of Julia's collapse, they didn't see Llewellyn sitting in the back in the shadows. He'd been waiting for them to go. He came out of the cafe. He was carrying a sketchbook in a plastic bag. He walked back to the fountain and took an A3 print of Oskar's photo of Julia out of the bag. Oskar had lent him the camera and he'd managed to find a place in Arca to make the copy. He placed the picture on the fountain wall, sat on the ground opposite it, opened his sketchbook and took out his pen. He wasn't sure why he'd needed to come back to Santa Irene to make the picture, he'd just followed his instincts. It wasn't so much he felt sorry for Julia, she'd gone - but for himself, he was still here. Her absence made his presence seem somehow more crucial. He had to get on with it, didn't he? Werner had been right about that at least - although he couldn't accept his battering of Ingrid. He could deal with, had dealt with, a few whose disturbance threatened violence, but the thing itself seemed beyond the pale. He suddenly found himself to be a prudish, purse-lipped, disapproving Welshman. Maybe that's what he really was, someone with an opinion, or even a purpose, and it was about time he faced up to it. He looked again at the photograph. Julia was, had been, gorgeous. He looked down at the blank sheet in his pad. He didn't want to picture her in death but in life, that's why he'd come to where she died. He couldn't really explain it but perhaps it was where something in him had died too, something he didn't want, and he felt like drawing himself back into life.

SANTIAGO DE COMPOSTELLA

Paul had walked on his own and he was ten kilometres away from the city. He was worried. Before they'd arrived in Spain Harry had taken into his head to write to the Bishop of Santiago asking if Paul could say a mass in the cathedral. The reply had been inconclusive, depends on schedules, visitors at the time etc., etc. Well what now if the Bishop said yes? If he said a mass he'd have to give a sermon. What would he say? Some half-assed crap that would avoid the point, or would he tell the truth? And what truth was that anyway? If his faith had been rocky before, Julia's death had been an earthquake. If he was going to be honest about it, he'd stand up there in that cathedral and tell them all there'd been doubts in his mind for as long as he could remember. OK, so he was weak according to Harry. Well, hell, that's what he was then, weak. How about your soul, Harry had said. He imagined his sermon. 'I'm here to tell you that the worm of doubt has eaten my soul.' And what is it, anyway, this soul? Just let me know when you work it out, will you, because I'd like to know; I'm not stupid and I want to use my mind if that's OK with you.

His anger and his thoughts were tumbling over each other in a rush to get out. He looked around. There was no beauty in his surroundings to help him; no shaded woods, or rippling brooks, or glorious, God-given sunsets. It was a grey day and he was standing in some kind of new-built holiday village. There were long, concrete and glass dormitories running either side of the road. Facilities for leisure everywhere; facilities for fun, dammit. What a shit hole. Why couldn't we just be happy without all this? It's not difficult. All we have to do is something good. We all know it already. Even a kid knows it. Do good, be happy. Every day just take a little suffering out of this world, you'll be happier than you can imagine. What's God got to do with that?

He realised he was hungry and went into what looked like an administration building which had a huge cafeteria in it. The place was empty. He ordered yet another bocadillo and a beer and sat alone surrounded by gleaming tables and chairs. A priest in a hard, shiny modern world with nowhere to go and nothing much to say, except to hell with it all. Julia's death had finally tipped him over, he had to admit that. If nothing else he had to be honest now, just for her. The meeting the night before had moved him, not the mass, the meeting, where a bunch of ordinary people he'd grown to know and love were sitting there trying to come to terms with something so unexpected, so arbitrary, so horrible and undeserved, and so damned impossible - with no help from God. He'd said the mass, the bread and wine had become Christ's body and blood, Christ here with us. It felt meaningless.

He hadn't slept last night, not for one second. He and Harry had moved down from the privado and they were all there in the municipal. He'd lain awake looking up at the bunk above him; there'd been a couple of snores, probably Stanislav, but not much else, just quiet. Maybe somewhere deep in their collective unconsciousness, after all these weeks on the road, they'd made a pact to co-operate, let their sleep be undisturbed. Perhaps they were all dreaming the same dream, or walking in and out of each other's, spreading a whisper here, a touch there, soothing everything, flattening it all out to peace in the night. Maybe down there in that subconscious lake we all float on they were slowly, unstoppably, creating Oskar's perfect world that Peter had told him about. And the next day they'd begin to make it happen without knowing they were doing it. Make it happen? Make what happen? His sour mood returned. Wait for damn death? What was so happy about that? Sweet kid. Dead. She was the key to something, he knew it. He looked round the cafeteria again, up at the doors, hoping someone would come in. A guy brought over his food, then he disappeared too. There wasn't even anyone behind the bar. He looked up at the sun refracting through the plate glass, creating bright shards of light on the hard wood floor, hurting his eyes as it sparked and dazzled off the legs of the aluminium chairs. And then the thought came to him. Why did it come then? He never knew. He stared at the Formica topped table in front of him, chewed a little on the sandwich, drank the beer as he turned the idea over in his mind, and then got up and left the cafeteria. He followed the concrete road through the holiday village and came to a brow of a hill with a radio mast on it. He stopped. Down below was Santiago. His first view of the city he'd spent a month walking to. It looked like any other big place. But in his mind, it wasn't; it was the destination for all of them, and if it was nothing other than that it meant it was the end of something, so it must also be the beginning of something else. He took a picture, then stood for a while, just looking. Now he knew what he was going to say in that damn cathedral.

* * * *

Ingrid was, of course, the first to arrive in Santiago. (Or at least she thought she was.) She'd left the Albergue in Arca early and come quickly into the city through its suburbs. The walk she'd had that day had been different from any other. She'd gone quickly as usual, but had then stopped and sat on a bench, or a wall, a fallen tree, and had sometimes remained there for a half an hour, her elbows resting on her knees, looking down at her feet, not knowing quite what she was thinking about. Then she'd get up, walked slowly and gradually picked up pace until she was almost running, then she'd stop again and sit. Stop, start, slow, fast. The walk mirrored her state of mind, uncertain, uneven and broken around the image of Julia she'd seen in Oskar's camera. Julia. She walked faster. Why Julia? Who was Julia? She didn't know Julia. Hadn't talked to her. Too pretty. Walking even faster now. Julia. Little girl Julia. Little girl Ingrid. Please you. Please me. Even faster. Julia dead. No. She pulled up sharply and sat on a wall. Her breathing was fast and shallow. Something in her was shaking. Like it was trying to shake loose. Like it was breaking up. She felt like crying. Didn't. Didn't cry. Held it. Looked up at the sun hidden by clouds. Breathed deeply. And again. Pushed herself up. Sat down again. Held her head in her hands. Looked at the ground through her fingers. Some grass in the stones. The shaking was worse. Breathed again and settled herself. Take some time. Take some time. Pushed herself up again and walked. Slowly now. Julia and then Ingrid, one step at a time. Slow now, keep it slow. She felt as if she almost stumbled the last kilometres into Santiago, unsure of who she was or where she'd been.

The city streets were old and narrow. Cobbled stone or renovated with slabs. The buildings either side were grey. She looked up and saw wrought iron balconies, which reminded her of women in bright, flounced dresses, a red rose in black hair, the stamp of flamenco, the old Spain of tall ships and leather. The shops under the balconies were small and old-fashioned and smelled of tobacco, coffee and chorizo. There were churches everywhere, and bells in towers too, though maybe she imagined those. Occasionally she crossed a main road and avoided the tyres on tarmac, the hard hush of traffic that could knock you and hurt. She dodged it the same as she'd have done anywhere, which seemed strange. Wasn't this supposed to be magic city? Did magic cities have roads and cars? She was dislocated, her mind here, there, nowhere. People passed old or young. It was weird they didn't acknowledge her, didn't know what she'd been through, didn't understand she'd walked eight hundred kilometres to come here. She wanted to shout. Don't you know what I've done, what's happened to me? They ignored her. Her pale bruised face. Her beating heart. She passed through the Porta do Camino into the old town. The streets even narrower. A huge stone wall to her right. No windows. Then a church, hard and permanent. Someone nudged her shoulder and said sorry in Spanish. She felt squeezed and wanted to cry.

She finally came to the Praza do Obradoiro. It was a broad, deep, stone square in front of the cathedral. There were other pilgrims there with packs on their backs. She didn't know any of them. She watched them turn in amazement at the sheer joy at having finally arrived. A group of cyclists rode past her, back wheels weighed down with overflowing panniers. One had a small flag with the scallop shell fluttering on the end of a high silver wire. They honked, shouted and rang their bells as they circled round her, she, Ingrid, standing still, pale face beating heart. A party of tourists followed a guide's raised umbrella; a souvenir seller was shouting. She didn't know any of it. She dumped her bag on the stone, sat on it and looked up the cathedral. She wasn't interested in it, but knew for some reason that escaped her that she needed to wait for the others to finish the journey. She watched silently for an hour as pilgrims she didn't know arrived in the square.

"The Palaccio de Rajoy!"

She looked round. Oskar was standing with his back to her pointing at the building behind. Next to him was Stanislav.

"I think you were contemplating!" He pointed to her left, "The Hostal de los Reyes Catolicas, pilgrim hospital. He said it slowly to Stanislav. Now hotel. Progress. Get the same bed, pay for it instead. Muchas dineros!"

Ingrid noticed vaguely he had no guidebook and must have studied all this.

He pointed to her left, "There convent. No." He thought about it. "I don't know. And there." He looked up at the massive, imposing facade of the cathedral with its two towers soaring up either side of the entrance. "The Catedral Santiago de Compostella." He inhaled happily.

Stanislav grinned.

"You know," Oskar looked down at Ingrid, "Whole catedral on the field where they found the grave of Saint James." He laughed. "So they tell me!" He looked serious again, "Church for one thousand years. Imagine. Old peregrino arrive, cloths rags, back turned over, no food, feet no shoes, come from little village, walk two thousand kilometres, no money, nothing, know nothing, never see nothing. Come here. Stand here. View this. Fall on the knees." He stopped and looked up at the vast, stone magnificence. "Power," he said. "Priest walk, big cloths, see peregrino, hold nose of stink, go into catedral. Old peregrino thanks God. Get up, don't walk maybe, still on knees, and goes up steps" He pointed to the grand entrance. "Go in. Fall in front altar. One metre away from Saint James. Apostle of Christ." He paused as if in amazement, then said, "Bullshit!" He guffawed and slapped Stanislav on the back.

But Stanislav wasn't listening. He was looking up at the high baroque stone of the cathedral, his head to one side, half quizzically, half in awe. "Power," he said. But he didn't share Oskar's contempt. "Very power."

"We wait," said Oskar. He put his pack by Ingrid and sat on it. It is tradition. You wait here for your friends." He pointed to the bruise on Ingrid's cheek. "Werner no good."

"Forget Werner," she said. "We are in Santiago."

She suddenly smiled feeling happier. There was something about Oskar. Whatever your doubts about the past or the future, he made the present clear.

"I have forgot!" he said. "I am ridiculous!" He leapt up, "Champagne! What I doing?" He did a little dance. "Champagne!"

He walked off towards the corner of the square. Ingrid noticed Stanislav watching him go. There was a love in his eye which clouded as he caught Ingrid's glance. She may not have been adequate to some of Oskar's wilder intellectual notions, but in other areas she was expert. She'd caught Oskar's looks at Stanislav, seen how he'd touched him when they talked, noticed the straightening of Stanislav's back, the tautening of his biceps as he'd returned Oskar's attention. These two were in love. If anyone knew it, she did, but she saw, with some amusement, that they hadn't worked it out for themselves.

By the time Oskar had returned with two bottle of champagne and a long thin stack of paper cups, Rhoda had arrived with Deena and Karen behind. Rhoda stood still as the two younger women circled, gasped, laughed, clapped their hands and sat on their packs staring up at the cathedral in the slowly expanding encampment in the middle of the square.

Deena had burst into tears, "Shit, I can't believe it." She took her mother's hand. "What about it, Ma?"

"I'm pleased we're here," Rhoda said sourly. She felt as if they were all blaming her for the disappearance of the boy who still hadn't been found. Her own daughter hadn't even wanted to walk with her on the last day, and here they were sitting right opposite the cathedral and she was still talking to that Korean, or Japanese American, whatever she was. Rhoda didn't like it at all. Like Paul she knew ends meant beginnings, and watching her daughter so deep in conversation with Karen, she had the horrible feeling that she could be in for one.

"Two bottles, Oskar?" said Deena.

"Why not three?" Oskar popped open the first and laughed.

Eva came soon after. Her head was pounding again; the closer she'd come to the cathedral the worse the pain. Now was the time, and she still didn't know what to do. She took a glass of champagne from Oskar and sat on her pack gazing up at the cathedral. She ignored Ingrid.

Deena and Karen talked, sprawled on the stone with their elbows propped on Karen's bag. Deena, walking a hundred metres behind her mother, had seen Karen sitting at a table in a picnic area. Wanting to be further behind Rhoda she'd gone over to her. She said she liked what Karen had said about Julia, "It was pretty wise."

Karen didn't mind the intrusion. Her path was almost done. She said to Deena, "Well we all got to be ourselves sometime. Or at least try to be."

"But what is it?' asked Deena. It was such a simple question, asked in Deena's usual straightforward and honest way, that Karen had laughed.

"Guess we spend our lives trying to find out," she'd said.

They walked together, Deena regretting all that time she'd spent with her mother, denying herself the opportunity of conversations like these. God, wasn't that what the Path was for? She began to open up to Karen in a way she'd never done before, because she needed to and because it was all pretty well over and she only had a few hours left. Karen didn't say much, didn't have to, it all poured out of Deena; how she'd put up with her mother for years, listening to those same damn boring stories and feeling sorry for her because she didn't seem to have much else except this recital of a past gone dead. But when Rhoda had been questioned by Oskar, she'd come alive. She'd had a damn past after all, and it was a pretty interesting and exciting one. What past was Deena going to have to look back on? A life spent trailing around after an old woman?

Karen didn't say anything. Maybe in other circumstances Deena would have expected a palliative, but it wasn't what she wanted. She needed the truth for once and Karen's silence wasn't an agreement or a denial, just an encouragement to go on.

"You know something," said Deena. "I feel like I've been deceived all my life."

They walked and they talked and they came to Santiago. They lay on their packs in front of the cathedral as they told each other more of their lives. Deena became more and more thoughtful. She could feel her mother glaring over at her. Karen sat up and started talking to Ingrid.

"Maria!" Oskar shouted.

Maria was coming towards them with Soon-ok. Behind them was Paul, as if shepherding a small flock. He'd walked with them for the last couple of kilometres. With their packs on their backs they were as slow as turtles. They say the last steps are the worst, and for both women they'd been agony. Their energy was gone and it seemed the closer they got the less they had. Sometimes it felt to Paul as if they were hardly moving, but they were, one foot at a time. Paul had kept talking to them to get their mind off it. They didn't answer. A Spaniard and a Korean, probably didn't understand what he was saying anyway. The cathedral got nearer like it was drawing them into itself. When they saw the others in the square the two women were so happy - they'd damn done it, they'd taken that weight, those sore feet all that way; done the impossible out of sheer will power and nothing else. And here they were standing beneath the bulk of that great building. Paul looked up at it. He was moved to tears.

The others all stood and applauded as the two women came painfully slowly across towards them. Oskar held up what was left of the champagne and began to shake it. He poured three cups. Maria took hers and slowly turned a complete circle then she began to cry.

Paul looked up at the cathedral and said, "My."

Soon-ok said, "My feet no good." She sat down heavily, spilling her champagne.

"Deena, I want to stay there!" Rhoda's was pointing at the Parador, the most expensive hotel in town. It felt like it was her last throw.

"OK, Ma."

"What? I said, in the big hotel."

"I said, OK."

Now Rhoda knew for a fact that something was wrong. They arranged to meet the others later, said their goodbyes, and went over to the hotel. Paul walked over to the cathedral. The rest went to the municipal. The first person they saw there, sitting patiently in the reception, as if he'd been waiting for them for hours, was Willi. He gave Oskar his usual ironic smile and said in German, "Where've you been?"

"I think I could say the same to you!" said Oskar.

Willi told them. He'd become lost in an eucalyptus wood and then seen a yellow arrow which he'd followed. He'd seen another one and followed that too. He'd gone through Arca as the light was falling and probably around the same time as Paul had been saying the mass for Julia. It had become dark, he'd become lost again, and slept in a bus shelter. Early the next day he'd seen more arrows and just kept walking. He was the first into Santiago, beating Ingrid by five hours. He hadn't bothered with the cathedral and kept following the arrows which led, as they always did in town centres, to the municipal albergue. He'd sat there and waited while they celebrated in the square.

Oskar called Heinrich who called the Guardia Civil who

called off the search. Then Oskar took Willi to a bar where he ate his last menu peregrino. He was cleaning out a plastic pot of icecream when Heinrich walked in and told him how stupid he'd been. Willi had heard that too many times in his life. He grinned and said, "Well you say I got to finish something. So I came to Santiago. I was first."

* * * *

Rhoda dumped her bag on the bed in the hotel room. Deena came in half an hour later, having gone across the municipal to pick up their bags, having had them, as usual, delivered to the wrong place. She sat looking out of the window.

"OK, what's wrong?" Rhoda faced her daughter's back with her hands on her hips.

"No more than usual, Ma."

"You didn't talk to me all the way from Arcola."

"Arca. Can you get the damn names of these towns right for once?"

"Don't take that tone with me. You had that tone all day."

"You just said I wasn't talking to you."

"I could see it in your posture. You been talking to that Japanese girl."

"She's from the States."

"And what's so fascinating she had to say?"

"We talked about a few things." The window faced away from the square. Didn't matter much, all you could see were churches anyway.

"You gonna tell me or not?"

"No." Although Deena knew she was going to.

"Is all this is about the boy?"

"He's at the alberg."

"They found him?"

"He's OK."

Rhoda hid her relief. "So what's the problem?"

Deena turned from the window. "The problem is, Ma, that

257

you were shooting your mouth off as usual, and you were wrong, as usual."

"He stole my purse!"

"He did not."

"Deena, it was right there!" Rhoda unzipped the pouch on the side of her pack. "He was sitting right next to it." Angrily she began taking things out of the pouch with her right hand and putting them into her left. "It's not there now, is it? There's my big purse, my glasses, this damn doll, don't know why I've got that, some lipstick," she grabbed another handful, "couple of brochures, my heart pills. That's it. See, Deena, nothing." She showed Deena the empty pouch."

"Ma."

"Nothing, empty."

"Look in your left hand."

"What?"

"Your left hand."

Rhoda looked. She was holding a small red purse. "Goddam." Deena turned back to the window.

"How'd that happen," said Rhoda, staring at the purse as if she'd been the victim of some kind of trick. "You put it back in there?"

"How much is in it?"

"I don't know."

"Look."

Rhoda opened the purse and prodded at the coins inside. "I don't know, a couple of euros."

"So that kid ran away, spent the night on his own, anything could have happened to him, all for a couple of euros."

"I didn't know, Deena." Rhoda began to whine.

"Don't start feeling sorry for yourself. You were wrong and you should apologise to Willi."

Rhoda sat on the bed holding the purse, "Wasn't there before."

Deena turned in fury, "Yes it damn well was!"

"Deena, can you keep your voice down?" Now Rhoda was being prim and proper.

Deena turned away. She'd had enough. "I was talking to Karen," she said quietly.

"Who?"

"The Japanese American."

"Uh huh." Rhoda knew it was coming now.

"She's going to Finnis Terre. It's another fifty miles."

"Deena, I'm not walking anymore."

"No, you're not."

"What are you saying?" Rhoda sounded panicky, "Deena we got a flight to catch."

"Finnis Terre means end of the world, Ma. It's on the edge of the ocean, where the old pilgrims used to go to finish off. They'd get there and know they couldn't go any further."

"So?"

"And they burnt all their clothes."

"And walked around naked?" Rhoda could see where this was going and didn't like it.

"It was a symbol. You know, get rid of the old." Deena hadn't meant it to sound that blunt. "Start again."

"What are you saying?"

"I'm going to Finnis Terre with Karen. You're going to Madrid to get the plane home." There, Deena had said it.

"You want me to go to Madrid on my own?"

"You lived in five countries, Ma. What's so difficult about Madrid?"

"I was young then," the self pity was creeping back into Rhoda's voice.

"I'm going to Finnis Terre, Ma. And you're not."

"You planned all this?"

"I just talked to Karen" Deena felt tears pricking her eyes. "I'm sorry. I'm going." She turned her back on her Rhoda. "Don't try and talk me out of it."

"Well, Deena, this is quite a shock." Rhoda was prim again.

"That's it," said Deena.

"Fifty miles," said Rhoda, "sure you can find your way?"

* * * *

Peter stood with his arms folded looking up at the towers of the cathedral. He felt flat and still angry at what Werner had said by the fountain. The excitement he'd imagined at finally arriving in Santiago hadn't materialised. As he'd walked in through the suburbs he'd done his best to pick himself up and congratulate himself on his achievement, after all he'd come nearly five hundred miles. Perhaps it had been the events of the last twenty-four hours that had deadened him, or maybe it was the depression that he'd heard often affected pilgrims as they completed their journey. Someone had said, one question answered, another one asked. He remembered Werner saying that depression was not being able to answer the question. Well he had news for Werner, depression is not knowing what the bloody question was.

He walked to the side of the square and sat on a low stone bench running the length of a wall. It was getting dark. He looked up at the cathedral silhouetted against a glowing sky. Maybe what Werner had said was true. Maybe he chased women because he was just a selfish bastard trying to save himself. The cathedral above him was rock solid. There was no maybe about it, that's exactly what he was. He looked down and away; having arrived, he didn't want to be there. Come on, admit it; the great pursuit had been a habit, deeply ingrained, his reason for being as Werner had said. And now this habit, if that's what it was, seemed to be not only dissolving, but actively daring him to destroy his reliance on it. Giant shadows were being thrown by the cathedral towers across the square, soon he'd be out of the light altogether. He felt he was beginning to doubt his shape as a man. If he lost this purpose what would he be then? Something that wasn't him? He wanted to stand and run from the encroaching darkness. How could he exist at all without this ideal, this female he couldn't touch, see, or even begin to describe? Werner was right, the chase was everything, he didn't give a damn about the end, didn't know what it was anyway; just some ephemeral notion that existed in his own unhappy mind. He suddenly had the image again of wiping the sick from his drunken mother's tit. You didn't have to be Freud to work that one out. But take it away, what was he then? It's what he was! He wanted to shout it. It wasn't what he wanted to be! He could have shouted that too, let it echo across the square. He crossed his arms and pulled them in tight against his chest. The Austrian had implied that in some way he'd been trying to save Ingrid. He wasn't trying to save Ingrid! He was engaging her, trying to know her! He breathed in harshly, squeezing himself inside the barrier of his arms as his anger grew. So what would he do when he succeeded in this knowing of her, when he'd broken the shell, got in there and saw it, the inner her; mushed, tender, uncertain, full of tears and joy; the heart and soul of another, all spread before him? What would he do then? Tread on it, eat it, love it? Or pass on again in this impossible search, for what? The equivalence in himself? The ideas were spinning around the axis of what he felt was something essential in him, something, he realised, with a rising panic, that was beginning to break. Muchas gracias, Werner, you brutal shit. Ingrid's face again, bruised and beaten, under the neon. He wished he had saved her, at least from that. Oh fuck it. He was an army officer, not required to think. He looked up. Hullo Santiago. It was dark now, the sun had slipped away behind the cathedral. He felt cold. He leaned down to pick up his pack. He hadn't even decided how he would get home. Maybe he'd concentrate on that. He heard a laugh and turned to his right. Chan was standing beside him. "Mission not so impossible!" The Korean grinned.

"Mission accomplished," said Peter trying to smile.

"Congratulation." Chan held out his hand.

Peter shook it, "And you, Chan. And you."

"I find Soon-ok," said Chan. "I worried about her feet." He pointed to a corner of the square. "Albergue that way."

"Thanks," said Peter. He watched Chan walk across the empty square. He looked up at the cathedral, now massive and grey against the night sky. He thought it looked ominous. There was something almost too powerful about it.

* * * *

There was a small praza outside the albergue. It was early evening and dark already. Ingrid was sitting on a bench with her legs spread wide and sticking straight out in front of her. She was lit by a street light, slowly chewing on an apple.

"Hello, Ingrid."

She turned, inclining her head slightly.

Eva stood awkwardly behind. She smiled, "We arrived."

"Yes." Ingrid looked away.

"Can I?" Eva indicated the bench.

"Why not?"

Eva sat down. They both stared ahead for a while. The air was cool, people moved slowly around the praza. Two kids on bikes raced each other and disappeared taking their shouts with them. Silence again.

"I don't like this, Ingrid," said Eva.

"And I don't."

"I'm sorry." Eva knew she'd been harsh.

"It's OK." Ingrid looked down.

The apology done, they were quiet again. Eva glanced at Ingrid and thought how quickly the bruises on her face had become part of her. They were still livid, but now somehow ordinary. Eva felt bad, not only at the way she'd treated Ingrid. They'd both come a long way but she didn't think she'd got anywhere at all. She said, "Do you think I am crazy?"

"Why?"

"The priest." Eva stopped. What Paul had said had deeply upset her. It had sent her spiralling down into a place full of jarring, pinching, jabbing ideas and feelings which she couldn't connect or make sense of. Seeing the cathedral had at least jolted her back into something she could understand; the harsh reality of leaving Geneva. She began to talk, mostly looking away at first, but slowly moving closer and closer towards her friend. She told her about her visions and what Paul had said.

"I see things all the time," said Ingrid.

"Do you?"

"Sometimes when I drink," she laughed.

Eva didn't. "Your face."

"I knew what I was doing."

"Aren't you angry?"

"Oh yes," Ingrid nodded her head. "Now I know."

"Know what?"

"I do it all the time, Eva. I pretend I don't know what's happening, that it's them that do it." She pouted like a child. "It's not. It's me too. I'm not a doll anymore." She was close to tears.

Eva took her hand, "What are you?"

"I don't know."

"Ingrid?"

Ingrid turned to her as the tears welled, "I am so lonely."

"And me."

Eva put her arms out. Ingrid cried on her shoulder. They sat close for a long time.

"Will you talk to him?" said Eva after a while.

"Werner? No." Ingrid wiped her eyes.

Eva said, "So. We've done it now."

"Have we," said Ingrid, "I don't think so."

"I mean, the Path," said Eva. "We've done it. We are in Santiago." But she knew Ingrid was right, it wasn't finished. She hadn't told her of the decision she still had to make. She'd called the Bishop's office after checking into the albergue and spoken to a Monsignor. He'd said there was a French nun she could talk to. She'd said she'd call him back.

* * * *

Harry had found Paul sitting at the back of the cathedral. He'd been there for nearly three hours. He seemed small under the high grey arches rising either side of him. Harry craned his neck to look up at the dome. Behind and around the altar was what he would later describe to his family when he finally gave his lecture, as one helluva mess of gold, the greatest thing I've ever seen. You wouldn't believe it, angels, saints, and I don't know what else, twizzles, and twirls. Around a ton of gold went into it I hear, and it was bigger than the front of that two-decker MacDonald's they built on the freeway. It dazzled you, gleaming there in the light like it had been there for hundreds of years, which it had. And in the middle of it all there's this life-size stone and gold Saint James, I take my hat off to the guy who made that. He was holding a scroll in one hand and what looked like a ball in the other. I tell you something, it reminded me of heaven, not that I've seen it, but it's what it reminded me of. Intricate and shining and going in and out of itself. Boy, that's what I call craftsmanship, that's what I call art. The absolute greatest. That's what I call a damn cathedral. And that's where the relics of the Apostle were too. Right under it all. You could go down the steps and stand next to them on the other side of this piece of glass. Imagine that, a foot and a half from the remains of an actual Apostle of Christ. You could even take a picture."

He wasn't exaggerating either. When he saw it at the other end of the nave from Paul, he just sat down and said, "Wow."

"Pretty impressive, huh?" said Paul.

"You talked to them?" Harry asked after a minute.

"They said I could say a midday mass." This was the international mass that all the pilgrim's went to as soon as they arrived in Santiago, a great honour for Paul to be asked. Bishop Rigson would have been very happy.

"You gonna do it?" Harry asked him. Above all else he needed to know this. He wanted to know if his prayers had been worth it.

"Sure, why not?"

"Jeez,' said Harry. "I thank God for that." He felt happier than if he'd retained the sole burger franchise for the whole camino. He touched Paul's knee with the side of his hand, "I knew you wouldn't let me down, old buddy."

"Thanks Harry. One thing you're not, is full of bullshit."

"I take it as a compliment." Harry grinned. He was still worried though. It was one thing Paul was going to say the mass, another thing what he felt about it.

264

Paul looked up and around, "Wonder how many men died constructing all this. How many others filled their pockets."

"Paul, you just told them you're going to say a mass."

"Didn't mean I changed my whole personality."

"You want me to comment on that?"

Paul laughed. "Nope. But I still don't know if that's the bones of Saint James sitting up there."

"You're not going to say that, are you?".

"Why not?" Paul turned to Harry and winked.

"How about saying thank you God for getting me here?"

* * * *

At a quarter to seven Werner was sitting opposite Ingrid in a small bar off the Rua do Franco in the old town. He'd been dreading Santiago. He hadn't come to the end of his path yet, he knew that. He'd entered the city and gone to the albergue, seen Ingrid sitting outside with Eva, turned round and gone to the tourist office and then to another bar. He was still there when Ingrid came in.

She and Eva had decided to go for a walk before meeting the others for dinner. It was Eva who'd seen Werner. He was sitting with his back to the door but his blond, curly head was unmistakable. Ingrid hardly hesitated. She told Eva she would see her later and went into the bar. She sat opposite Werner. It was the first time they'd been alone together since the night he'd hit her. She sat erect in her chair as he looked carefully at her seeming to examine what he'd done. He apologised tersely then looked away.

"You're still drinking," she said.

"You want one?"

"No."

He took a long pull on his beer.

"Did you use a condom?"

"Don't you remember?" The question was a challenge.

"No, I don't."

"You drunk as much as me."

"It was anaesthetic." She said it with a degree of contempt, though whether it was for him or herself wasn't clear.

"Did you knock me out of the bed?"

"Yes."

"Good." He paused. "No condom."

"Thank you."

He shrugged.

"Are you coming to eat tonight?" she said.

"With you?"

"No, everyone. Oskar has found a place."

"You want me to?"

She shrugged.

"I'm getting the night bus to Lisboa. Tomorrow morning I begin the Camino Portugues."

"How long is it?" she asked.

"Around five hundred back to Santiago." He rubbed his face. "You want to come?" He grinned.

"She smiled, "No, thank you."

"I'm not finished."

"I'm going home," she said.

He nodded. She got up.

"Goodbye Werner."

"You can tell the police if you want."

"No, I don't want."

"I deserve it."

"That's your problem."

"Ja." He nodded, looking away from her. "You see Lew, tell him goodbye from me."

"OK." She stood over him for a few seconds as if she was observing something distant from her, witnessing the cause of an event that had never happened. She left the bar. Eva was still waiting.

"You OK?" she asked.

"Oh yes."

266

Oskar led them all to a bar in the old town. "Rua Bella. It's cheaps!" he shouted as he took them under the colonnade on the street and then into the bar. There was a life-sized, brightly coloured papier mache figure of a pilgrim with a blue and yellow striped shirt, drinking a beer by the door. They went through to the restaurant at the back. There was the inevitable television high in the corner over a group of tables that had been pushed together to form a large square with places laid for fifteen.

Rhoda raised her hand and said in a loud voice as everybody began to sit down, "Wait, everybody wait. Willi come here." She took the boy's arm. "You sit at the head of the table." She led him to a place. "Just want to say," she announced, "there was a purse missing the other day and I thought Willi might have known where it was." Deena covered her eyes with her hands. Only her mother could do something like this. "But he didn't. He didn't know anything about it. Sit down, Willi. Guest of honour, the first one into Santiago!"

They all applauded Willi as he sat down.

Heinrich said, "Thank you, Rhoda.'

"How could you do that?" Deena whispered as she sat down.

"What I do now?"

Peter was at the other end of the table with Oskar, Paul and Harry. "Where's Lew?" asked Harry.

"And Werner?" said Paul.

"Gone to Portugal." Ingrid told them about Werner's new camino.

"Didn't he want to see us?" asked Paul. He seemed hurt.

Ingrid shrugged and raised her glass. "I forgot him already. Can I have some wine please?"

"Vino tinto!" Oskar shouted and began to fill their glasses from the bottles already opened on the table. Heinrich did the same the other end.

Rhoda leaned across Deena to Karen, "So you're going to Finish Terra with my daughter?"

"I don't know. Is she?" said Karen.

"Yeah, I'm coming," said Deena. She turned back to her mother and said through compressed lips. "That's enough now. OK?"

"Just asking."

They read the menus and began to order.

Paul touched Eva's arm and said quietly, "Sorry Eva, I was a little hard on you the other day. If you want to speak to the Bishop I can arrange it."

"It's OK," she said, "I have spoken to them myself."

"Uh huh?" He was asking the question.

"We will find out," she smiled.

Paul didn't push it.

Oskar raised his glass. "To Heinrich! For making the Path and finding his boy!"

"To Oskar for finding this place!" Peter raised his.

And so it went on. They ordered and were half way through the main course when Llewellyn came in with his pack on. "I couldn't find you."

"So you been checking all the bars?" Harry made a space between him and Peter.

Fifteen minutes later the Italians came in. They'd been busking on the Rua do Franco. They didn't eat too much, but they drank, and Francesco occasionally plucked at his ukulele, as various dishes came and went, more wine was ordered, and the noise got louder in a curious atmosphere of celebration and regret; friends gained would soon be friends departed.

Peter looked over at Karen. She was deep in conversation with Deena. He wondered what she was saying. She wouldn't be revealing anything, he thought. The only time he'd seen her show any feelings was when Oskar had questioned her about leaving Hollywood. Her anger had been real enough then. Maybe it was only that glimpse of her vulnerability that had interested him and when she'd closed down again that interest had evaporated. He noticed that Ingrid was watching her too. She turned towards him and smiled. For a moment the marks on her face seemed to disappear. Must be the angle of the light, he thought. Eva said something to her and she leaned back in her chair and into the shadow.

Pina asked Maria, "You have good camino?"

"Trente kilos" said Maria.

"That's how far you walked?" asked Rhoda. "It's more than that."

"That's how much weight she lost!" said Deena. "That's amazing, Maria!" She raised her glass. "Here's to you."

As the last dishes were cleared away Stanislav began to sing. The Italians gave him an enthusiastic if sometimes a little uneven backing. Fabian hadn't brought his guitar but he sadly joined in the Beatles medley which ended predictably enough with a sentimental chorus of With A Little Help From My Friends."

The party broke up. Oskar divided the bill and insisted on paying for the Italians. "For the music," he said.

"Say goodbye now, we may not see each other in the morning," said Deena.

There were hugs and kisses and a few tears. Paul announced his mass at twelve the following day and added as usual, "If anyone's interested," and they began to leave.

As Fabian went to the door Llewellyn fumbled in his pack and took out a rolled up piece of paper. "This is a picture of Julia," he said. "No, don't look at it now."

Too late. Fabian had unrolled the paper. He looked at Llewellyn's drawing for a long time. Then with tears in his eyes he said, "Merci, mon ami," and gave the Welshman a hug that was worth more than all the commissions he'd ever had.

Peter stood, shook hands with and then embraced Heinrich. He wished Willi good luck.

Karen came over to him. "I'm pleased I met you, Peter," she said.

"Thank you for the meditation," he said.

"It takes a lot of practice." She smiled and brushed his cheek with hers. "Good luck." She gave Paul a perfunctory handshake and left. Peter watched her go, as enigmatic to him now as she was when he met her.   She passed Ingrid by the door with Eva. Ingrid smiled, gave him a small wave and then went out.   He wanted to follow her, hold her, and tell her that everything was alright.   But he didn't.   He sat heavily feeling more than a little drunk.   He was left with Oskar and Llewellyn.   Oskar leant forward and put his elbows on the table, "I know what we must do.   Get another bottle!"

"I think I've had enough," said Peter.

"Never!"

The wine was brought.   They drank the bottle and then another one.

"I want to play your virtual reality game,' said Peter now too drunk to care.

'It's not a game, it's real."

"I'm not me.   I'm someone else.   What room am I in?"

"You can't be someone else."

"Well that's what I am, Oskar."

Oskar went along with it, "What room do you want to be in?"

"A bedroom."

"So you see it on the screen in front of you."

"I am in the room.   Not me, this is another person," Peter added, beginning to slur.   "I'm on the bed, listening to music. Very loud."   He was staring at an imaginary computer screen on front of him on the table.

"No problem."

"I see myself on the screen."

"Thought you weren't you," said Llewellyn.

"I'm not.   I see him.   I am him.   I get up and go to the door, I open it."

"OK.   We have to make this other place," said Oskar.   "Where do you want to go?"

"I want drugs," said Peter.

"Drugs?"

"I want heroin."

"Where do you buy your heroin?"

"I don't know.   In a bar, alleyway, doesn't matter."

"I can make the bar. But first you must see yourself wanting the heroin."

"I do see myself for Christ's sake!" Peter pointed to the imaginary screen. "There!"

"What are you doing?"

"Going to the door." Peter stared fixedly ahead. "I want heroin."

"It don't open. We don't know yet where you go."

"I kick it."

"It still don't open." Oskar was looking at him as if evaluating him.

"Then," said Peter, "I go insane." He looked away from the screen for a long time, took a drink and began to cry. "I have to say, Oskar, your reality game is very successful." He began to sob. Just couldn't stop it, slobbering down into his chest, all the retched up gobs of his fucking miserable life.

Oskar put his arm round him.

"If I was in a room," said Llewellyn, "It'd be a little studio somewhere. And I'd drink like a fish." He held up his empty glass.

"Ha!" said Oskar, "So would I!" With his other hand he filled Llewellyn's glass, then raised his own. "To us."

Peter managed a last toast, "To us," he said, his eyes still wet.

"Werner never even said goodbye," said Llewellyn.

* * * *

At six the next morning Deena began to do up the straps on her pack hoping she wouldn't wake Rhoda. There was no hope of that.

"Don't put your sleeping roll on top," said Rhoda from her bed.

"Ma, I packed this every day for five weeks." This was the moment Deena had been dreading. She pulled the pack onto her back.

"Bye, Ma. I'll call you."

"I'll be there, Deena."

"Oh don't, Ma. Please don't cry."

"I won't. I been around long enough."

Deena bent to kiss her. The weight of the pack unbalanced her and she half fell onto Rhoda's bed.

"And you think you're gonna get to this place?" Rhoda laughed.

"I will, Ma."

She kissed her mother, stood up, went to the door and opened it. A shaft of light fell across Rhoda. "Bye, Ma."

"Bye, hon."

Deena closed the door. She met Karen in the square in front of the cathedral. They walked together down the Rua das Hortas and began their camino to Finnis Terre, and as was the tradition, once there, they burnt some clothes they didn't want, to say goodbye to something they didn't need. A couple of hours after Deena had left Rhoda took a taxi to the station and a train to Madrid. She felt sad, and somehow freer than she'd ever been. She sat opposite an English girl on the train and told her about her five countries and three husbands. As soon as she got home, she rang Edwina Matthews and told her that the camino had been the best thing she'd ever done.

* * * *

At ten that morning Oskar walked with Stanislav to the end of the Rua do Franco to get a taxi. He watched Stanislav put his pack on the back seat of the cab. They embraced. For a second they looked into each other's eyes.

"Sorry, Oskar," said Stanislav. "I am Catolica."

He got into the taxi. At first Oskar didn't think he was going to look back. Then he did.

Oskar watched the taxi until it was out of sight, then walked over the road to a park and wandered along a path under the trees. He saw a life-size, bronze statue of a man with a long beard. The inscription said the man was a famous academic. Oskar said conversationally. "You and me." Then he laughed and walked away to the train station. He was thinking that maybe he'd take a sabbatical to work on his idea.

* * * *

At just before midday Harry sat towards the back of the cathedral. He was as nervous as hell for Paul. Saying a mass in a place like this could be scary. But mainly he was nervous because he was dreading what Paul might say in the sermon. The place was half full, he hoped it didn't get any fuller. He clasped his hands together in his lap and prayed under his breath, "Dear God, please make that dumb bastard realise where he is and see some sense." He looked up. There were already priests moving around the sanctuary getting the altar ready for the mass. A party of schoolkids in green uniforms sat near the front and some old guys in a kind of costume with sashes over their shoulders were sitting behind them. Maybe from one of the orders of the Knights Templar, thought Harry. More of the congregation were filing in; mainly pilgrims, but most of the rest looked older and from the city. He hoped to hell they didn't speak too much English. The bishop didn't seem to be there anyhow which was a relief.

A nun came to the lectern by the side of the altar. She said a few words in Spanish, then began to sing, and God, was that beautiful. She had a small microphone in front of her, but she didn't need any amplification, her voice soared, filling the cathedral and taking Harry's heart with it.

Eva, sitting in the pew behind him couldn't take her eyes off the nun either. She was a middle-aged woman, not particularly beautiful, or angelic, or adoring, or even intense. She was quite matter of fact. She glanced round the cathedral as she sung, as if these extraordinary sounds were coming out of her involuntarily and all she had to do was open her mouth. You do nothing, and let God take you, thought Eva. In front of her Maria was singing too. Her voice was not as powerful as the nun's, and not amplified, but if anything was more pure. Standing close to her Eva could hear it, slightly higher than the nun like a faint breeze

273

playing on top of a stronger one. Maria was here to offer her gratitude. She had no doubts as to who'd taken her up those hills and across that plain; it was her patroness, her adored namesake, Maria the Virgin.

Paul came down the narrow stairs from the vestry followed by two other priests. He crossed to the altar and stood behind it. Harry guessed he'd had to borrow the vestments; all the visiting priests probably did that, but Paul cut a fine figure. Harry raised his camera over the heads of the congregation in front of him, zoomed to his longest lens, and took a picture. Paul began the mass.

Sitting a few rows behind Eva were Fabian, Peter and Llewellyn. Fabian was going to begin the long walk back to Nancy straight after the mass. It was close to fifteen hundred kilometres and would take him three months through the winter. It was what he'd always planned to do; the only person who could have stopped him was Julia. Now he wanted to leave Santiago as soon as he could. He was only at the mass because of what Paul had asked him to do. He knew it wouldn't be easy, but he'd do it for her, and he hoped that he could then walk her away from those terrible moments by the fountain and into another place in his memory. He'd planned to make a memorial to her somewhere along the camino. Not at Santa Irene where she'd died, but where he'd caught up with her on the day after he'd met her in that square in Pamplona with Werner; where he'd fallen in love with her. He didn't know quite what he'd make the memorial out of but was sure he'd find something. He'd thought about leaving his guitar for her but didn't think she'd want him to do that.

Llewellyn was there because he couldn't quite make the decision to leave Santiago and had to be somewhere while he made up his mind. A woman came to the lectern and read an epistle in Spanish, which Llewellyn didn't understand. He wondered how Werner was getting on. He'd be walking out of Lisbon by now, probably sat in a bar. Llewellyn knew Wern would be at the mass if he was in Santiago; his faith was strong. Llewellyn's wasn't; he knew he couldn't live as he wanted if he was tied to anything as unyielding as that. But there was no harm in a little prayer. He put his hands together and prayed for Werner. Then he looked up, Paul was coming down to the lectern.

Harry prayed, "Please God, keep his damn mouth shut."

Paul looked round at the congregation. Since the beginning of the mass more pilgrims had come in, many of them directly from the path. Their packs were in huge piles against the pillars in the side aisles. They'd taken four, five, six weeks to get there. Paul didn't see any way he couldn't tell them the truth.

"Welcome," he said. "Welcome to you all and congratulations to many of you on the completion of your path. It's a long walk, a very long walk. I know because I've done it myself. And I'll tell you the first thing I learned," he smiled. "Look at me, I'm a sixty-five year old man with a big fat gut. I didn't think I could walk five hundred miles, but let me tell you there were a lot of people in worse shape than I am, people with illness, people with big problems who went up those hills and crossed those plains. Just ordinary people, like you and me, and we all did it. And that was the first thing I learned, we're all capable of more than we think we are." He smiled again and adopted his very easy, folksy way of talking. He didn't seem to have anything prepared, there were no notes, it was as if he was just chatting to them.

Harry sat back, maybe he didn't have anything to worry about.

Paul went on. "Now let me tell you a little about myself. I'm from the United States of America. I'm a parish priest in Jefferson City, Missouri. I came to the priesthood late. I wasn't very brave, I wasn't very clever, but I did have one thing, I had my faith in God. And I took that faith into my work. And now fifteen years later, here I am in this beautiful cathedral in Santiago, privileged to be asked to say this mass, and I have to say something to you. You may find it shocking."

Harry clasped his hands tighter than he'd ever done, "Oh God, please, please..."

"I don't know if there is a God."

Harry wanted to crawl away. There was a silence in the cathedral. Several priests sitting behind Paul were looking at each

275

other. One was whispering a translation to another who looked deeply shocked. Many pilgrims turned to one another. Peter, still suffering a terrible hangover and only there because Paul had asked him, thought that for a priest to say that in the middle of a mass in the Cathedral of Santiago de Compostella was about the most extraordinary thing he'd ever heard.

"Many times in my life that idea has found its way into my mind, but I always repressed it. But it came back, and kept coming back, and maybe this is the wrong place to say it, but it's where it has arrived, and I can't keep lying to myself, and I'm not going to lie to you either."

He stopped again, looked around, then stood firmer, as though he was settling himself in to what he had to say.

"See, something else I learned on that walk was that to find out about this world you got to be honest with yourself first. I'm a man, nothing else, pretty ordinary, and I'm trying to tell you the truth, which is about all a man can do, I guess. Now if I'm telling you that I don't know whether there is a God, you have a right to ask, what do I believe in? Well the first thing is, that the question doesn't matter. It doesn't matter, you say? How can that be? Didn't it matter to all those who built this cathedral? And the hundreds of thousands, maybe millions, who have walked here on the greatest pilgrimage of their lives? Didn't it matter to them? Yes it did, but there's something that matters even more. Every single one of those wonderful people had a question to ask. Sometimes those questions were small, you know, should I change my job, should I get a new girlfriend? Sometimes they were too big to handle, how do I live without my father, or, in my case, is there a God? Whatever the questions, these people put one foot in front of the other on their own path to find their own answers. And what was I supposed to do? Say I'm a priest and I know it all?

There was growing consternation amongst the priests in the sanctuary behind him. Paul turned back to them and smiled, then back to the congregation

"Maybe I'm going to get stopped in a minute. But before I am,

I just want to tell you this. It's about something that happened to me and those people I travelled with. A young Australian woman died."

The priests behind him quietened. If they were going to stop him they couldn't do it now. Not even they could interfere with a story about death. It was their principle purpose, to ameliorate our terror at the thought of extinction. They sat back in their chairs, watchful and suspicious.

Paul went on, "She died of a massive and unexpected coronary. She was twenty-two, beautiful, a unique human being, just like the rest of us, with something to do with her life. And now she's gone. It upset me a lot. Didn't seem right to me. I sat in a cafeteria yesterday, on the last day of the walk. I was depressed. I asked myself, had God done this? And if He hadn't, then why didn't He stop it, protect her, save everyone from this damn misery? Then I has this crazy idea. Don't know where I got it from, but I began to think of miracles. There have been many of them that we've believed in, but it came to me that maybe death is the greatest one of all. Death is the greatest miracle? I know that sounds as if I've lost my mind. I'm not talking about a miracle like the loaves and fishes, or water into the wine, or even the raising of Lazarus, or any other of those bible stories, I'm talking about the real thing, a miracle of life. Death, a miracle of life? How in hell do I work that one out? Well I'll tell you. Most of us have experienced the death of a loved one; we've been there, felt the pain. We all know too that death brings us together. It brings us together, in my opinion, because we all know we're going to die, and we all know that everyone else is going to die too. There's not one of us that is exempt from that terrible knowledge."

He was speaking from his heart. Even Peter, one of the least believing, was hooked.

"Let me tell you this, the night after she died I was sleeping in a bunkroom with maybe fifteen or twenty people who'd walked with this young woman. I lay there listening to the sounds of their sleep. And I felt the greatest love for them because I knew that no matter what they did, whatever they made, however great their ambition, their success, their goodness, their evil maybe, every one of them lived with this knowledge of death lying there, solid and immutable in the centre of their minds like a cancer growing bigger every day, until finally it would envelope each and every one of them and take them away leaving the rest of us bereft and grieving and wondering why. How in hell do we live with that? Pretend we don't know it? Try and ignore it? Distract ourselves with the toys of life? Well how we deal with that knowledge is the miracle. We laugh, that's what we do, we cry too, and we make things; a cake for our kid's birthday, a house, an irrigation system, a pile of money, a philosophy, a rocket to the Moon, a nuclear bomb, anything we can think of which, in each of our crazy ways, we think will make the world a better place. Sure, and every day we make a million mistakes too, but it doesn't matter, we're trying, and that's the important thing. And why do we do all this? Because we love each other and we love ourselves. And why do we love each other so much? Because we know we're all together in this; all so bravely marching towards the ultimate, the end of the road, dead, done, gone. And we stand together. And we face it."

He stopped again, looking round.

"What sheer, utter, damn courage we all have. And we all love each other because we all know we have this courage, because we all know that we are all walking unstoppably towards our own extinction. And the closer we get to it, either in thought or understanding or age, the more we love each other. And that means that death is the ultimate cause of love. That's the miracle. It's the greatest miracle of all time. Death makes love. If love is the most natural thing there is, so is death, and you can't have the one without the other."

He waited for a moment as if considering the question he was about to ask.

"So how does that affect how we live our lives? Well first it means that if we can accept that the end of life has reason and a cause that unites us all, then maybe we can stop being so damn pernickety about living it. And in the light of this, everybody is right, and always has been; the Christians, the Jews, the Moslems, Hindus, the Buddhists, and whatever interdenominational, agnostic, atheistic, and crazy cult that has ever existed; because they have each in their own misguided, no doubt corrupt, stupid and beautiful way, looked to increase love. What a people we are! And I'm so proud to be part of it. So damn proud."

His voice cracked for a second. He cleared his throat. His voice was lower.

"You know, on that path there are many conversations about the spirit, and what it is. Well I'll tell you what the spirit is. Just another way of describing this love we feel. You don't believe me? Take a look at the person standing next to you. Look hard and you'll see the miracle, right there, walking towards their death with courage and love. Did God make this miracle? I don't know. Does he exist? I don't know. Do we know what happens after death? No. And, does it matter? No. All those questions just get in the way. We know what we know. That's it. Nothing else. The beauty of death, the creation of love. The miracle is within us. We live it. We don't need a God. We don't need an excuse. We have each other. I know that and I've always known it. We all know it. And if you ask me, I'd say it was pretty good."

He looked up into the great vaults of the cathedral and as if in comment on its majesty and said quietly, "There isn't anything else. There doesn't need to be. Thank you for listening to me."

He stood still for a second. The cathedral was silent. No-one moved.

If Peter knew anything about procedure, power, and how those who held it and protected it, he knew that Paul had probably ended his career in the church. You couldn't say those things in the Cathedral of Santiago. Personally he'd never been so moved in his life.

Paul turned and went back towards the altar. Behind it sat the six priests. Two of them glared at him with the utmost contempt, one walked to the back of the sanctuary, turned and stared at him as though he was the devil himself; two younger priests looked at him with the greatest concern, though whether that was for him or themselves wasn't clear. One of them had tears in his eyes. The last of the six, a middle-aged man with a bald head got up and walked sternly to the altar. The mass would continue no matter what anyone thought. Or said.

Harry said later, the communion took place in the thickest atmosphere he'd ever known in a church. Not many went to Paul to receive the host. At the end of the mass, after the blessing Paul stepped forward again. He said, "I mentioned to you a young woman who died. I've asked a man who knew her well to sing something in memory of her."

Fabian went to the front with his guitar and stood behind the microphone on the lectern. He sang Julia. He didn't sing it well, his voice cracked and he was too far back from the microphone. But the congregation sat and listened. Tears streamed down Llewellyn's face. Eva cried too.

The mass was over but the congregation hadn't moved. Peter couldn't understand why, then he remembered, the famous butafumeira. There seemed to be some consternation in the sanctuary; several of the priests were arguing. Finally the two younger ones came forward and were joined by five others. Peter didn't know who or what they were, they'd suddenly appeared in clerical dress from the side. They went to a pillar at the front and left of the altar where a rope at least two inches in diameter was tied round a heavy iron bracket. Several of them took the strain as the rope was released and the great censor was lowered from the roof. It came down slowly and stopped about four feet from the ground in front of the altar. This was the butafumeira. It was an ornate, sliver incense burner about two feet from top to bottom and judging by the expressions on the faces of those bearing the rope it must have been very heavy. The bald priest who'd served at the mass took the top off it and inserted a tray of smoking incense, then he swung it gently across the altar as the rope bearers began to haul it up again. As it rose it swung further left and then right like a giant pendulum across the transept, emitting pungent smoke as it went. The more the bearers jerked on the rope the higher it went and the greater its swing across the face of the altar as it flew high above the heads of the congregation either side, almost reaching the fifty foot high vault of the cathedral above them on the extremities of its arc. The sweet smell of the burning incense pervaded the cathedral, the flames of the silver burner were reflected in the gold statue of Saint James. It was certainly spectacular, but for all its smoke and fire it seemed an almost empty gesture after what Paul had said.

Peter and Eva waited for him outside in the square. Llewellyn had already gone, sloped away for a quick fag. Paul came out with Harry behind. Harry seemed lost for words. He didn't know what to make of any it. His faith was like a rock in a stream; his life flowed over it, and there it remained, getting a little worn maybe, but that just made it more comfortable. He just didn't get Paul. Mostly he'd have liked to have punched him in the mouth, but then there was this feeling he couldn't put into words.

Eva gave Paul a bemused look and kissed his cheek.

"Au revoir, Papa. I will pray for you."

"Thank you, Eva."

Fabian strapped his guitar to his pack to start his long walk home. "Au revoir." He couldn't think of anything else to say and walked sadly away, disappearing slowly through the last of the crowd still coming out of the cathedral, many of whom were giving Paul looks of either admiration or disgust, but mainly sheer bewilderment.

"Come on, Harry, don't be so frosty," said Paul.

"I'm not frosty."

"How would you like a defrocked priest on the board of this charity of yours?"

"What charity?"

"The one we're going to set up together."

"I don't know about that." It was the first time Peter had ever seen a look of confusion on Harry's face.

"I'm scared as hell, Harry," said Paul suddenly.

"Well, what you want to say all that for?"

"Had to."

"Talk about it later." Harry looked away then back to Peter. "Been an education." He shook hands and walked across the square towards the albergue.

Paul looked sheepishly at Peter who could see the hurt in his eyes. Peter told him how much he admired him. Paul nodded as if he wasn't sure he deserved it.

"Stay in touch." He gave Peter a hug, then Eva, and went after Harry.

Peter watched him go then turned to Eva, "Has Ingrid gone?"

"No, I am meeting her to say goodbye." Eva smiled, "Why don't you come?"

* * * *

Peter went back to the albergue to pick up his pack. Eva already had hers. She sat at a table outside a restaurant not far from the cathedral waiting for him and Ingrid. Her flight back to Geneva was in a couple of hours. The weight had lifted. She was not going to follow the path of seclusion. She was going home. She'd made up her mind last night waiting outside the bar while Ingrid talked to Werner. Watching her friend sitting opposite the man who'd beat her, with her face so vulnerable, but somehow accepting of both him and herself, she'd seen that Ingrid was facing down her demon and would accept the loneliness she dreaded. Eva had seen that her desire to isolate herself within a holy community had been perversely to defeat the same thing in herself. In Geneva all she'd ever done was hide; her idea of further separation was only to wrap herself tighter against everything she wanted. But whatever those visions on the path had been they'd emanated from a faith deep inside of her; a faith she now felt that didn't have to be exclusive, that needn't condemn her to a life of solitude, but one that could open her out and be shared, and as she'd listened to the nun's voice soar into the vaults of the cathedral, she'd realised with a sudden intense surge of joy, that she need never be lonely again. She would be a woman fully immersed in a real world of pain and happiness, chestnut trees and laughter, even a legal practice, even children, and in the heart of it would be her own true faith. What did solitude have to do with that?

Peter came and ordered a beer. "What did you think of Paul?"

"Sometimes it's not so good to be brave only. You have to be true."

"Maria didn't come out to see us."

Eva shrugged as if the answer to that was obvious.

She didn't really want to talk about it. Peter's beer arrived, and then Ingrid.

"I'm sorry I'm late, I went to Santa Irene. I went to the fountain, I wanted to say goodbye to Julia." She said.

"All the way to Santa Irene?" Eva asked.

"I can't stop walking." Ingrid laughed. "But I come back in a taxi. Julia is important, you know?" She tilted her head as if she was expecting them to argue.

"You are so strange," said Eva.

"Maybe I want to be like her." Ingrid said it in her sometimes vague way, and then looked over shoulder at the cathedral, closing the subject.

Peter told her about Fabian singing Julia, and about Paul's sermon.

"If every priest was like him I might go to church," she said.

"There wouldn't be a church anymore," said Eva.

"Perhaps Paul will build a new one," said Peter.

"I want a beer," said Ingrid. She waved to the waiter. "You know this is like the first night. You remember our dinner in St Jean and I went out to talk to Siri?"

Peter thought it seemed like a hundred years ago.

"Many things are different now," said Eva smiling at Ingrid. That morning she'd told her of the decision she'd made.

"I know," said Ingrid. She leant forward and kissed Eva. The two women held each other for a moment.

"I have to go now to the airport," Eva said.

She stood and lifted her pack onto her back. "Goodbye Peter." She kissed his cheek and squeezed his arm, then blew a kiss to

Ingrid who sat with tears in her eyes. "I will email." She went to the end of the street to find a taxi.

Peter and Ingrid sat in silence for a while. Her beer came. She sipped it, then raised her face to the pale afternoon sun. Peter noticed again how the bruises seemed to disappear in a certain light. The city seemed very quiet.

"When are you going home?" They both said it at the same time.

Ingrid laughed, "We came on the same plane to Biarritz."

"I know. I'm going back this evening."

"Me, tomorrow," she said, then hesitated, "Would you like to come and see me in Danmark?"

"I didn't think you'd want me to."

"Why not? At least I wouldn't have to explain anything to you."

"That's true." He laughed, then paused. "There's something I have to do."

"Oh it's OK," she said. "I say these things and only bad things happen anyway."

"Ingrid, I'd like to, but..."

She didn't let him finish. "You know I'm going to tell my daughter that she can see her father whenever she want. He's the only one she's got. And I'm her only mother." she giggled. "Poor Siri."

"Perhaps not so poor." He smiled.

"Thank you, kind gentleman." She touched her face with her finger, prodding to see if it still hurt.

"I'm sorry."

"It wasn't you."

"I somehow feel it was."

"Why?"

"Difficult to explain."

She leaned forward and took his hand. "You don't have to come to Copenhagen. I understand. Anyway maybe I won't be there."

"Where will you be?"

Her usually pale eyes were dark. "I don't know. Maybe something comes from this anyhow. Something good." She smiled, let go of his hand, leant back and put her face up to the sun.

* * * *

Peter took the plane from Santiago to Stansted a couple of hours later. In the taxi to the airport he saw Chan and Soon-ok sitting in a cafe. He waved but they didn't see him. As he sat on the plane he felt he was rejoining another world, some foreign place where bills had to be paid and conversation was difficult. On the camino they were children, allowed to do nothing but let thoughts rise without thinking them; now he'd need to know what he was doing. He looked out of the window, another coastline was approaching. England. He wondered if they'd pass over Salisbury Plain where many years ago he'd been on exercises with the army. Life in bits, live in pieces. Whatever those pieces were, they were the qualities that made him what he was, nothing more or less. Could you make the stronger qualities more effective? A little maybe. Could you diminish the weaker? A little maybe. He realised now that the Path didn't answer questions, but maybe the person asking them was different. That was enough. As soon as he'd cleared customs, he called Gemma and asked her if she'd meet him. "I'd like to talk about Sam," he said.

* * * *

Ingrid picked up her pack from the albergue and went on to the street outside to find a taxi to the airport; but in that mysterious way she had of making decisions without knowing she was making them, she walked instead to the tourist office to ask about buses to Lisbon. She called Siri and left a message saying she wouldn't be home for a while, then she went to the bus station. She knew she was a day behind Werner, but that was no problem. Ingrid could catch anyone.

285

* * * *

Llewellyn got on the boat to Plymouth from Santander. On the crossing he drank too much and was sick twice. Halfway across the channel he thought he'd start that picture of his niece his brother-in-law had commissioned. He took out his camera to look through the photographs he'd taken of her before he left and discovered that somehow he'd deleted them, and all the photos of his work too. Oh well, he thought, they'll all be there when I get back. He looked out of the window at the sea and said a little thank you to Julia. Her life and definitely her death had changed them all. Maybe Paul was right, if you saw it for what it was, it was beautiful. He saw a seagull flying about twenty feet up. It suddenly dropped down over the sea, floated for a while as the waves undulated beneath it, then ducked its head down beneath the water and came up with a small fish. Llewellyn laughed out loud.

ends

Printed in Great Britain
by Amazon.co.uk, Ltd.,
Marston Gate.